CW00829266

TRANSGRESSIONS: CULTURAL STUD
Volume 64

TRANSGRESSIONS: CULTURAL STUDIES AND EDUCATION

Cultural studies provides an analytical toolbox for both making sense of educational practice and extending the insights of educational professionals into their labors. In this context *Transgressions: Cultural Studies and Education* provides a collection of books in the domain that specify this assertion. Crafted for an audience of teachers, teacher educators, scholars and students of cultural studies and others interested in cultural studies and pedagogy, the series documents both the possibilities of and the controversies surrounding the intersection of cultural studies and education. The editors and the authors of this series do not assume that the interaction of cultural studies and education devalues other types of knowledge and analytical forms. Rather the intersection of these knowledge disciplines offers a rejuvenating, optimistic, and positive perspective on education and educational institutions. Some might describe its contribution as democratic, emancipatory, and transformative. The editors and authors maintain that cultural studies helps free educators from sterile, monolithic analyses that have for too long undermined efforts to think of educational practices by providing other words, new languages, and fresh metaphors. Operating in an interdisciplinary cosmos, Transgressions: Cultural Studies and Education is dedicated to exploring the ways cultural studies enhances the study and practice of education. With this in mind the series focuses in a non-exclusive way on popular culture as well as other dimensions of cultural studies including social theory, social justice and positionality, cultural dimensions of technological innovation, new media and media literacy, new forms of oppression emerging in an electronic hyperreality, and postcolonial global concerns. With these concerns in mind cultural studies scholars often argue that the realm of popular culture is the most powerful educational force in contemporary culture. Indeed, in the twenty-first century this pedagogical dynamic is sweeping through the entire world. Educators, they believe, must understand these emerging realities in order to gain an important voice in the pedagogical conversation.

Without an understanding of cultural pedagogy's (education that takes place outside of formal schooling) role in the shaping of individual identity–youth identity in particular–the role educators play in the lives of their students will continue to fade. Why do so many of our students feel that life is incomprehensible and devoid of meaning? What does it mean, teachers wonder, when young people are unable to describe their moods, their affective affiliation to the society around them. Meanings provided young people by mainstream institutions often do little to help them deal with their affective complexity, their difficulty negotiating the rift between meaning and affect. School knowledge and educational expectations seem as anachronistic as a ditto machine, not that learning ways of rational thought and making sense of the world are unimportant.

But school knowledge and educational expectations often have little to offer students about making sense of the way they feel, the way their affective lives are shaped. In no way do we argue that analysis of the production of youth in an electronic mediated world demands some "touchy-feely" educational superficiality. What is needed in this context is a rigorous analysis of the interrelationship between pedagogy, popular culture, meaning making, and youth subjectivity. In an era marked by youth depression, violence, and suicide such insights become extremely important, even life saving. Pessimism about the future is the common sense of many contemporary youth with its concomitant feeling that no one can make a difference.

If affective production can be shaped to reflect these perspectives, then it can be reshaped to lay the groundwork for optimism, passionate commitment, and transformative educational and political activity. In these ways cultural studies adds a dimension to the work of education unfilled by any other sub-discipline. This is what Transgressions: Cultural Studies and Education seeks to produce—literature on these issues that makes a difference. It seeks to publish studies that help those who work with young people, those individuals involved in the disciplines that study children and youth, and young people themselves improve their lives in these bizarre times.

Re-Symbolization of the Self

Human Development and Tarot Hermeneutic

Inna Semetsky
University of Newcastle, Australia

SENSE PUBLISHERS
ROTTERDAM/BOSTON/TAIPEI

A C.I.P. record for this book is available from the Library of Congress.

ISBN: 978-94-6091-419-5 (paperback)
ISBN: 978-94-6091-420-1 (hardback)
ISBN: 978-94-6091-421-8 (e-book)

Published by: Sense Publishers,
P.O. Box 21858,
3001 AW Rotterdam,
The Netherlands
www.sensepublishers.com

Printed on acid-free paper

Cover: "The White Bird", artist Michail Grobman. Painting, gouache on paper, 1987.
Reproduced with the artist's permission.

and:

Illustrations of Tarot pictures are from the Rider-Waite Tarot Deck.
Reproduced by permission of US Games Systems Inc., Stamford, CT, USA. ©
1971 US Games Systems, Inc. Further reproduction prohibited.

TABLE OF CONTENTS

ACKNOWLEDGMENTS

I would like to express my gratitude to Shirley R. Steinberg and Michel Lokhorst for making the intangible idea of this book a reality. I am grateful for the editorial assistance of Proof This in Melbourne, Australia, during the writing process. I wish to thank the Faculty of Education and Arts at the University of Newcastle, Australia for the 5 months special study period in 2010 that allowed me to lead this project to completion. I am immensely grateful to Nel Noddings whose remarkable scholarship and care remain a source of intellectual inspiration and emotional support for a number of my research efforts. Last but not least my thanks go to my sons David and Eugene and to my colleague Roger.

ACKNOWLEDGMENTS

WHY THIS BOOK?

This book originated as an action-research project conducted between 1992 and 1994 under the auspices of the California Board of Behavioral Sciences when I was a postgraduate student enrolled in the Masters of Arts degree program in the area of Marriage, Family and Child Counseling and Human Development at Pacific Oaks College in Pasadena. Unbeknown to me at the time, my study was to be a type of research analogous to what Jungian scholar Robert Romanyshyn will have called more than a decade later "research with soul in mind" (Romanyshyn, 2007). Yet back then in 1992 I was not only ten years away from the subject matter of my future doctorate in the area of philosophy of education and cultural studies, but also quite undecided on the topic of my Masters thesis that was eventually to be called "Introduction of Tarot readings into clinical psychotherapy: a naturalistic inquiry".

Interestingly enough, and once again in accordance with Romanyshyn's *imaginal* approach, my topic was about *to choose me* rather than the other way around! Referring to the *imaginal*, Romanyshyn emphasizes the role of this "third" dimension between the senses and the intellect as enabling an embodied way of being in the world within the context of complex mind reaching into the whole of nature. It was Henry Corbin who coined the *imaginal world* – *Mundus Imaginalis* or *mundus archetypus*, the archetypal world – as a distinct order of reality corresponding to a distinct mode of perception in contrast to purely *imaginary* as the unreal or just utopian. Yet, it is our cognitive function enriched with imagination that provides access to the imaginal world with a rigor of knowledge specified as knowing by analogy.

The method of analogy that mystics around the world have practiced for centuries defies the privileged role allotted to the conscious subject that observes the surrounding world of objects – from which he is forever detached – with the cool "scientific" gaze of an independent spectator so as to obtain a certain and indubitable knowledge, or *episteme*.

Mystics and poets (from whom Plato used to withhold academic status) historically played a *participatory*, embodied role in the relational network that forms an interdependent holistic fabric with the world thus overcoming the separation between subject and object. This dualistic split has been haunting us since the time of Descartes, confining us to what Corbin calls the "banal dualism" of matter versus spirit.

As for the "socialization" of consciousness, it pretends to resolve the dilemma by making, according to Corbin, a *fatal* choice: either myth or historical reality. Either facts or fiction! This book avoids the binary fatality of either/or choice: we will see in Chapter 3 that Tarot renders itself to explication in *both* mythical *and* real historic, cultural, terms.

The sociological dimension is significant: Philip Wexler (1996, 2000, 2008), pointing out the current importance of religion and spirituality for socio-cultural life, ascribed the status of symbolic movement to sociology of education that aims to bring spirituality to secular, long-disenchanted and alienated, contexts so as to satisfy their hunger for meaning.

Wexler emphasizes an approach from within long-standing religious tradition and focuses specifically on Jewish mysticism. He calls for the "broad-scale revitalization...of the culture of modernity, a re-articulation of ancient religious traditions, and...the anti-institutional, but religiously-oriented movements of everyday life that we often referred to as instances and heralds of a 'new age'" (Wexler, 2008, p. 9).

I share with Wexler his conviction that our present postmodern age calls for revision of the pre-modern traditions of theory, interpretation and understanding and especially in terms of following "the new age...tendency [by means of] opening the reservoir of the cultural resources of traditional, religious understanding... [in] mystical, experiential and spiritual aspects: from Hinduism, Tantra; from Islam, Sufism; from Christianity, mysticism; from Judaism, Kabbalah and Hasidism" (Wexler, 2008, p. 10).

This book will not only have added Tarot as a spiritual, both metaphysical and practical, system to Wexler's list of multicultural traditions but will focus specifically on Tarot hermeneutic or on the art of, using the term from popular culture, Tarot readings. Etymologically, the Greek words *hermeneuein* and *hermeneia* for interpreting and interpretation are related to the mythic god Hermes, a messenger and mediator between gods and mortals, who crosses the thresholds and traverses the boundaries because he can "speak" and understand both "languages", the divine and the human, even if they appear totally alien to each other.

As a practical method, Tarot hermeneutic allows us to *relate* to something essentially *other* but nevertheless understandable, knowable and, ultimately, known. The *relation* thus established between the generic "Self" and "Other" in our real practical life is significant and has both epistemological and ontological implications. The dimension of the foremost importance is however ethical, considering that we live in a time of the multiculturalism and globalization when different values appear incommensurable and continuously compete, conflict, and clash!

In our current global climate permeated by diverse beliefs, disparate values, and cultural conflicts, understanding ourselves and others and learning to share each other's values is paramount for the survival of our species. This requires an expansion of our consciousness using all available means, including the knowledge of the symbolic language of Tarot pictures that are worth more, as the saying goes, than many thousands of words. Classical Russian author Ivan Turgenev pointed out that a picture shows at a glance what it can take dozens of pages of a book to expound. Without making grand metaphysical claims concerning Tarot, this book will focus on its practical side as comprising my empirical research data. Yet, important theoretical stepping stones will be laid down through chapter 1 to chapter 7 to ground the empirical data that will be presented in minute detail in chapter 8. Chapter 8 will comprise the fifteen actual Tarot readings that have been documented as constituting the core of my research and published with the written consent of all participants.

So, coming back to 1992, I remember the day when I took the November-December issue of *The California Therapist* out of my mailbox and my eyes fell on the letter to the editor. The author of the letter was interested in learning of other professionals who were encountering in their practice people who were more interested in learning about their past lives and going to psychics, as the author put it, rather than discussing their parents and more recent childhood. The author felt that she and other therapists working with quite a number of "new age" clients needed more publicity.

When I read the letter written by a qualified mental health professional and published in a respected professional periodical, my first feeling was that of belonging. Wow! I am not alone in my pursuits! At that stage, being a postgraduate student, I did not widely publicize the fact that I was a Tarot reader. Yet the very fact of being a reader is what originally motivated me to want to become a professional counselor and to invest my time, money, mind and soul into the intensive research culminating in the book you are now reading.

Many years ago, eager to listen to anyone who would have provided any guidance to me in my seemingly vicious circle of then current life-tasks, problems and issues, I turned to readers. Nothing seemed to help, and I found myself going from crisis to crisis and losing the thread of connection with not only the external world but myself as well. Moving from one counseling room to another, I did not feel understood, and more and more doubts about my own integrity started to occupy my mind, further contributing to the loss of that connection, that fragile link, which enables one to know oneself.

It was the ancient "Know Thyself" maxim that was inscribed on the temple of Apollo at Delphi and, as philosopher of education Nel Noddings (2006) reminds us, still remains the necessary, even if often disregarded, goal of education. It was the quest for meanings and evaluation of life-experience – an examined versus unexamined life – that Socrates was calling for.

Noddings is adamant about the importance of self-knowledge as the very core of education: "when we claim to *educate*, we must take Socrates seriously. Unexamined lives may well be valuable and worth living, but an *education* that does not invite such examination may not be worthy of the label education" (Noddings, 2006, p. 10, italics in original). Still more often than not education is equated with formal schooling (for children) or perpetual training (for adults) thus *a priori* marginalizing the realm of lifelong human development and experiential learning situated amidst real-life situations.

For me, such an informal – or, rather, post-formal (Steinberg, Kincheloe, and Hinchey, 1999) – education grounded in an existing cultural practice began when, on the verge of despair, I found myself sitting opposite a man who was a genuine Tarot reader. It was his reading that precipitated a catharsis: something that sub-consciously I did not want to know or accept, that was repressed and stored away in my unconscious mind and thus not dealt with, was brought to my awareness, then explored and discussed by my reader and me, becoming in this process a meaningful reality.

I left that reading session fully aware that I had to deal with the emergent information as this new knowledge was me, my selfhood that so far has been denied, displaced, or sublimated. This process of informal guidance by means of a Tarot reading, that transgressed the boundaries between education and therapy, facilitated a process of development and personal transformation. This developmental, at once healing and learning, process is still going on, and in this quest I was and still am accompanied by the wonderful world of Tarot: I became a reader, in the parlance of popular culture. Or, in terms of academic discourse, a "bilingual interpreter" who can translate the "language" of the unconscious, projected in the array of Tarot pictures (chapter 7), into verbal expressions; and I consider this one of the richest and most liberating experiences a person can have in life.

The word education derives from Latin *educare* that means to lead out as well as to bring out something that is within. The word therapy derives from the Greek *therapeia* in terms of human service to those who need it. Education and counseling alike involve either implicit or explicit inquiry into the nature of the self and self-other relations. Carol Witherell notices that, ideally, each professional activity "furthers another's capacity to find meaning and integrity" (1991, p. 84) in lived experience. Importantly both practices are "designed to change or guide human lives" (Witherell, 1991, p. 84).

In the area of human development, which is the focus of this book, the rigid boundaries between those apparently separate, in the contemporary context, disciplines of education and therapy become blurred: both are oriented to creating meanings for our experience that includes the realm of the yet unknown and unconscious. The role of unconscious learning has been systematically addressed by the Australian higher educator Marian de Souza (2008, 2009) especially as a means for focusing on emotional and spiritual intelligence grounded in "the processes of feeling and intuiting" (de Souza, 2009, p. 681) in the combined context of education and mental health.

Tarot hermeneutic provides an unorthodox epistemic access to the realm of the unconscious analogous to Carl Gustav Jung's analytical or depth psychology, to be addressed in chapter 2, when the effects of the archetypal dynamics comprising the field of the collective unconscious – a theoretical construct posited by Jung – is analyzed in practice. Jung's biographer Laurens van der Post, in his introduction to Sallie Nichols' book *Jung and Tarot: An archetypal journey* notices her contribution to analytical psychology by virtue of the "profound investigation of Tarot, and her illuminated exegesis of its pattern as an authentic attempt at enlargement of possibilities of human perceptions" (in Nichols, 1980, p. xv).

Contemporary post-Jungian scholar Andrew Samuels mentions "systems such as that of the I Ching, Tarot and astrology" (Samuels, 1985, p. 123) as possible even if questionable resources in analytical psychology, and quotes Jung who wrote in 1945: "I found the I Ching very interesting…I have not used it for more than two years now, feeling that one must learn to walk in the dark, or try to discover (as when one is learning to swim) whether the water will carry one" (p. 123). Irene Gad connected Tarot pictures with the stages of human development in the context of Kabbalistic teachings and alongside the Jungian process of individuation towards becoming authentic selves. She considered their archetypal images "to be…trigger symbols, appearing and disappearing throughout history in times of transition and need" (1994, p. xxxiv). Such historical and socio-cultural value of Tarot hermeneutic in the context of collective – not solely individual, but social – consciousness will be addressed in Chapter 9.

This book will demonstrate that Tarot, as an existing, albeit marginal, cultural practice traditionally located at the "low" end of popular culture, plays a significant role in the process of self-formation or construction of human subjectivity, thus becoming a means for the re-symbolization of the Self. Philip Wexler introduced the concept "resymbolization" as focused on the "*collective* symbolic or cultural work" (1996, p. 115; italics in original) constituting a process of cultural, societal change due to the reinterpretation of human subjectivity as grounded in "the inter-active dynamics of relationality" (Wexler, 1996, p. 115) especially as it pertains to Jewish mystical teachings, Kabbalah, which is literally translated as *Tradition*. It is a *relation* as ontologically basic (versus an isolated and self-centered moral agent) that is also central to Nel Noddings' ethics of care in education.

Hasidic philosopher Martin Buber, whose concepts were instrumental for Noddings, referred to the "wordless depths [when we] experience an undivided unity" (1971, p. 24; brackets mine) between the two people at the soul-level in the form of the famous *I-Thou* relation. These depths are filled not with words but with images, and the task of this book is to elucidate the images, to articulate them, to appreciate their role in the re-symbolization of the *relational* Self at both individual and collective levels.

For Buber, it is the lived world that engenders the personality of a particular individual. It is the world comprising the whole environment, both natural and social, that "'educates' the human being: it draws out his powers and makes him grasp and penetrate its objections" (Buber, 1971, p. 89). Buber deliberately puts the word *educate* in quotation marks to distinguish his new mode of the relational, shared, erotic educational experience from the old one-sided model based on the will to power and authority that neglects "experiencing the other side" (p. 96). It is the integrative dynamics between self and other, between consciousness and the unconscious, between I and Thou that constitutes an element of inclusion comprising education in which educator "is set in the midst of the service" (p. 103).

A relational, integrative approach is also a formidable *Zeitgest* in the area of another human service profession, that of psychological counseling and therapy (Corey, 1991). In the early '90s, Corey has been already advocating an integrative perspective taking into consideration therapists' willingness to look into the expansion of their own outlook and into possibility of widening the range of techniques to accommodate a diverse population. Including rapprochement, convergence, and integration in the psychotherapeutic Zeitgeist, Corey envisaged that the current "Zeitgeist…will continue with this trend toward convergence and integration and that there will also be an increased emphasis on a spiritual perspective" (p. 429).

Michael Murphy (1993) also called for the *integral practices* that encompass a wide variety of domains in human nature in a comprehensive way; including somatic, affective, cognitive, volitional and, importantly, transpersonal dimensions. Edward Whitmont (1985), in the context of post-Jungian practices of psychotherapy, pointed out that solely verbal or reflective methods may not be sufficient. Acknowledging the limitations of just "talking therapy", he emphasized that the development of psychic awareness achieved a new quality in terms of a novel relation to spiritual meaning. Whitmont pointed out a new developmental phase in the evolution of consciousness that demands a broader scope of awareness encompassing but not reducible to intellect alone.

Understanding that human consciousness undergoes evolution, growth, and expansion is an important premise in the present approaches to education for spirituality, care and wellbeing (De Souza, M., Francis, L., O'Higgins-Norman, J., and D. Scott, 2009; Gidley, 2009). Jean Gebser, a French polymath, referred to the evolution of human consciousness in terms of its intensification by means of progressively going though the archaic, mythic, magic, and mental structures to be finally superseded by the *integral* consciousness, which will have incorporated a spiritual dimension. Gebser pointed out that mythical bards like Homer are represented as being blind because their task was not to observe the visible world with the organ of sight, the eye, but to use insight, "a sight turned inward to contemplate the inner images of the soul" (Gebser, 1991, p. 271). It is an insight into the meanings of Tarot images, as this book will demonstrate, that leads to intensification, expansion, and re-symbolization of consciousness.

Another memory comes to mind. It is summer of 1993. I am busy working in my clinical internship in West Hollywood. The client population in the area, and accordingly in the agency I am working for, consists of mostly gay men. I am having a counseling session with "John", in his thirties, and HIV positive. We are discussing his outbursts of sudden anger in the relationship with his live-in boyfriend, when abruptly John switches the issue: "I saw my spiritual guru yesterday," he says. "She said she didn't see a speck of death in me."

The impact of that phrase on me, and the timing of it, was like a turning point. It brought a paradigm shift in my professional relationship with John. The session became illuminated by what was of paramount importance, significance and value in John's painful and uncertain internal world. It redistributed the weights of issues he was overwhelmed with. It indicated that John was reaching out to whoever could understand his hopes and fears, acknowledge them, reflect back and help him in working through his problems. It happened to be his spiritual guru who cared about him and was able to provide him with the necessary reassurance.

This emotional desire as "the longing to be cared for…is manifested as a need for love, physical care, respect or mere recognition – [and] is the fundamental starting point for the ethics of care" (Noddings, 1998, p. 188). Such was John's internal subjective reality – and this reality was addressed and mirrored in his spiritual quest. I began to wonder about the ambiguity of my professional role in this situation: what response or intervention could I, in my capacity as a counselor, provide in agreement with the framework of the behavioral-cognitive approach advocated by the agency I was working for?

What could one do within the limitations of a solely cognitive orientation aiming to behavior modification for this particular person whose initial assessment, according to his intake form, indicated an early stage of dementia? Desperate and overwhelmed by the turn of events in his personal experience, he turned to somebody outside this formal counseling room, to somebody he perceived as a spiritual guru. My immediate feeling was: if only I could introduce into our counseling sessions a spiritual dimension – and specifically by means of Tarot readings – John may very well benefit! At the very least his world view, which obviously included spiritual aspects, would be validated; at the very best, the meanings of the events in his life and the value of his personal experience, however tragic, would become open to his awareness.

Slowly the idea emerged. Nothing should prevent an existing phenomenon from becoming the subject of inquiry. The phenomenon of Tarot readings does exist; the shelves in the bookstores are crowded with popular publications; there are more than two hundred and fifty various decks available. There is a variety of advertising in popular media. TV channels have their own "psychic networks"; yet all of this exists mainly at the level of popular culture.

As noticed by Emily Auger (2004) in her research on Tarot and other meditation decks in the context of aesthetics, Tarot decks represent a popular, or "low", rather than "high" art forms such as painting, architecture, or sculpture. Yet, it is Tarot that was to become the subject matter of my postgraduate research in the area of behavioral sciences, thus transgressing the borders between popular and academic cultures. Similar to Robert Romanyshyn's "wounded researcher" (Romanyshyn, 2007) I was ready to step into the untapped unconscious field and to explore the many "wounds" underlying our perceptions and judgments.

There was no aim to prove or disprove anything, to qualify or disqualify, to compare or contrast. This study grew out of a desire to bring light to the often misunderstood realm of Tarot which is so much richer and valuable than its reductive popular role as a fortune-telling device, yet which is more often than not considered as such. The main "objective" of my study was, is, and will remain, the wellbeing of those who are seeking Tarot counsel.

A Tarot deck consists of seventy-eight pictorial cards, or Arcana. The meaning of Arcana (or Arcanum, singular) is that creative, but often missing, element in our lives, which is necessary to know, to discover in experience so as to be fruitful and creative in our approach to multiple life-tasks situated in the midst of experiential situations, events and our complex relationships with others. If and when discovered – that is, made available to consciousness – it becomes a powerful motivational force to facilitate a change for the better at our emotional, cognitive or behavioral levels and thus to accomplish an important ethical objective.

What is called a Tarot layout or spread is a particular pattern of the picturesque cards with a variety of images that are full of rich symbolism. Each position in the sequence of pictures constituting a particular layout has some specific connotations that will be addressed in detail in chapters 7 and 8. Tarot pictorial symbolism embodies intellectual, moral, and spiritual "lessons" derived from collective human experiences across times, places and cultures.

As such, Tarot "speaks" in a mythic format of symbols, the metaphorical universal language full of deep, even if initially opaque, meanings. The interpretation of Tarot images and pictures indicates a specific "hermeneutic, composed from the juxtaposition of disparate elements, [or] what Freud called pictographic" (Grumet, 1991, p. 75). As a symbolic system of reading and interpretation, Tarot is oriented toward the discovery of meanings for the multiplicity of experiences that would have otherwise appeared to lack meaning and significance. Thus the readings necessarily "honor the spontaneity, complexity and ambiguity of human experience" (p. 67).

The educational function derives from the holistic dimension embedded in experience that transcends the dualistic mind-body split and the scope of which expands to also incorporate the spiritual, transpersonal, domain. We thus acquire a better ability for self-reflection, self-knowledge, and a sense of value, purpose and meaningfulness of our experiences. Importantly we achieve a better understanding of what may appear to be the otherwise irresolvable moral dilemmas and which subsequently leads to the choice of right action and developing a better-informed, intelligent, decision-making ability.

In their monumental study, Crawford and Rossiter (2006) equate young people's search for meaning, identity and spirituality with their very *reasons for living* and point out that

> meaning and identity are the same psychological reality looked at from different perspectives. From the viewpoint of meaning, it is an explanation of individual intentionality. From the viewpoint of identity, it is the individual's distinctive self-understanding and self-expression (p. 33)

Noticing the link between the search for meaning, personal identity and spirituality, Crawford and Rossiter suggest that teachers should help their students "to look on their experience of education with a greater sense of its value" (2006, p. 321).

It is a noble task, indeed, but it should be performed by teachers equipped with at least an equal if not greater sense of value and meaning of their own professional practice and their own personal development in terms of what Jung called *self-education* (chapter 2). Nel Noddings (2002) keeps reminding us that the aim of moral, holistic, education is to contribute to the continuous education of both students and teachers, in the dynamics between selves and others embedded in the *caring* relation.

"The attitude of care" (Noddings, 1991, p. 161) is characterized by the presence of attention or engrossment and is especially significant in the context of Tarot. Noddings refers to the story of the Holy Grail as told by Simone Weil (1951):

> In the first legend of the Grail, it is said that the Grail...belongs to the first comer who asks the guardian of the vessel, a king three quarters paralyzed by the most painful wound, "What are you going through?"... It is a recognition that the sufferer exists, not only as a unit in a collection, or a specimen from the social category labeled "unfortunate," but as a man, exactly

like us. ... This way of looking is first of all attentive. The soul empties itself of its own contents in order to receive into itself the being it is looking at, just as he is, in all his truth. Only he who is capable of attention can do this (p. 115).

Yet, John was not asked the question, "What are you going through?" within the agency's behavior-modification approach. Nor that he would have been able to – consciously – answer this straightforward question anyway or wanted to engage in an explicit dialogue so as to intentionally share his pain and suffering with me. The counseling sessions under the adage of behavioral modification of the agency were supposed to "instruct" John to not get into arguments with his boyfriend. John's referring to a conversation with his spiritual guru was an indication that he was looking for an alternative way to be cared for, to get attention especially because the probability of his early passing was his very reality.

To connect with the Other at the soul level means to connect via *corpus subtile* – the subtle, spiritual, "body" of emotions and feelings that are so often difficult to articulate precisely because they are buried deep in the unconscious, in the *psyche*. Their expressive language exceeds and spills over the limitations of our conscious discourse. It is the Tarot hermeneutic as the metaphorical, symbolic, quest for the Holy Grail that helps us in articulating what otherwise betrays words. This takes place because of the symbols' functioning to bring the unconscious wounds and pains to the level of cognitive awareness, therefore engaging with the psyche and making it whole, healing it.

The psyche becomes filled with the new meanings of experiences and the acquired sense of not only interpersonal connection but, ultimately, spiritual communion. The plurality of evolving meanings express themselves indirectly, in symbolic form, and symbols act as transformers capable of raising the unconscious contents to the level of consciousness, therefore ultimately performing what Jung called the transcendent function when the implicit meanings become explicit by virtue of "becoming conscious and by being perceived" (Jung in Pauli, 1994, p. 159).

The readings described in chapter 8 of this book were conducted in the spirit of what Jean Watson (1985) called, in the area of nurse education, the occasions of caring. Noddings explains that the occasions of caring constitute the moments when nurse and patient, or teacher and student, meet and must decide what to do with the moment, what to share, which needs to express, or whether to remain silent. This encounter "needs to be a guiding spirit of what we do in education" (Noddings, 1991, p. 168); such a guiding, relational and caring, spirit ontologically preeminent in Tarot hermeneutic.

Referring to "a hermeneutic lag [as] a poor reading of cultural tendencies" (Wexler, 1996, p. 5) that have become frozen in the dominant structures of the over-rationalization of knowledge, Wexler calls for the cultural, theoretical, and educational renaissance. His intent is to gather the holy sparks of the Kabbalistic creation myth told in the mystical Judaism as "the vital residue of an uncontainable supernal light [that] remain glowing in the dross of fragments of worldly vessels unable to contain them. So it is with…reinterpret[ing] ancient traditions in contemporary fields of thought. We have some glimmering, but only within the prevailing cover of opaque and limiting fragments. What I hope for…is an opening toward those premodern traditions, and their inspirational 'sparks.'" (Wexler, 1996, p. 113)

To reclaim the divine sparks at the level of human cultural practices is a challenge that this book intends to meet. The restored light as the central metaphor will have contributed not to the over-rational *Enlightenment* of modernity but to a postmodern spiritual *Illumination* that would defy pessimism and the frequent fatalistic resignation currently permeating individual and collective consciousness, locally and globally.

In the remarkable book *Educating for Intelligent Belief or Unbelief*, Nel Noddings (1993a) comments that some of the new age criticism appears superficial and "lacks the intelligence" (p. 39) which she encourages in her work. Noddings points out that this type of education will put "great emphasis on self-knowledge… that… must come to grips with the emotional and spiritual as well as the intellectual and psychological" (p. xiv). Analogously I encourage an intelligent and open attitude in the book you are going to read.

Furthermore, you will discover that Tarot hermeneutic paves a road toward such expanded self-knowledge and that using Tarot symbolic system as an educational and counseling "aid" enables us to learn from life-experiences hence becoming able to acquire intelligence and wisdom, indeed urged by Noddings. Philip Wexler suggested that many of the assumptions underlying the new age culture should be deeply deconstructed into the ancient core religious traditions from which they perform their *bricolage*. The next chapter 2 will focus on the notion of bricolage *per se* as constituting a theory-practice nexus in which the Tarot hermeneutic is embedded.

CHAPTER 2

DOING BRICOLAGE

Addressing a significant role in the process of identity-formation of post-formal education and cultural pedagogy, Kincheloe (2005; 2008; also Kincheloe and Berry, 2005) conceptualized *bricolage* as drawing from multiple theoretical and methodological resources, including hermeneutics, phenomenology, and narratology, while retaining the rigor of the best critical thought. The term *bricolage* was coined by French anthropologist Claude Lévi-Strauss (1966) with regard to spontaneous human action grounded in the characteristic patterns of mythological thinking and in the context of structuralism defined as the search for the underlying patterns of thought in all forms of human activity. Gilles Deleuze and Felix Guattari referred to the bricolage as a "schizoanalytic" (1972), transgressive, mode of production.

Deleuze's post-structuralist philosophy, which has been inspirational for expanding the range of qualitative methods in educational research (St. Pierre, 1997a, 1997b) and has made a significant contribution to educational theory (Semetsky, 2006; 2008), will be addressed in detail in chapter 6 as it pertains to Tarot hermeneutic. A *bricoleur* constructs the object of study paying particular attention to the webs of relationships, processes, and interconnections among phenomena within which he himself is situated.

For Kincheloe, *doing bricolage* involves marginalized practices and the development of transgressive conceptual tools as well as exploring the breadth and wealth of typically underestimated human cognitive capacities. A *bricoleur* embedded in phenomenology of lived experience acts as the first explorer to discover new territories, trying new strategies, and opening new avenues for research while aiming to help people in reshaping their lives. While hermeneutics came to connote the ambiguity of meanings, the bricolage implies the fictive and imaginative elements present in research methodologies.

From this perspective, Tarot hermeneutic represents the work of a bricoleur. A bricoleur – a genuine Tarot reader – makes a creative and resourceful use of the "material at hand" that is, the images and symbols on Tarot pictures. My research was grounded in the broad material provided within the framework of Carl Gustav Jung's analytical, or *depth,* psychology. As for the empirical data presented in chapter 8, they were grounded in naturalistic inquiry employing both phenomenology and hermeneutics.

The essential identity of human experiences reflected in worldwide myths and folklore led Jung to postulate the existence of the collective unconscious as *objective psyche,* which is shared at the deepest level by all members of humankind and manifests itself through archetypal, symbolic and latent, images. Jung called the deepest level *psychoid* and asserted that it is at this level where, in a holistic manner, body and mind, *physis* and *psyche,* become united as two different aspects of one world, *Unus Mundus.*

The archetypes underlying our subjective perceptions and judgements are "located" at the unitary level of objective reality that transcends both the human mind and the external physical world. Jung's great achievement was his anti-dualistic and unifying approach to what we today call human sciences. He insisted on the multiplicity of inner, spiritual, meanings for the unconscious that would have exceeded its overt, even if latent, meaning posited by Freud as merely repressed.

These deep evolving meanings express themselves through archetypal images that act as symbolic transformers capable of making unconscious contents manifest at the level of conscious awareness. Archetype is seen by Jung as a skeletal pattern, filled in with imagery and motifs that are "mediated to us by the unconscious" (Jung, CW 8, 417), the variable contents of which form different archetypal images. In his memoirs, *Memories, Dreams, Reflections*, reflecting on his own development as an adult and on his own "second half of life", Jung said that the years when he was pursuing his *inner images* were the most important in his life; it is via images that the essential decisions were made.

The unconscious is capable of spontaneously producing images "irrespective of wishes and fears of the conscious mind" (Jung, CW 11, 745). *Typos*, as the composite of the archetype, means imprint, stamp or pattern. As the multiplicity of dynamic patterns "acting" in the collective unconscious, archetypes exist *in potentia* and are beckoned forth by our experiences. The unconscious "archetypes [as] ...structural elements of the psyche ...possess a certain autonomy and specific energy which enables them to attract, out of the conscious mind, those contents which are better suited to themselves" (Jung, CW 5, 232), thus helping us achieve much wider scope of awareness than rational thinking, in terms of solely cognitive reasoning deprived of what Jung called feeling-tones, is capable of providing.

The actualized archetypes are charged with psychic or spiritual energy, exceeding Freud's solely sexual libido. For Jung, "psychic energy is a very fastidious thing which insists on fulfilment of its own conditions" (Jung, CW 7, 76). Archetypes "reside" in the dynamic field of the collective unconscious and form an unorthodox virtual foundation upon which many individual real-life experiences lay down their own structures. Multiple combinations of innumerable experiences – the constella-tions of the actualized archetypes – produce diverse archetypal images that manifest overtly through their effects at the level of the body in the form of particular behavioral unconscious patterns.

The activity of archetypal dynamics determines where an individual stands within the process of individuation, the goal of which, for Jung, is the achievement of a greater personality culminating in the Self, the archetype of wholeness. Whole-ness as the integration of the unconscious into consciousness is marked by a change of attitude when the centre of the personality shifts its position from the Ego to the Self. We will see the unfoldment of archetypal dynamics in real-life individual experiences expressed by the constellations of Tarot pictures in chapter 8 as symbolic stopovers in the individuation process. We will also see the elements pertaining to the change in attitude and the connection of the latter with the individual ability to *learn* from her experience.

Individuation as an analytic and healing, therapeutic, process was defined by Jung in terms of *self-education* during which both unconscious and conscious aspects of life-experiences become integrated. Jung was explicit that education should not be confined to schools nor should education stop when a child grows up. Presenting his depth psychology as a method of/for self-education, Jung (1954) was adamant that self-knowledge remains an indispensable basis of adult self-education and emphasized an indirect method for attaining such inner self-knowledge by means of its symbolic mediation in the analytic process:

> There are...many extremely psychic processes which are unconscious, or only indirectly conscious...there is... something as impersonal as a product of nature that enables us to know the truth about ourselves ...Of the un-conscious we can learn nothing directly, but indirectly we can perceive the effects that come into consciousness (Jung, 1954, p. 49).

To bring the multiple, and often painful, effects of the unconscious processes into our consciousness is the task of depth psychology and Tarot hermeneutic alike. While human development potentially tends toward the Self, this archetype is fully actualized only when the unconscious becomes completely integrated into conscious-ness. We will encounter multiple archetypes of transformation in the series of images of the Major Arcana in chapter 4.

Human development engenders itself via the symbolism of the pictures as the expressions of the unconscious that precedes and exceeds the verbal expressions of the conscious mind: "it is not the personal human being who is making the statement, but the archetype speaking through him" (Jung, 1963, p. 352). Jung asserted that the real communication becomes possible when the conscious Ego acknowledges the existence of an unconscious partner. It is through a symbolic dialogue with this virtual partner represented by the archetype of the Self, which is present only implicitly, *in potentia* – yet will have been actualized during the journey through the constellation of Tarot images – that we can achieve this critical level of self-knowledge that forms a threshold for self-education and manifests in the individuation process.

When I started my project in the early 1990s, Jung's depth psychology as the analysis of the unconscious has existed not only just on the margins amidst many theoretical orientations in clinical or counselling practice but also was rather foreign to mainstream educational discourse. It is only recently that several pioneering studies (for example, Neville, 2005; Main, 2008; Mayes, 2003, 2004, 2005, 2007; Semetsky, in press) have focused on the implicit value of Jung's analytical psycho-logy for the field of *education* as a powerful complement to its *therapeutic* value, crossing the boundaries between two disciplines, both oriented toward development and individuation and blurring therefore the absolute line of division between pedagogical and clinical aspects.

Robert Romanyshyn (in press) addresses Jungian psychology as a mode of ethical pedagogy and showcases a Jungian classroom modeled on the paradigm of

"The Wounded Researcher" (Romanyshyn, 2007). Undercutting the Cartesian dream of reason, Romanyshyn weaves together phenomenology, hermeneutics and Jung's psychology so as to analyze the unconscious dynamics between a teacher and a student as leading to ethical ways of knowing and being. Romanyshyn points out that educators indeed have an ethical obligation to take responsibility for their own unconscious prejudices that form complex "characters" implicit in the transference field in a classroom as a deep unconscious connection arising in a genuine relationship.

Laura Huxley, the widow of the famous author and herself an Honorary Doctor of Human Services and recipient of the World Health Foundation for Development Peace Prize in 1990, was asked whether she had found any psychological techniques to be especially valuable or whether the success of a particular method varies for different persons (Brown and Novick, 1993). Her answer was that, despite many existing techniques being effective in the hands of a capable practitioner, the most important factor remains the relationship between the guide and the client. From this standpoint, the *relationship* per se as developed with fifteen participants in my study became a significant therapeutic and pedagogical component. Some of my participants have benefited from even a single session, as will be seen from their feedback; some, however, were not yet ready for a therapeutic change.

The effect of any session depends on many factors, a particular modality being only one of several. I always follow these timeless guidelines (Paul, 1967): *what* method, by *whom*, is the most effective for *this* particular individual with *this* specific problem and under *what* set of particular circumstances. However the multiple *what* and *this* are being conveyed in Tarot hermeneutic with clarity and accuracy so as to ensure a professional and ethical approach.

I agree with Romanyshyn that we have to master metaphors – in other words, to become *bricoleurs* – in our very practice, and that education understood as ethical should become a vocation oriented towards human development, that is, bringing up individuated and caring human beings who can take up the universal conditions of human existence in a manner that is transformative both of themselves and also of those very existential conditions. In order to fulfil Romanyshyn's intent to cultivate a special, even if uncertain, *metaphorical sensibility* so as to lead us out of linear and literal ways of thinking, we should learn to read and interpret the metaphorical pictorial language "spoken" by Tarot images that represent this extra, *imaginal*, dimension of *real*, both actual and potential, human experiences.

Jung observed that a relationship situated in the transference field between an analyst and analysand can "lead to parapsychological phenomena" (Bolen, 1979, p. 33), *I Ching* and Tarot notwithstanding. As existential psychologist Rollo May stated, "therapists cut themselves off from a great deal of reality if they do not leave themselves open to other way of communication that human reason" (1991, p. 163). Freud pointed out that a relationship developed in psychoanalysis at times comes close to a telepathic connection; and Jung's intuition during dream analysis in his analytical practice "bordered on being psychic" (Bolen, 1979, p. 13).

A renowned Tarot author Mary Greer[1] comments that Jung wrote in one of his letters, "Yes, I know of the Tarot. It is, as far as I know, the pack of cards originally used by the Spanish gypsies..." and has referred to Tarot cards as the descendants from the archetypes of transformation. Importantly, for Jung,

> The symbolic process is an experience *in images* and *of images*. Its development usually shows an enantiodromian structure like the text of the I Ching... Its beginning is...characterized by one's getting stuck in a blind alley or in some impossible situation and its goal is, broadly speaking, illumination of higher consciousness, by means of which the initial situation is overcome (Jung, CW 9i, 82).

The term *enantiodromia* (from the Greek *enantios*, opposite + *dromos*, running course) has been used by Jung to refer to the unconscious acting against the wishes of the conscious mind, but in accord with the psyche's grand, yet inaccessible, plan on the basis of which the unconscious life is constructed.

Respectively, our customary perception of a given situation being "impossible" and our lack of control over such an insolvable problem persist. In chapter 8 we will see many of the initially impossible situations embedded in the Tarot layouts that become resolved when the transcendent function implicit in Tarot hermeneutic enables one to get out of the "blind alley" of habitual narrow ego-consciousness thus empowering people with the revealed feeling of value and meaning when what seemed to be an impossible, really problematic, situation has been overcome.

Jung was adamant that the impossible situation produced in the unconscious is the means to abandon one's personal will reduced to the ego-consciousness and to begin trusting the impersonal power of the unconscious as the means for growth and adult development. Jungian psychology postulates that typical situations in life are the reflections of archetypes as patterns of spontaneous behavior which are practically engraved in the psychic constitution.

As primordial images embedded in the Tarot Major Arcana (chapter 4), archetypes can inflict strong psychological pain. An emotional situation that corresponds to a particular archetypal constellation may develop, and mental pressure may become too strong to be contained within one's coping abilities: "Colloquial expressions acknowledge this change in psychological level: 'What the devil got in him anyway?' or 'He got caught in the grip of an idea' or 'She went out of her mind with fear or rage'" (Bolen, 1979, p. 19). Tarot symbols hold together contents that individual consciousness alone is incapable of holding at the rational level, but which nonetheless express themselves at a subtle emotional level.

Archetypes do have two complementary poles, one expressing a "positive, favorable, bright side [and the other a] partly negative...partly chtonic" (Jung, CW 9i, 413). It is "a natural process [as] a manifestation of [psychic] energy that springs from the tension of opposites" (Jung, CW 7, 121) expressed in the dark and light archetypal aspects, both pertaining to Tarot imagery (not unlike yin and yang as an interplay of opposites in the Chinese Book of Changes) that give rise to the transcendent function performed by symbols embedded in Tarot hermeneutic.

By bringing to awareness many initially unperceived, unconscious and latent, meanings, the pictures serve the function of what Jung called amplification. The meanings, even if implicit, are nonetheless highly structured or organized, and a

Tarot layout (such as the Celtic Cross shown in chapter 7) amplifies the unconscious contents of the archetypal images via their representation in the material medium of the pictures. Because of the amplifying, synthesizing, nature of symbols, the meanings expressed in the multitude of images hiding in the unconscious can be elucidated, interpreted, narrated and potentially integrated into consciousness.

The amplifying and synthetic character of symbols reflects the dynamical and evolutionary approach to knowledge and, for Jung, a "psychological fact...as a living phenomenon...is always indissolubly bound up with the continuity of the vital process, so that it is not only something evolved but also continually evolving and creative" (Jung, CW 6, 717) as a function of our life-long learning from experience *per se* in the process of individuation and re-symbolization of the Self.

The Tarot pictures that are full of interpretable symbols relate to archetypal ideas; thus they are subject to hermeneutic interpretation involving intuition, insight and creative imagination. Jim Garrison, a philosopher of education, suggests *sympathetic data* as a term describing intuitions and perceptions that enable our understanding of others, and expresses his regret that "our culture has not evolved highly refined methods of collecting [those] data... researchers do not perform careful interpersonal experiments, [and] the theories of human thought, feeling, and action remain... remarkably underdeveloped" (Garrison, 1997, p. 35).

There is a sad irony here with regard to the fact that it is precisely sympathetic, inter-subjective, data that are maximally "relevant to the topic of teaching" (Garrison, 1997, p. 36) as well as to counseling, which are a central concern in the present context of Tarot hermeneutic grounded in relational dynamics. An expert reader as a genuine bricoleur can translate the pictorial language of symbols and signs into spoken word, thus creating a wealth of sympathetic, emotional data embodied in the unfolding narrative for the subject of a particular reading.

Many typical life experiences are represented in the patterns that appear and can be discerned when the pictures are being spread in this or that layout, and a person can learn from her experience when it is being unfolded in front of her eyes in the array of images. Respectively, the latent meanings of experience become available to human consciousness, and a person can discover in practice a deeper, spiritual and *numinous*, as Jung would say, dimension of experience. Thus Tarot, in terms of its archetypal dynamics, and despite being traditionally considered irrational and illogical, helps us achieve an intense scope of awareness exceeding narrow instrumental rationality.

It is what educational psychologist Jerome Bruner called an intuitive sense of rightness that allows a genuine reader to articulate the implicit meanings of Tarot images and symbols. For Bruner, intuition "implies the act of grasping the meaning or significance or structure of a problem without explicit reliance on the analytic apparatus of one's craft" (Bruner, 1966, p. 61). A symbolic, intuitive, approach creates a dialectical relationship between consciousness and the unconscious. In this respect Tarot images may be viewed as a bridge between the personal unconscious, via the archetypal field of the collective unconscious, to the conscious mind.

Similar to the interpretations of dreams in Jungian analysis, Tarot hermeneutic as reading and interpreting pictorial images becomes the core means assisting people in the process of individuation. The task of the reader is to make the information concealed in the unconscious available; thus to facilitate a growth-promoting process for the subject of the reading who is an equal participant in the emerging, therapeutic and learning, relation. Like in any relationship, human subjective experience is critical. The human factor is a precondition for us experiencing what Jung, in collaboration with physicist and Nobel laureate Wolfgang Pauli, called *synchronicity* (Jung and Pauli, 1955).

Synchronicity is defined as a meaningful coincidence when "an unexpected [mental] content which is directly or indirectly connected with some objective external event coincides with the ordinary psychic state" (Koestler, 1972, pp. 96–97). The ability of mind to be about something, to have mental content, constitutes intentionality as a subject-matter of phenomenology. According to its founder Edmund Husserl, a faithful description of any phenomenon as it presents itself within one's concrete experience represents a prime objective of phenomenology.

Husserl's phenomenological method supports the very process of Tarot readings during which *noemata* and *noiesis* are related in such ways that the archetypal structures embedded in the unconscious become intuitively present to consciousness. Noiesis as intuition is an operation of the *Nous*, or Intelligence, and represents the highest portion of human knowledge. In Eastern Orthodox Christianity human *nous* is described as the "eye of the heart or soul" or the "mind of the heart". *Noema* is a structure of experience that appears to consciousness in the form of implicit, as yet unconscious, pre-linguistic meanings embedded in the patterns of experience. We arrive at the noematic structures through self-reflection mediated by symbols.

For Husserl, the noetic and noematic are ideally two sides of the same experience, and it is the bricolage of Tarot as a mix of phenomenology with hermeneutics that enables us to see – in the form of sensible material patterns – that which otherwise would have remained outside of sense-experience, in the intelligible realm of Platonic Ideas, or archetypes to which we have no direct access. Yes, the archetypes *per se* cannot be known *directly*, but can be transcended – or brought "down to earth", so to speak – when being *mediated* by the images and symbols embedded in the Tarot pictures.

Understanding the symbolic meanings embodied in the archetypal images of Tarot Arcana and bringing them to consciousness contributes to re-symbolization of the Self in the process of gradually removing the Ego from its privileged, egocentric, position and enriching the human mind with other ways of knowing that complement its solely rational functions. For Jung, an *intuitive* function is non-rational, and the contents of intuition "have the character of being given in contrast to the 'derived' or 'deduced' character" (Noddings and Shore, 1984, p. 25) pertaining to two other Jungian functions of thinking and feeling. Feeling is considered by Jung to be a rational function as determining our value judgements.

Jung insisted on intuition's unconscious nature. While the "fostering of intuition as an aid to learning and knowing was not on [Jung's] agenda" (Noddings and Shore, 1984, p. 27), it is the Tarot symbolism that triggers the stream of the unconscious and serves as a device to educate and strengthen the human intuitive function invaluable for meaning-making. Noddings and Shore (1984) notice that phenomenology has contributed a *dynamic* quality to the notion of intuition in terms of its sense-fulfilling (that is, meaning-making) feature so that intuition becomes essential to the acquisition of knowledge. Husserl referred to intuition as *"a source of authority…for knowledge,* that *whatever presents itself…in primordial form…is simply to be accepted"* (Husserl, 1962, p. 83 quoted in Noddings and Shore, 1984, p. 31; italics in original).

Implementing a phenomenological approach means to accurately describe a "given phenomenon as it presents itself in one's own experience – not [to explain] its genesis through reference to antecedent causal factors" (Casey, 1976, p. 9). Such absence of a direct, unmediated causal link pertaining to phenomenology relates to Jung's *a-causal* principle of synchronicity as it manifest itself in Tarot. It is synchronicity that indicates the *"unitary aspect of existence"* (von Franz, 1992, p. 40; italics in original) which is difficult to explain rationally, especially since our thinking is heavily conditioned by deductive reasoning from premise to conclusion and the linear cause-effect connection prevalent in classical mechanics.

Still synchronicity is primarily connected with psychical and not physical conditions, that is, with the archetypal dynamics of the unconscious mind. Archetypes are the constellations of psychic energy dispersed in the collective unconscious, not unlike the "holy sparks" of the Kabbalistic vessels. Jung described synchronicity not only in terms of a coincidence between mental content, or a dream, or a vision with the physical event, but also as a premonition about an event, *"a foreknowledge of some kind"* (Jung, CW 8, 931; italics in original). The reality of this implicit "self-subsistent 'unconscious' knowledge" (Jung, CW 8, 931) of what we are meant to be and where we stand within the individuation process demonstrates itself *empirically* in the archetypal constellations of Tarot images as will be seen in chapters 7 and 8.

It is the archetypal symbolism of the images that presents us with those inner unconscious meanings that, while being *outside* of the conscious thought, are nonetheless "located" *inside* our intensified experiences. We learn from our very experience, the archetypal patterns of which unfold in front of our eyes in this or that layout. Tarot therefore performs two functions, existential and educational, the latter focusing on the ethical and spiritual dimension of experience and the former on the construction of identity – in terms of the re-symbolization of the Self – within experience itself which is symbolically represented in the pictures.

In terms of its archetypal dynamics, and despite being traditionally considered irrational and illogical, Tarot helps us achieve an intensified and expanded scope of awareness exceeding narrow rationality. The bricolage of Tarot as a theory-practice nexus is a process of the education of the Self: self-education that encompasses two processes, that of learning and counseling. Since Aristotle, the relationship between theory and practice has been controversial. Theory is derived from *theoria* defined as a philosophical contemplation of higher truths and as such disengaged from practical, political, contexts and social life; that is from *praxis*, which is defined as the process of putting theoretical knowledge into practice and is embedded in actions, relationships, and experiences that by definition have an ethical or moral dimension.

This detachment, in modern times, has led to a spectator theory of knowledge and strict disciplinary boundaries between sciences and humanities. The detached gazing at the "spectacle" in antiquity is, quite ironically, a precursor to modernity's scientific method. Scientific, intellectually certain, knowledge (or cognitive *episteme*, in Greek) became distinguished from, and opposed to, the creative arts (as *techne* or τέχνη).

Tarot pictures are artistic productions – *techne*; the pictures mastered by a human skill inspired in turn by the creative imagination of a particular artist, who designed this or that deck. Techne is often translated as craftsmanship, handicraft or skill; the products of techne are artifacts, such as Tarot pictures. In its dimension as a *techne*, Tarot becomes a powerful, albeit alternative, educational aid in the context of post-formal holistic education and mental health alike. But Tarot as *praxis* is equally if not more important.

In Greek mythology, *Praxis* is also another name for Aphrodite, the goddess of love who was a central character in the story of Eros and Psyche. The myth tells us that it is by virtue of active learning from novel life-experiences imposed on her by Praxis/Aphrodite – rather than by a theoretical contemplation of the objects of knowledge already possessed by the conscious mind – that Psyche, as a personification of *human* soul, was eventually able to reunite with Aphrodite's son, *divine* Eros.

For Plato, the highest philosophical vision is achievable only by one with the temperament of a lover, a lover of wisdom, who will allow himself to be grasped by, and to grasp in turn, the erotic passion in the process of recollecting true ideas. In Plato's *Symposium*, Diotima the Priestess teaches Socrates that Eros or Love is "located" *in-between* lack and plenty; it is a spirit or daimon that, importantly, can hold two opposites together as a whole, therefore to eventually reconcile that what analytic thinking habitually perceives dualistically, that is, as binary *irreconcilable* opposites. Jung used the Latin term *coincidentia oppositorum* for the apparently mystical coincidence of opposites, such as psyche and matter, which takes place in synchronistic experiences.

The term *philosopher* literally translates as a lover of wisdom who has a passionate desire for deep inner knowledge, *Gnosis* (from the Greek for *knowing*). It was Hermes, the messenger of gods, who finally summoned human Psyche to Olympus where she reunited with her beloved, divine Eros, having been granted a godlike immortality in this loving union. It is through being driven by Eros/Love that Psyche was able to meet the multiple challenges and win over the obstacles created by Praxis.

And it is only through love and compassion for the often suffering human spirit that an expert Tarot reader can intuit, understand, and narrate the subtle meanings encoded in the symbolism of the pictures, hence making each reading a precious learning experience.

The art of using Tarot lies in the knowledge of its symbolic language as the means of communication between another pair of supposedly binary opposites, consciousness and the unconscious. Jungian psychology postulates that all products and expressions of the unconscious are symbolic and thus carry or guide messages. The symbolic messages can be perceived by a reader as the information implicit in the collective unconscious because one's personality and life circumstances at any given moment reflect the actualized archetype or the constellation of archetypes.

Jung insisted that it is through the integration of the unconscious that we might have a reasonable chance to make experiences of an archetypal nature provide us with a feeling of continuity not only throughout our life-experiences but also, in a spiritual sense, before and after our existence, in virtue of the *immortal* soul. The better our understanding of the reality of the archetypes, the more we can participate in this reality, progressively realizing the archetypes' eternity and timelessness.

We learn from the constellation of Tarot pictures that embody real events, thoughts, and feelings implicit in the problematic situation (or, as it is called in the context of counseling-reading sessions in chapter 8, *presenting problem*) and become able to understand the situation better when it is amplified, clarified and brought to consciousness by means of the Tarot hermeneutic. The interpretation of symbols not only enriches a session with information but also makes this information meaningful. Many experiences start making sense for us when their disjointed fragments assembled in the bricolage of pictures ultimately form a unified meaningful whole, hence contributing to our self-education and meaning-making.

The experience of Tarot readings is both learning and therapeutic in terms of providing insight into the archetypal dynamics, thus enabling better communication and a greater understanding between a person and her potential Self. The actualized Self is fully individuated, yet it strongly contradicts "individualism". Vice versa, "the Self" always involves "the Other". As the archetype of wholeness, it is inherently inter-subjective and transpersonal, encompassing many experiences that the human soul learned in the "school of life", which is full of diverse situations, relationships with significant others, and ever-varied empirical contexts.

Jungian self-education therefore should be understood as constituting the developmental and learning, individuating, process towards achieving a "greater personality" (Jung, CW 7, 136) ultimately reaching towards the re-symbolized, integrated Self. Referring to self-education, Jung said:

> At present we educate people only up to the point where they can earn a living and marry: then education ceases altogether, as though a complete mental outfit has been acquired... Innumerable ill-advised and unhappy marriages, innumerable professional disappointments, are due to this lack of adult education. (Jung, 1954, p. 47)

Jung was adamant that "the education of the educator... will eventually rebound to the good of [the] pupils" (Jung, 1954, p. 47). Such self-education, however, should not be defined in terms of the currently popular professional development or life-long training, but "should make him properly conscious of himself" (Jung, 1954, p. 46).

The adults *are* educable; however such education should not proceed along the lines of compulsory "schooling". Jung considered the analysis of dreams whose constancy of meanings is exhibited by archetypal images to be "an eminently educational activity" (Jung, 1954, p. 94). It is becoming conscious of the archetypal field of dynamic forces-in-action that constitutes the method of indirect post-formal adult education as a "process resulting from the independent activity of the un-conscious" (Jung, 1954, p. 49); and Tarot hermeneutic represents but one example of post-formal pedagogy.

It is our learning from life experiences embodied in the symbolism of the pictures that not only leads to human development and eventual individuation but can also reconnect an individual *psyche* with its symbolic origin in *Anima Mundi*, the soul of the world, because our unconscious ideas are archetypal in nature and partake of the collective unconscious. Jung noticed that such conceptualization

> is particularly true of religious ideas, but the central concepts of science, philosophy, and ethics are no exception to this rule. In their present form they are variants of archetypal ideas created by consciously applying and adapting these ideas to reality. For it is the function of consciousness not only to recognize and assimilate the external world through the gateway of the senses, but to translate into visible reality the world within us (Jung, CW 8, 342).

This is the ultimate function of Tarot hermeneutic: to *translate into visible reality the deep and invisible, internal world within us.*

The Tarot hermeneutic via the mediation or embodiment of archetypal ideas in the material medium of pictures makes the invisible visible, and the expressive, yet silent, "voice" of the symbols and images becomes articulated with the help of creative imagination during constructions of specific narratives as will be demons-trated in chapter 8. The correlation between inner and outer realities has to make sense and become meaningful; but not because a particular cause has brought about a specific effect as in the case of mechanistic causality.

In the next chapter 3 we will address the Hermetic tradition that posits the existence of relations, correlations, analogies and correspondences akin to Jung's synchronicity principle that enables meaningful connections between a person's individual psyche and the collective unconscious. Like a genuine bricoleur, Hermes – the messenger of gods – crosses borders and transgresses boundaries; inhabiting a liminal in-between place, the *Imaginal* world.

NOTES

[1] See http://marygreer.wordpress.com/2008/03/31/carl-jung-and-tarot/

MYTHS AND REALITY

Tarot myths abound: the Greek god of communication, the messenger Hermes, has been identified with the Egyptian mystical god Thoth who is said to have "given" his name to a Tarot deck known as The Book of Thoth. Yet, there does not exist a single certain and proven origin of Tarot cards. Different sources mention variety of geographical and historical roots: in Europe in the south of France, or Italy, or Spain; in the Far East, or in Egypt. Tarot richness derives from the fact of it encompassing the elements in common with so many different cultures and ethnic groups.

There does not seem to be a straight or direct line of its descent from any particular area. When exactly Tarot first appeared in its functioning form remains unknown too, even if it is understandable that it is unlikely for Tarot in its current format to manifest its presence before the invention of the printing press. The imaginary point of the birth of Tarot does not seem to have a fixed position in the space-time system of coordinates. The migration of nations throughout history could have easily caused a migration of ideas, but these ideas happened to survive amidst their movement along the globe.

It seems that on several occasions during the history of humankind one or another civilization gave birth to Tarot; hence such discrepancy in opinions of where and when Tarot originated. This chapter will go through some of the cultural memory traces left in history by the ancient Hermetic tradition and revived during the Renaissance (Yates, 1964, Faivre, 1994; 1995). The messages encoded in the format of pictures were made more accessible to the public in an age when writing was a restricted act. Even if a singular linear descent is problematic, there remains some factual evidence regarding the origins of Tarot, as a produced *deck* in the form of the seventeen exquisitely painted cards, which are now located in the Bibliotheque Nationale in Paris and dating back to 1392, as has been documented in the French Court ledger. A current collection in Pierpont Morgan Library in New York comprises thirty five pictures from the full deck of the seventy eight, whose origin is believed to go back to around middle of fifteenth century.

As a system of universal Gnostic knowledge, Tarot may be as old as the world or as young as the world; different civilizations, through generations, may have used various means, pictorial or otherwise, for encoding the same ancient, universal knowledge. Quite likely Tarot went through its own rebirth several times during its existence. The *ideas* inscribed in Tarot Arcana might have been circulating through-out the world since earlier times and may have only surfaced and attracted attention at the time of the Renaissance and the revival of Gnosticism.

The Egyptian-born Plotinus reconstructed ancient Greek metaphysics by in-corporating elements of the Hermetic tradition, thereby founding the system that was in modern times called Neoplatonism as a synthesis of Plato's ideas with other philosophical systems including pagan beliefs as well as the mystical teachings of Judaism, Christianity and Islam. Plato himself was viewed by Neoplatonists as a transmitter of the earlier ideas of Pythagoras who, while remembered mainly as mathematician, was considered in ancient Greece to be a human incarnation of the god Apollo and sharing his divine powers.

Plato's *Republic* tells a story of prisoners living in illusion among the shadows on the walls of the infamous cave while remaining unaware of the bright light produced by the sun as the metaphor for true, real, knowledge. The soul's quest to unite with what is missing parallels a hero's journey away from the cave towards the sun, to which he is drawn by his love for light, for wisdom. This knowledge of the real is to be shared with those who are still chained to the walls; and this is the most challenging part of Plato's story. We will see in chapter 4 that many images of the Major Arcana in the deck relate to celestial images, culminating in the Arcanum called The Sun indeed.

In Plato's *Symposium,* he elaborated on the erotic desire for the good and the beautiful as the highest aspiration of the soul's quest. For Plotinus, the soul's memories could be either in words or in images, and the feminine principle of the World Soul or *Psyche* is accompanied by a masculine one, *Nous,* as the World Intelligence. Still, they are but aspects of the ultimate unity, the One.

Frances Yates notices that the "great forward movements of the Renaissance… derive their vigour…from looking backwards" (Yates, 1964, p. 1) to the Hermetic tradition and the harmonious, peaceful and prosperous Golden Age presided over by the virgin goddess *Astraea* and filled with Justice as the guiding archetype. The passing of the Golden Age is characterized by modern over-rationalization following the mythical death of the god Pan, or rational Apollo taking over nature-bound Dionysus. As a form of thought, which transforms beliefs into inner knowledge, or Gnosis, the Hermetic tradition survived many centuries into the Christian era. Revived by Marsilo Ficino, Pico della Mirandelo and Giordano Bruno, it informed the Renaissance, since then being manifested in a plurality of forms, including the pictorial representation of this knowledge in the symbols of Tarot.

Ficino, who believed in the Egyptian roots of Hermes, has translated the *Corpus Hermeticus* into Latin. Giordano Bruno took the Egyptian revival even further: for him, the mind works solely through archetypal images that are reflecting the universe in the human mind. In the middle of fifteenth century the Jewish Kabbalah "penetrated Christian milieus and celebrated surprising nuptials with …Hermeticism" (Faivre, 1994, p. 7). The Kabbalistic Tree of Life is a metaphor for consciousness when the supreme unity, the One, not unlike in Plotinus' scheme of things, incorporates both masculine and feminine principles as intelligence and wisdom.

Russian philosopher and professor of law Valentin Tomberg, the author of the "magisterial work" (Faivre, 1994, p. 98) devoted to the meditations on the twenty-two Major Arcana of Tarot in the light of Christian Mysticism (published as Anonymous, 2002), cites sources as diverse as Plato and St. John of the Cross, Jewish *Zohar* and Christian St. Paul, Bergson and Ouspensky, Dionysus and Leibniz, St. Augustine and Teihard de Chardin, as representatives of the ancient mystical, Hermetic, form of thought.

In his Afterword to the latest edition of Tomberg's opus, the late Vatican Cardinal Hans Urs von Balthasar considered the twenty-two images of Major Arcana to be the expressions of the all-embracing wisdom of the Catholic Mystery, while tracing its history back to the revival of Greek, Arabic, and Jewish philosophies during the Renaissance, followed by the accommodation of Hermetic and Kabbalistic teachings into Biblical and Christian thought.

While Tomberg related Tarot Arcana to Jungian archetypes, von Balthasar pointed out, as Jung also did, the *objective* character of the psyche in terms of the "principles of the objective cosmos" (in Anonymous, 2002, p. 661) akin to Biblical "powers". Von Balthasar emphasized the certainty provided by Tarot symbolism with regard to "the depth of existence [where] there is an interrelationship between all things by way of analogy" (in Anonymous, 2002, p. 663). He referred to the conception of the world by woman-mystic Saint Hildergard of Bingen, for whom "the cosmic powers...are incorporated in the great Cristocentric drama between creation and redemption" (p. 665). Pointing out that during the Renaissance Hermes Trismegistus was celebrated as the father of the wisdom of the Greeks, von Balthasar also brought into the conversation Martin Buber's modern transposition of Jewish Hasidism, which was deeply influenced by the oral tradition of Kabbalah dating back to the time of Moses.

Non-incidentally, Buber's famous *I-Thou* relation was instrumental in Nel Noddings developing her ethical theory in the area of educational philosophy - an ethics of care (Noddings, 1984). Commenting on the importance of addressing philosophical and theological questions of immortality, pre-existence and life after death in the educational context, Noddings reminds us that "Eastern European [Hasidic] Jews believed that every soul exists from creation and that memory of this existence is wiped out by a slap just before birth" (1993a, p. 84) so that a human soul has this implicit desire to reconnect, to return to its eternal "home" just like in the mythical story of Eros and Psyche that we referred to in the preceding chapter 2.

Still the task remains to create a *good* life here on earth, in the here-and-now of our ordinary human existence, and to put love and compassion to a good end. Jim Garrison, an educational philosopher, emphasizes the human desire "to possess what is good [and] to live a life of ever-expanding meaning and value" (Garrison, 1997, p. 1). All subsequent chapters in this book are devoted to elucidating the means for living such a life, all its messiness and frailty notwithstanding, when it becomes enriched with the symbolism of Tarot that serves the function of the re-symbolization of our very selves. It is not only that Psyche eventually succeeds in her *ascent* upward to Olympus. James Hillman reversed the direction, imagining a divine soul's *descent* "downward toward human affairs. This is the Tree of the Kabbalah in the Jewish and also Christian mystical tradition" (Hillman, 1997, p. 43).

Hillman points out that in the main Kabbalistic text, the *Zohar*, the descent is portrayed as tough and the soul appears to be "reluctant to come down and get messed in the world" (Hillman, 1997, p. 43). The branches on the Kabbalistic Tree of Life represent the gradual descent of the soul in accordance with the creation

CHAPTER 3

myths of both biblical and Platonic thoughts. In the Bible, God spends six days till the concrete is created from the abstract in its progressing "downward from the transcendent to the teeming here of immanence" (Hillman, 1997, p. 44). We will see in many of the subsequent chapters, and especially in chapter 6, how Tarot hermeneutic indeed overcomes the immanence-transcendence split, as well as other dichotomies of modern discourse.

In the *Republic,* Plato tells the Myth of Er, in which the soul is attracted by her "lot", her place in the overall cosmic order of things so as to eventually become able to recognize her true calling, or what she, an individual human soul, is meant to be in the realm of human affairs. Love is the name for the desire and pursuit of wholeness. We will see in chapter 4 that it is the image of Judgement in the Tarot Major Arcana which is a symbolic representation for the true calling when a soul is resurrected to life. For Hillman, it is human soul that "selects the image I live" (1997, p. 45), and each image is what Plato called a *paradeigma* or pattern.

When we "look upon" the patterns created by the Tarot pictures, we enter what Noddings and Shore (1984) call *an intuitive mode* of perception. Etymologically, intuition is derived from the Latin verb *intueri*, which means *to look upon*. In the Middle Ages, the word *intuition* was used "to describe an ineffable mystical experience of identification with God" (Noddings and Shore, 1984, p. 11). Tarot hermeneutic is a process of reading and interpreting these implicit patterns embodied in the images of the Arcana and as yet concealed by the unconscious; the readings that encompass an intuitive mode of perception reveal them; making them explicit and integrated in consciousness.

An appealing hypothesis about the origins of Tarot in its present form is that it served a means of keeping and protecting esoteric knowledge which was considered a heresy in the eyes of the medieval Church. Any deviant groups such as Cathars or Jewish Mystics were persecuted to the point of near eradication. As a matter of fact, Jews running away from the Spanish Inquisition were welcomed in the Cathars' communities. As Guirdham (1993) points out, the Cathars' degree of tolerance was unusually high in the Middle Ages. Elsewhere in Europe Jews stayed in ghettos and remained there well into the twentieth century in many countries. In France – specifically in the city called Languedoc – they were not only well tolerated but even achieved positions of eminence and social recognition. Guirdham suggests that such an atmosphere of tolerance and sophistication provided a supportive environment for the implantation of alternative belief systems, combining elements of both mysticism and practical applications.

Perhaps the fact that Tarot surfaced in Europe among French heretics, a politically incorrect population who provided asylum to the persecuted Jews, may be considered as a possible key to open the doors to the Tarot origins. History appears to having repeated itself, backtracking to times when Jews were running away from the Egyptian pharaohs, perhaps carrying with them even then their ancient knowledge, in an attempt to save and preserve it.

Languedoc was a place in the south of France where Tarot cards surfaced and where the Kabbalists and Cathars had founded the centers of development that, as Gad (1994) notices, had also become the traditional gathering place for Gypsies.

The philosophical school of Cathars, the Kabbalists, and the Gypsies' (of Egyptian descent) fortune-tellers thus gathered in the same place at around the same time, and it is possible that the survival of the alternative mystical beliefs encoded in the cards' pictorial symbolism could have been safeguarded by their appearing in the guise of traditional fortune-telling by the Gypsies.

It should be noted, however, that eminent British historian and philosopher of language Michael Dummett, in the course of his research, has found "virtually no evidence for Gypsies telling fortunes with Tarot cards, or indeed with playing cards of any kind, from before the twentieth century" (Dummett, 1980, p. 144). Dummett presents Tarot as belonging to a family of card games, integral to specific cultures. Tarot images survived through the ages and, although their exact origins continue to be debated, appear to have been in existence in their modern form, according to Dummett (1980, p. 20), since the fourteenth century.

It was in 1781 when French author Court de Gébelin introduced his ideas of the Egyptian origins of Tarot as grounded in the teaching of the sage Hermes Trismegistus who is said to have lived before, or alongside, the time of Moses. De Gébelin's nine-volume encyclopaedia was called *Primitive World* (*Le Monde Primitif*) and devoted to the Golden Age of ancient civilization when people were united by one language and one religion. Indeed, as the Biblical account of Genesis (11:1) tells us, once upon a time the whole earth was of one language and of one speech, united by the same understanding of the nature of the universe.

Later, Arthur Edward Waite, whose 1910s Tarot deck, designed by the artist Pamela Colman Smith, I used for my empirical case studies (Chapter 8), will have referred to this belief system as an example of perennial philosophy. Pamela Colman Smith's creative work was inspired by her acquaintance with William Butler Yeats, an Irish poet and mystic, a proponent of Celtic Christianity and the unity of culture as "the goal of religious reconciliation" (Hederman, 2003, p. 64). There exists a correlation between the Tarots, whether or not wearing the mask of fortune telling, and the Jewish mystical tradition, Kabbalah.

In the nineteenth century, the French scholar Eliphas Levi who was influenced by de Gébelin's beliefs, has uncovered such a connection even if it may appear to be insufficiently supported: Dummett points to the "lack in precision of intellectual substance" (1980, p. 115) in Levi's work on occult phenomena, up to the point of his even submitting to a "climax of fantasy" (Dummett, 1980, p. 119). It was Levi who first developed the correspondence between the twenty-two images of Major Arcana and the twenty-two letters of Hebrew alphabet. The meanings of the cards *per se* were said to have been decoded in a systematic manner in 1889 by a French physician known as Papus who, by describing the meaning of each picture, has aligned Tarot symbolism with its keywords.

Tarot has been linked to *I Ching* – the Chinese Book of Changes – to Indian Tantra, to Jewish Torah. It has been noted (Blank, 1991), that the Rider-Waite deck includes the word "Tora" (even if the correct spelling should be Torah) as it appears on two major cards. In chapter 4 we will see that the imagery of The High Priestess depicts her holding an enfolded scroll on which "Tora" is written, indicating sacred and secret knowledge that needs to be *unfolded* in order to be perceived.

The imagery of the Wheel of Fortune indicates a circle that has neither beginning nor end, but represents eternal spinning; and Latin for wheel is ROTA, an anagram of Tarot. The letters T, A, O and R inscribed in the picture can be combined into either Tora or Tarot and permutated indefinitely between the both.

The Russian-born Peotr Ouspensky, a mathematics student in Moscow University who went on to become a journalist, was the follower of Gurdjieff's spiritual teachings. Ouspensky (2008) thought that all allusions to the Hebrew letters simply further obscure the significance of Tarot, which he posited primarily as a metaphysical system indicating the three-folded relation between a human soul, the physical or phenomenal world, and the world of ideas or the noumenal, divine or spiritual, world. Ouspensky pointed out that Tarot symbolism cannot be learned in the same way as one learns to build bridges or speak a foreign language: the interpretation of symbols requires the power of creative thought and a developed imagination.

It is true that in order to practice Tarot hermeneutic one has to first of all see *through* the images; that is, to experience their symbolism in the course of real life; to learn their symbolic lessons and feel their effects on one's own skin, so to speak. Still, Tarot "speaks" a language of sorts, a language of symbols; and it is my intent and purpose to make this language understood by the time you will have finished reading this book. While Gnosis is indeed "a type of experiential transformative knowledge that does not include book learning" (Place, 2005, p. 45), the particular path paved by Tarot hermeneutic will inadvertently lead us closer to Gnosis.

The interpretation of images, in dreams or in Tarot alike, exceeds the world of facts "known" by a solely "cognitive act [that] has 'grasped' it" (Jung, CW 11, 417). As enriched with imagination and intuition, interpretation, according to Jung, "reflects a higher level of intellect and, by not forcibly representing the unknowable as known, gives a more faithful picture of the real state of affairs" (Jung, CW 11, 417). The images and symbols, when interpreted, create "something that is…in the process of formation. If we reduce this by analysis to something that is generally known, we destroy the true value of the symbol; but to attribute hermeneutic significance to it is consistent with its value and meaning" (Jung, CW 7, 492).

In Richard Roberts' (1987) verbatim account of Tarot readings, that includes a reading for, and a dialogue with, Joseph Campbell, he suggests that it is rather pointless to construct hypotheses "about Tarot origins… because the ultimate importance of Tarot is that it is a symbolic system of *cosmic, moral,* and *natural* laws, each of which has the same underlying principle, *operating in all areas relevant to human endeavor,* and which ties together all three systems" (p. 7; italics in original). The very fact that Tarot is alive and well today confirms its resilience. For the purpose of my study it matters little who, where and when gave birth to Tarot pictures because the "essence of their importance for us is that a very real and transforming human emotion must have brought them to birth. It seems apparent that these old cards were conceived deep in the guts of human experience, at the most profound level of the human psyche. It is to this level in ourselves that they will speak" (Nichols, 1980, p. 5).

Still, the many correlations – symbolic, numerical and interpretive – between the different cultures, separated by time and space, indicate that Tarot as a metaphysical system may have had a common hypothetical origin, perhaps dating back to the famous Hermetic text, the *Emerald Tablet* (*Tabula Smaragdina*). It is there where the famous axiom "as above so below" first appears. For it is the second verse of Hermes' *Emerald Table* that proclaims the ancient formula of analogy or the doctrine of correspondences: *That which is above is like to that which is below and that which is below is like to that which is above, to accomplish the miracles of (the) one thing.*

Robert Place (2005), a Tarot scholar, lists six specific qualities that characterise the esoteric tradition in accordance with Antoine Faivre's (1994) original research. Faivre notices that the term "esoterism" conjures up the idea of secret – indeed, *arcane* – or hidden knowledge. We can "access understanding of a symbol...by a personal effort of progressive elucidation through several successive levels, i.e., by a form of hermeneutics" (Faivre, 1994, p. 5). In the chapters that follow, and especially in chapter 8, I will be using the hermeneutic method in order to take away the veil of secrecy pertaining to Tarot while retaining yet another meaning relative to esoterism, that of a type of knowledge "to be attained after transcending the... ways and techniques...that can lead to it" (Faivre, 1994, p. 5).

This type of knowledge is invaluable with regard to diverse educational contexts: as Gnosis, it is at once intellectual and spiritual, *integrative,* activity. As a process of knowing, Gnosis involves both "intuition and the certainty of possessing a method permitting access to such [deep, inner] knowledge" (Faivre, 1994, p. 19). In the Gnostic Gospel of Mary, she refers to Jesus' teaching as focusing on *nous,* on intelligence, because it is within the *nous* where the treasure of Gnostic knowledge lies. When Mary asks her Teacher whether it is through the soul (*psyche*) or thorough the spirit (*pneuma*) that we can meet with the divine, he answers that it is through the *nous* which is *between* the two. Thus true intelligence cannot be reduced to a rational understanding alone; it is our human experience that can bring a soul to life and enrich education with its spiritual dimension.

Antoine Faivre (1994) traces the Western esoteric tradition from its ancient and medieval sources to Christian theosophy up to the twentieth-century philosophers of science, physicists and university scholars described as "gnostics of Princeton and Pasadena" (1994, p. 280) and does refer to Tarot as one of the forms of esoteric knowledge. Faivre lists six fundamental elements of the esoteric form of thought (Faivre, 1994, p. 10–15), and Place presents six Hermetic qualities as specific for esoterism (Place, 2005, pp. 50–52). I will briefly address this belief system in the context of this study so as to structure the necessary background for the conceptual understanding of Tarot and its practical functioning as a method for acquiring Gnosis.

In what follows, I will summarize the important beliefs underlying the esoteric world view that in fact create a whole culture that would have embraced the esoteric tradition.

- The principle of interdependence, analogy, or correspondences between phenomena or, in other words, the *relational* world view. Yet many correspondences are unseen or "veiled" and require our subjective effort to discover them; to read and interpret them so that they begin making sense for us. In contemporary education, a relational approach most strongly manifests in the ethics of care (Noddings, 1984; 2002) as well as in the approach promoting the faculty of "the inner eye" as the means for cultivating intuition in education (Noddings and Shore, 1982). In chapter 2 we have seen that it is a correlation or interrelation between matter and psyche, body and mind, implicit in Tarot that manifests at the level of human experiences due to Jungian *synchronicity* as an unorthodox acausal connection; the principle of correspondence.

– The role of imagination and mediation in using symbols and images to discern their deeper meanings by means of connecting theory with practice, in other words, to actively discover the interrelations and correspondences in our practical experience. According to Henry Corbin, who was a professor of Islamic Studies at the Sorbonne in Paris prior to his death in 1978, there is an intermediate realm between micro- and macrocosm called *mesocosm* (the *Imaginal* world that we referred to in chapter 1). Corbin's spiritual theology combined the religions of Judaism, Christianity and Sufism as a manifestation of the analogical story about the relationship between the human and the divine, between the individual and God. Developing a creative or active imagination becomes a soul's inner means for achieving spiritual Gnosis which exceeds the factual knowledge obtained by modernity's "scientific method", leaving no room for imagination. In Jungian psychology, it is the method of active imagination and dream work that can reach the depths of the unconscious at the level of psyche or soul.

– The possibility of transmutation. This alchemical concept should be understood metaphorically. It describes not a magical transformation of basic matter in the form of metal like lead into "noble" gold, but human spiritual development that involves a whole person including her *psyche*. It is a soul-based process of Jungian individuation of the Self. The process of gradual transformation is inscribed in the archetypal journey through Tarot Arcana. Joseph Campbell, for example, equates the spiritual quest with a Hero's journey that transcends cultural differences and manifests in common myths created and told from generation to generation across diverse cultures and times.

– The practice of concordance or what, in contemporary discourse, we may call tolerance. And it is Gnosis that would allow us to see beyond the veil of religious, cultural, language and other differences and barriers. Because the deepest level of the unconscious is, according to Jung, shared by all members of humankind, we indeed can connect with each other and develop inter-communication and mutual understanding if we find the means for interpreting the archetypal symbolism through which the collective unconscious expresses itself in the form of typical patterns at the level of human experiences. It is the hermeneutic of Tarot that provides us with the opportunity of understanding this common, even if hypothetical, symbolic language, which is said to be spoken by Adam before the Fall.

– A specific pedagogy, which is irreducible to direct instruction. Esoteric tradition has its own means of transmitting Hermetic teachings. Therapeutic and counseling practices notwithstanding, contemporary moral education indirectly advocates some of the methods traditionally used by sages and mystics, such as initiation, facilitation, guidance, as well as inculcating virtues that result in creating values-based practices. Specifically, it is an experiential character as a feature of post-formal, cultural, pedagogy taking place outside formal settings that pertains to the bricolage of Tarot, which we addressed in the preceding chapter 2, and especially in terms of the existential function of identity-formation and meaning-making, in addition to the Jungian transcendent function. Non-incidentally, Noddings (2006) says that the field of education as a professional practice should employ teachers who have a broad knowledge not only of disciplines and "subject matters" but, like the Renaissance people, of perennial questions as well. Tarot functions both as the *method* and as the *knowledge* obtained by this very method; and the knowing of the Self is embodied in *praxis* and *theoria* at once. Gnosis aims not to a single scientific truth but to new values and meanings implicit in practical life with all its multiple contexts. Yet in chapter 10 we will see that a new science of complexity and self-organization is not opposed to mysticism or Hermeticism but forms with it one organic whole while simultaneously explaining – as science, sure enough, is supposed to do – the functioning of Tarot.

– The natural world is not reduced to "dead matter" but is alive, even if "hiero-glyphic", grounded in hidden interrelations. The symbols, full of implicit meanings, should be deciphered; the invisible relations and correspondences should be made visible; then it will be possible to "read" Nature as a book, to understand its multileveled complex structure. In chapter 2 we singled out Tarot as a tool whose function is indeed to make the invisible visible. The world's *quintessential* soul, *Anima Mundi*, is what holds together the four physical, material, elements, namely air, earth, fire and water; itself being a fifth, invisible, "element". In the next chapter, we will encounter the symbol for the world's soul in the imagery of the last Arcanum in the Tarot deck called The World, which is also a symbol for the Jungian archetype of the individuated Self.

I share von Balthasar's sentiments that expert training, serious moral responsibility and, not the least, a certain "sixth sense" – the developed intuition and creative imagination – should be absolute requirements for our meditations on, and the journey through, the Tarot symbols and images. The book that you are now reading has been written with keeping those requirements both in mind and in the heart; and the sentiments have been exercised through many events and encounters comprising my personal and professional life.

As recently noted by philosopher and abbot Mark Patrick Hederman in his remarkable book *Tarot: Talisman or Taboo? Reading the World as Symbol*, Tarot provides us with the system to fill the gaps produced by the area "where education and trained sensibility are in short supply" (2003, p. 86). Hederman is adamant that "each of us should be given at least the rudiments of one of the most elusive and important symbolic systems if we are even to begin to understand human relation-ships. This would require tapping into a wavelength and a communication system other than the cerebral, reaching what has been called the 'sympathetic system' as opposed to the cerebro-spinal one which covers the three Rs of traditional education" (Hederman, 2003, p. 87).

In the next chapter we will go through the symbolic process of human development, individuation, and re-symbolization of ourselves in terms of learning from archetypal experiences expressed in the imagery of Tarot Major Arcana.

CHAPTER 4

HUMAN EXPERIENCE AND TAROT SYMBOLISM

In front of me there are twenty-two pictures, the twenty-two Major Arcana of Tarot. The word *Arcana* derives from Latin *arca* as a chest; *arcere* as a verb means to shut or to close; symbolically, *Arcanum* (singular) is a tightly shut treasure chest holding a secret: its implicit meaning. In reference to Greek etymology, Arcana relate to *arce* that means origin or inception. Jung conceptualized the archetypes of the collective unconscious as primordial, *original*, images engraved in our psychic constitution; these archaic images may have inspired the artists who designed the Tarot pictures.

The pictures, following each other in a Tarot deck, resemble the illustrations to a fairy tale with its classical theme of a hero's (or a simpleton's) journey in his quest for a hidden treasure. The journey is usually full of challenges yet the hero learns from his very experiences; he becomes capable of overcoming obstacles, defeating adversaries or, more importantly, winning over his own complexes, anxieties, and fears personified in the variety of adversaries he meets along his symbolic journey; he becomes wiser and more resilient. For Jung, symbols express themselves via the "images of contents which…transcend consciousness. … [The] contents are real… they are agents with which it is not only possible but absolutely necessary for us to come to terms" (Jung, CW 5, 114).

Sallie Nichols (1980) in her book on Jung and Tarot commented on the correlations between Petrarch's sonnets and the Tarot Major Arcana, the images of which are sometimes called Trumps. Trumps means Triumphs, and in Petrarch's sonnets a series of allegorical characters each fought and triumphed over the weaker preceding one, each image symbolically winning over its own precursor by the characters becoming emotionally stronger, more resilient and more conscious after overcoming the challenges of emerging life cycle issues. Mystical allegories are usually based on the eternal motif of virtues "trumping" vices, eventually "triumphing" in reaching the mystical truth, symbolized by the Holy Grail. The same happens during the course of the Tarot archetypal journey where and when an individual Ego is given an opportunity to become the real Self, a whole person.

An isolated human soul as a fragmented spark of primordial Adam whose soul, according to the Jewish Kabbalah, embraced all the souls of humanity, has a chance to recollect with others within the soul of the world, *Anima Mundi,* thus to become whole, to be healed. As Nichols (1980) reminds us, the word "whole" is etymologically synonymous with "holy", and the original meaning of the word "to heal" was "to make whole". Jung thought that contemporary neuroses relate to humanity's lost capacity for holiness and the wholeness of spiritual traditions. Many Hasidic tales tell archetypal stories, in which a person has to go on a journey and carry necessary, even if seemingly insignificant, tasks that eventually contribute to rescuing the holy sparks held in captivity.

Laurens van der Post, Jung's biographer, who called him the greatest among the great, pointed out that to consider Jung's concept of the collective unconscious to be his main interest and his main contribution, is a misunderstanding. A far greater mystery for Jung remained the realm of human consciousness and its profound relationship with the universal unconscious as the connection between the individual psyche and the world. This connection expresses itself by means of the subtle language of the unconscious. This expressive language is different from, and appears to be alien to, the orderly ways we usually process information consciously. It draws from what Freud used to call the *archaic* means of communication prior to our logical reasoning that employs "grown-up" conscious thoughts expressed in verbal language.

The reductive meaning of consciousness as merely an intellectual and rational state of mind has been challenged by Jung. Identifying consciousness with just an ability of logical reasoning and rational thought is a simplified linear approach that goes back to the days of Descartes' motto, "I think, therefore I am". Here we are, sick and deprived of meaning (van der Post in Nichols, 1980); overwhelmed by the mental disorientation and alienation caused by the narrow boundaries of our ego-consciousness reduced to an isolated Cartesian *Cogito*. Yet, becoming conscious of our many unconscious issues helps; also "recognizing what we are doing, helps, and …our self-understanding can expand the realm of our choices and possibilities" (Viorst, 1992, p. 4).

In the due course of the archetypal journey through the array of the Tarot pictures, the life situations and the feelings associated with them are being externalized and provide an opportunity to literally look at them as if from the outside while they are spread on a table in one or other pictorial layout. The journey through Tarot images is practically a dynamic search for identity and the discovery of meaning and value in our lives via creative encounters with the unconscious in the process of individuation. Even if symbols constituting the journey may appear to be (as we said in chapter 3) of "obscure origin and significance [they remind us of] the set of pictures in the Tarot cards [that] were distantly descended from the archetypes of transformation" (Jung, CW 9i, 81, cited in Gad, 1994, p. 179).

So here they are, the twenty-two pictures of the Major Arcana (Fig. 4.1), the archetypal images of transformation. At the outset, I would to like to emphasize that the descriptions presented below are only *general*. In chapter 8 we will see how the same images situated in different contexts and pertaining to different people acquire specific connotations, thus combining universality with particularity. Another caveat is that even if the Arcana follow each other in a seemingly linear sequence, it does not mean that human development proceeds exactly through these *successive* stages, one after another. The specific layouts for the 15 participants, in chapter 8, will have demonstrated the archetypal constellations of both Major and Minor Arcana in a variety of unpredictable combinations.

Real lives are not fairy tales; individual circumstances and free will do play important roles. The archetypes do provide a ground for our spontaneous actions

Figure 4.1. Major Arcana.

but lifetime experiences accumulate and create recurrent habitual structures that sink into the collective unconscious, thus inadvertently further restructuring the archetypal bricolage. It becomes even more important to address the interplay of diverse factors, each of which will have added yet another layer to individual psycho-dynamics. Each image can be interpreted at a variety of levels: feelings, emotions, thoughts, actions, spiritual aspirations, etc. We will see in chapter 8 the powerful effects and *affects* produced by the archetypes in the psyche of this study's partici-pants and the frequent havoc they tend to wreak.

Tomberg (Anonymous, 2002) comments that the Major Arcana as authentic symbols must be presented to consciousness so as to "render us capable of making discoveries, engendering new ideas" (p. 4). Nearly each one of the pictures has an image of a living being, a human figure, printed on it. This figure is not just a physical body but mind, soul and spirit as well. And while a body goes through different life cycles and accomplishes different life tasks, a psyche too goes through transfor-mation, as life itself keeps its demands of constant renewal, enlargement and intensification of our consciousness.

The human figure travels from picture to picture, from one stage in life to another, from one life task to another. This journey is both learning and therapeutic, as each new experience heals the psyche in the process of individuation and self-realization. The traveler – the subject of the reading – carries a past that "with all of its glamorous wishes and terrors and passions, inhabits the present" (Viorst, 1992, p. 4), and shapes the future.

The first picture in the series, numbered zero, is called The Fool; that is where the archetypal journey starts. The human soul has just been born, it is innocent and open to suggestion. A lot of choices are ahead of this archetypal Wanderer; he perceives himself as being on top of the world. The Fool is driven into a world of new experiences and trusts that this world is here for him. At times, though, he may be too trustful and naive – the archetypal eternal child, *puer aeternus*, a symbol of new potential and unlimited possibilities in the "abyss of freedom" just a step away.

In the Tarot picture the Fool stands on top of the mountain, yet at the edge of the abyss. One wrong step and he may fall down. This step may be one of many choices in front of this Wanderer with his head high in the clouds. His self-reflective consciousness has not yet been developed and, according to Jung, the ego may be standing on a shaky ground. Yet, asked Jung, how "can one …attain wisdom without foolishness?" (Jung, CW 11, 953).

What if the Fool takes a risk and makes a step ahead? He will find himself in the abyss amidst novel, yet unknown experiences. Still, even if many unexpected life lessons appear to lie ahead among unlimited possibilities, the Fool will take a chance. He will be transformed into The Magician, Arcanum I, a symbol of practical wisdom and successful accomplishment of goals; equipped with many tools and capable of using them properly. While the Magician's right hand holding the wand points upwards, to the skies, his left hand is pointing to the earth as a symbol for *putting into practice* the Hermetic maxim, *as above so below*. The number I associated with this Arcanum is a prime number as indivisible unity and is related to *aleph* – the letter of Hebrew alphabet that means breath of life.

In the journey through subsequent experiences from Arcanum I to XXI, the Fool's very identity will be contested and will reappear in the guise of the names of other Major Arcana in the deck. For Jung, each archetype embodies both light and dark aspects as a bipolar pair of opposites. The qualities associated with the Magician are deep knowledge, insight, and vision. The Magician's "dark" side, however, is that of the Trickster, capricious, incomprehensible, and manipulative. The psychology of the Trickster reflects not knowledge but cleverness, not insight but wit, not vision but voyeurism. While the Magician's actions are wise and ethical, his counterpart the Trickster may coerce people into playing his games and performing his tricks.

The four tools on the Magician's table represent four suits in a Tarot deck: wands, pentacles, swords and cups. They symbolize the four Jungian functions, feeling, sensing, thinking and intuiting, used by the wise Magician in a holistic manner. They also symbolize the four elements available to the Magician in his alchemical laboratory: fire, earth, water and air, all the elements of nature brought together to serve the aim of enriching the physical world with a fifth, quintessential element or, in the Gnostic tradition, freeing a human spirit from the constraints and limitations of the material world. The Magician is a symbol for our guardian angel or the saint who can protect us in our real lives.

The next image is called The High Priestess. The Arcanum II is a symbol of female intuition and spiritual life. The High Priestess represents the "return of the Goddess" (Whitmont, 1984) as a feminine principle complementary to the essentially masculine instrumental rationality prevalent in the modern world. Her task is to unfold the scroll so as to reveal to the Fool the symbols of hidden and secret, Gnostic, knowledge. The High Priestess is a symbol for Sophia (in Greek philosophy) or Shekhinah (in Jewish mythology) representing Wisdom "written" in the scroll on her lap. Jung associated Wisdom with the Hebrew Chochma, one of the Sephirot on the Kabbalistic Tree of Life. The Tree is a symbol of the divine descending into our human, material world. It is the High Priestess who can eventually unfold the scroll she holds in order to reveal to the Fool the secrets of Gnostic knowledge lost in the scientific (read: overly masculine) rationality, thus to unite the human with the divine.

Sophia is a concept equally important for Hellenistic philosophy and religion, for Platonism and Gnosticism, as well as for Orthodox Christianity and Christian mysticism. In the Hebrew Bible Wisdom/Sophia is personified in the Proverbs (8:22–31). The principle of Wisdom was considered by medieval alchemists to be identical with the Holy Spirit. It is the union of God with his beloved, Shekhinah, or the union of Logos with Sophia that produces the sought-after union of *coincidentia oppositorum* manifested in the ultimate Jungian archetype of the Self.

The High Priestess signifies the invisible and secret knowledge as opposed to the sensible and empirical; yet she can potentially express herself, thus making the invisible present. This is the very prerogative of Tarot hermeneutic as we said earlier: to translate the invisible into visible. The lost speech may manifest itself in the unconscious contents such as the slip of the tongue in Freudian psychoanalysis, in dreams, or in Jungian word associations. In the image of The High Priestess, the Fool is now accompanied by the archetypal Kore, a maiden that "as the daughter of the Great Earth Mother, ...is connected to the bounty of the Self and is the [potential] agent of the soul's fulfillment" (Hopcke, 1992, p. 111).

The archetype of the Great Mother is represented by Arcanum III, The Empress who can teach the Fool a lesson of healing with her abundance of feelings and the ability to give love and always understand her children unconditionally. In the Kabbalistic Tree of Life it is a Sephirah called Binah, translated as *understanding*; and that at a deeper level means Mother of the world. Binah is the place in which the Tree of Life has its roots: it is creation enabled by the eternal Mother. In the reading, The Empress often indicates pregnancy.

The word *sephir* as the root for Sephirah (singular) and Sephirot (plural) can be translated as letter or number; yet its underlying idea is information or pattern – analogous to Jungian archetypal patterns embedded in the collective unconscious. Jung, addressing the aspects of the feminine, stated that women's psychology is grounded in the principle of *Eros*, as the great binder, while from the ancient times the ruling masculine principle has been *Logos*. The concept of Eros expresses itself as psychic relatedness; and Logos – as objective detached rationality. In the image of The Empress the Fool can learn the lesson of Love, so as to become capable of intimacy and relatedness. Yet, the dark, chthonic aspect of the Mother archetype may manifest in real life as being excessively overprotective or vice versa, too demanding for the Fool who, at the psychological level, may as a result demonstrate arrested development, lack of confidence, and the tendency to regress to the developmentally preceding archetype of the immature Ego.

Here comes The Emperor, Arcanum IV, the omniscient and powerful Father archetype, a symbolic guide of the superego that the Fool needs right now. The Fool stops being a victim of his own weak ego; he exercises the Logos principle, he is learning to assert himself, sometimes even to the point of aggression, as power or control issues may become dominant in his psyche. Confusion between sex roles may take place as the Emperor and the Empress may be manifestations of the archetypes of anima and animus, two sub-personalities that, according to Jung, exist at the level of the unconscious. Etymologically, anima and animus have their origin in Latin as the words designating "soul" and "spirit" respectively; still they can manifest in our actual lives by the modes of perception and behavior represented by the figures of the opposite sex in each individual psychic template.

As the actualized archetypes, The Empress and The Emperor function as the dominant character traits; but the unconscious anima and animus may demonstrate an inferior, in Jung's classification, psychological function. For Jung, thinking and feeling are Judging functions; while sensing and intuition are Perceiving functions; all four functions – if the psyche is unbalanced – classified as the "dominant", "auxiliary", "tertiary" and "inferior", with the inferior function being the least developed and the deepest in the unconscious. Certain psychopathology may surface for individuals affected by those two archetypes. In the case of being "anima/animus ridden" (Hopcke, 1992, p. 91) men may become moody and hysterical as if demonstrating a negative stereotype for women, and women "possessed" by the archetype of animus may display the male's stereotypical hunger for power.

At this level the archetypal figures turn into social roles; the innocent Fool, while traveling, has lost his spirit; he put on a mask and has become what Jung called a Persona. Was it part of his defense mechanism? Or perhaps he felt like wearing a mask when living in a conservative world of orthodox beliefs, strict requirements and traditional schooling, represented by Arcanum V, The Hierophant. The term *persona* derives from the Latin for "mask" or "false face", and Jung considered Persona to be the archetype of conformity.

To adjust to societal standards the Fool must learn a lesson of conformity and to follow traditions of those who make rules in the establishment. The Hierophant, or The Pope as a masculine counterpart to The High Priestess, is a symbol of law and order, establishment, and fundamentalism. Psychologically, the personality behind Persona may be of an obsessive-compulsive type, intolerant or passive-aggressive, and in the captivity of one's own ideas. A socially adapted mask may become over-used to the extent of becoming a second face, to the total detriment of personality, to the neglect of inner life. Jung called this process persona identification and considered it to be a frequent cause of psychological disorders. At the deeper level, the soul put on a mask as well and became the False Self. To win over his False Self, the Fool must continue on his way of accomplishing new life-tasks and learning more experiential lessons.

The imagery of The Lovers, Arcanum VI, represents temptation and duality, a time for choice. Even if the Fool may be guided by the Jungian archetype of the union as the ultimate mystical conjunction of opposites existing in perpetual tension, this tension persists in the image of The Lovers. Standing at the crossroads, the Fool has to make a choice so as to adequately meet The Lovers even if he may be facing a moral dilemma. In the story of Eden, the knowledge of good and evil – that is, our capacity for ethical decision-making – is symbolically related to the Tree of Knowledge, with the verb "to know" having sexual, erotic, overtones. For Jung, "Eros is a questionable fellow [who] belongs on one side to man's primordial animal nature [and] [o]n the other side...is related to the highest forms of the spirit. But he only thrives when spirit and instinct are in right harmony" (Jung, CW 7, 32). The Lovers indicate that the Fool is likely to make a right choice, a "good" decision; especially when symbolically carried forward by The Chariot, Arcanum VII.

The Fool started his journey like a "magical child" (Pearce, 1977) but is now being transformed into the Jungian archetype of the Hero. Commenting on the symbolism of The Chariot in the context of Jung's process of individuation, Tomberg (Anonymous, 2002) related this image to the phenomenon of ego-inflation or "the epiphany of the hero" (Jung and Kerenyi, 1951, p. 137). This is the negative, dark, aspect of the archetype of the Hero, analogous to the negative aspect of The Magician as the Trickster. It is only in the actual practical context of the hermeneutic process embedded in Tarot readings that we can distinguish between the light and dark aspects of the archetypes, as will be demonstrated in chapter 8.

For the charioteer, it isn't easy to control his instinctual nature or to differentiate between fantasy and reality represented by the two horses, but the Hero-Fool is learning to apply his volition to balance the constant tension of opposites and thus triumphs trough self-discipline. The Chariot carries our Fool out of the constricted environment, out of inhibitions. The Chariot is a symbol of controlling one's emotions and "correcting" one's present course of action, by means of keeping the two horses, as the forces of creative and destructive psychic energy, in balance. A Greek myth tells the story of souls that, in their disembodied state, have chariots, and a charioteer must gain control of the unruly horses in a pair (an appetitive versus spirited element), as indeed portrayed in The Chariot picture.

Mastering the unconscious part of oneself is equivalent to acquiring inner Strength, symbolized by Arcanum VIII. With the newly found strength the Fool is able to also acquire interpersonal skills, even if he may need some professional counseling help as often happens when Strength appears in a particular layout of Tarot pictures for an individual. The Hero can now tame any beast that distracts him from learning what his real strengths, values, skills and limitations can be. For Jung, lion is a "fiery" animal that symbolizes being "swallowed by the unconscious" (CW 12, 277). In this Tarot picture the female figure is portrayed as mastering the lion with her bare hands. According to Abraham Maslow, without accepting oneself one can not accept others: the Strength image is the symbol for self-acceptance that highly developed individuals can possess.

Winning over the fiery lion in oneself, The Fool is ready to meet The Hermit, Arcanum IX. That's where – at the beginning of the "mid-life" cycle of the Jungian individuation process – examination and self-reflection produce an examined vs. unexamined (read: lacking meaning) life! That is, authentic experiences reach their critical mass when the Fool has to symbolically stop so as to reflect back on them, to reflect on oneself: the lantern in the picture symbolizes this search, via inward knowledge, for the authentic Self. It is the Hermit who can teach the Fool the ancient "Know Thyself" principle.

The Hermit is a symbol for solitude and withdrawal, as part of every mystical training, and observing a period of isolation and silence. The lesson of "knowing thyself' is, importantly, self-reflection but not in the form of subjective inward introspection. In solitude, one becomes closer to Nature and has a chance to feel the harmony with Nature as the universal intelligence *(Nous)*. The Fool is ready for meditation, temporary stopover and solitude in order to learn to reflect on his experiences so far. He is learning the lesson of integration. He is presented with "evocative challenge...concerned with inward resolution and outward relatedness" (Hopche, 1992, p. 126). It is a deep spiritual meaning that from now on will guide the Hero along the road to individuation; and he who seeks shall find. The Hermit represents the Jungian archetype of the Wise Old Man related to the figure of the ghost, Philemon, who appeared often in Jung's dreams and who dictated to him "The Seven Sermons to the Dead".

Self-search is an infinite process; many pictures include a symbol for infinity; and the Fool is still quite a dilettante regarding such qualities as insight, intuition, or self-knowledge as the lesson of the Hermit. The Hermit's lantern illuminates and brings into consciousness the seeds of Gnostic knowledge available now for the Fool. The Wheel of Fortune, Arcanum X, starts to turn, indeed, as the Hero-Fool has reached a turning point. The movement of the wheel is not brought about by force. The wheel is turning effortlessly, so that the old is discarded, giving room to the new.

The turning point can occur during any life cycle; in fact it determines the very existence of any current cycle. As the wheel turns, the archetypal Hero acquires a sense of self accompanied by a possible change in luck. It is karmic laws – luck or fortune – that now accompany the Hero on his journey. His own actions, though, may help or hinder the turning of the wheel, and the Hero needs both luck and perseverance to maintain his integrity and self-awareness, otherwise a current life cycle may turn into a vicious circle and the Hero's victory into defeat.

Perhaps it is time for the retribution of karma or, alternatively, for distributive justice, represented by Arcanum XI, Justice. It is necessary to maintain a balance and to weigh up and give a fair and balanced evaluation to experiences. The image of the blindfolded female figure holding the scales, carries the message that she knows justice not by means of logical reasoning, but with her heart. She is putting into practice the Jungian function of feeling, leading to a wise decision based on precise value-judgement in the context of a particular situation. Justice will be done according to individual integrity, and there are fair consequences for human actions.

Jung used to say that a person should live according to his own nature and concentrate on self-knowledge. Then he should live in accordance with this truth about oneself. Jung asked a sacramental question: what would one say about a tiger who was a vegetarian? The correct answer is that he was a bad tiger. The conclusion is that everyone must live in harmony with his or her nature. Our Hero may now need to work on the issues of fairness. He is longing for harmony and balance. The lesson of Justice is to learn to apply both intellectual eyesight and spiritual insight, combined harmoniously, so as to achieve the state of psychological balance. It is not that Justice rules blindly in accord with the universal moral law. For Jung, "morality was not brought down on tables of stones from Sinai and imposed on people, but is a function of the human soul, as old as humanity itself" (Jung, CW 7, 30).

The most difficult task of course remains becoming aware of one's soul-function, hence become conscious of what one is meant to be. At some point it might be necessary to face a sacrifice; perhaps something is counterproductive to the journey ahead; such is the lesson of The Hanged Man, Arcanum XII, with its imagery of the figure as if suspended between the sky and the ground without a solid foundation under his feet. The battles and obstacles represented by many life-tasks may have exhausted the archetypal Wanderer. This is a testing period accompanied by the feeling of the loss of direction.

The Hanged Man presents a challenge of a helpless moment that we face now and then in certain life cycles. Perhaps a change in priorities will teach the Hero that it is worth letting go of old concepts, and a new level of awareness will be his reward upon completion of this transitory period. Russian movie director Andrey Tarkovsky made a film called *The Sacrifice* which happened to be his last; he died shortly after, in 1986. The idea was to present a character that is capable of sacrificing himself and his habitual way of life.

Tarkovsky affirmed that it is out of sacrifice that harmony is born. For Tarkovsky, this phenomenon exists "regardless of whether that sacrifice is made in the name of spiritual values, or for the sake of someone else, or of his own salvation, or of all these things together. Such behavior precludes, by its very nature, all of those selfish interests that make up a 'normal' rationale for action; it refutes the laws of a materialistic world view... And yet...the man who acts in that way brings about fundamental changes" (Tarkovsky, 1989, p. 217). Jung would have agreed: "A great reversal of standpoint, calling for much sacrifice, is needed before we can see the world as 'given' by the very nature of the psyche" (Jung, CW, 11, 841). Jung pointed out that many initiation rites often include a figurative death as a symbol for the reversal of values so as "to restore to the soul the divinity it lost at birth" (Jung, CW 11, 842).

Indeed Arcanum XIII that directly follows The Hanged Man is called Death, with its symbolism of transition and passage, but also change and renewal. As noted by Christine Downing, "Eros-love is transformative [for the psyche] and all serious transformations involve death" (2005, p. 202; brackets mine). Old and restrictive viewpoints, a stagnant environment, whatever was *status quo* for the Hero are now in the process of evolution and transformation. He must leave his old self behind, and the dynamics of this process may be quite painful.

Rollo May (1991) was certain that it is the whole history of humankind that teaches us that only by going through hell does one have any chance of reaching heaven. This trump carries an idea of pain and suffering, and exploring its meaning in a reading brings to consciousness the world of suffering through emotions, feelings, and affects. In is in Death that one's present self encounters a confrontation with one's own potential, fully integrated, Self. Still, undergoing the death of a previous state of mind brings awareness of success. The Hero is close to the realization of the existential meaning of life because many lessons have been learned and during the course of his archetypal journey he suffered a great deal.

But do not rush, advises Arcanum XIV, Temperance; there is the danger of the ego being fragmented; control your ego. The maxim that said "Nothing in excess" as the virtue of Temperance was as much celebrated in the Hellenic world as the "Know Thyself" principle; both were inscribed on the Temple of Apollo at Delphi. This picture is the image of moderation as the Hero needs to collect his thoughts and to consciously put together the jigsaw puzzle pieces of his experiences. Temperance is also one of seven virtues that in Medieval and Renaissance Christianity "were presented as a model of spiritual excellence: temperance, strength, justice, prudence, faith, hope and charity" (Place, 2005, p. 19). We have earlier encountered Strength and Justice through the Fool's archetypal journey. However, as the Hero's soul expands to accommodate new qualities, as his consciousness grows, the challenge of the task of the personal Ego transcending toward the Self can usurp power from the Hero.

He now feels enslaved by a symbolic image of The Devil, Arcanum XV, as the Jungian archetype of the Shadow, the fallen angel, a symbol of evil as "darkened matter." The Devil's world is the world of ignorance: bad things happen to good people because people know not what they do! Self-destructive tendencies may pull one back as if distracting the soul from its original purpose. What is holding the Hero in bondage? How to overcome the fear of one's own future Self? Rollo May noticed that his patients often, towards the end, were frightened by the possibility of making a decision about whether to take chances by completing the quest they have begun in therapy. The conscious brightness of ego-centeredness always casts its own shadow that consists of impulses, complexes, shameful desires, denials, self-indulgence, or being a slave to one's own primitive instincts.

The chains in the picture are symbolic of sexual compulsion, poor impulse control or low frustration tolerance. It may be a fear, a superficial complex of superiority when in fact one feels inferior. In the context of interpersonal relationships The Devil may point onto co-dependency issues. Intra-psychically it may be a deeply ingrained fear of breaking loose, like battered spouses afraid to leave and who, overwhelmed by submissiveness or sexual/economic dependency, continue to stay in an abusive relationship. As an archetypal figure, the Shadow calls for a deep exploration so that its psychosocial presence and poisonous quality is recognized and integrated into consciousness. Otherwise it may fall deeper and deeper into the unconscious where it will continue to work even if repressed or denied to oneself. Here is a poem written by my older son, then in his teens, and published in the volume *Journey to the Point, Poetry by Young Australians*, 1994.

THE NIGHT

It's this intoxicating night
Whose foreign smell and melting light
And steaming sounds at every pore
Entice me to the devil's door

The beating heart sweet poison craves
As groaning muscles in their graves
Are roused, and ancient flesh is thawed
By tongues of fire that long ignored

The taste of wine, the candle's flame
A glimpse of skin, the naked shame
Of heaving beasts! A sleeping snake
In darkness strikes! Alive! Awake!

The hiss of death, the kiss of birth
Both writhe entwined beneath the earth
That promised cooling midnight rain
But brings forth deadly weeds, again

Again, the first bleak rays of dawn
Will open weary wounds to scorn
And mock the bloody, sweat-drenched fight
In this intoxicating night

Rollo May recalls the movie *Platoon* as communicating messages that speak both to our conscious mind and the unconscious. The movie turns into "a soul-shaking narration in which 'we are not fighting the enemy but fighting ourselves', as one of the characters in *Platoon* remarks near the end... The film...presents what

CHAPTER 4

Jung would call the 'shadow' and I have called in *Love and Will* the 'daimonic'" (May, 1991, p. 27). The Shadow-projection is one of the most powerful symptoms, when we may attribute to others those undesirable qualities that we may be tempted to deny in ourselves.

The awareness of the collective Shadow is equally necessary, and we will address it in chapter 9 in the context of Tarot cultural pedagogy. How to overcome the daimonic fear of the unknown that may accompany the process of individuation? Recognition of any bondage is required for the Hero to go forward and to continue his search for meaning and identity. Who knows what evil lurks in the hearts of men? The Shadow knows! The Devil is one of the most powerful symbols in the Tarot deck and a detailed exploration of its connotations, if this card comes up in a reading, will in turn empower the person! The Hero will break the chains of old habits and he will understand those aspects of himself that kept him in a self-destructive pattern.

Yes, the realization comes forward, but because it is not so easy to break out of the Devil's chains, it may come in the form of a shock. The Tower, the next Arcanum XVI, breaks everything in the Hero's life that is counterproductive for the journey ahead. At the level of the mind, overthrowing of false consciousness takes place, sometimes as a catharsis. A rapid, and painful, intensification of consciousness is transmitted by the symbolism of this picture: it is the lightning that hits the ivory tower one imprisoned oneself in! It might be a moment of sudden truth shaking basic security – perhaps it was a false security – but providing illumination, a light of awakening, represented by The Star, Arcanum XVII.

The naked woman pouring waters is in the midst of organic growth, surrounded by all four elements of nature that appear together for the first time in this Arcanum in their real and not symbolic form, like in the image of The Magician. The soul is being purified by the stream of the unconscious washing away the remnants of "dark matter", the explosion of which manifested itself to the maximum in the imagery of the preceding Arcanum, The Tower. The Star of hope and healing is now accompanying the Hero in his journey. It inspires the Hero to focus his energy on realizing his talents and fulfilling his dreams. For Jung, just "as evening gives birth to morning, so from the darkness arises a new light, the *stella matutina*" (Jung, CW 13, 299), rising up from the ruins of The Tower that precedes it.

The lights from the stars in the sky reflect actualized archetypes encountered during the Fool's journey that "have about them a certain effulgence or quasi-consciousness, and…numinosity entails luminosity" (Jung, CW 8, 388). The symbolism of The Star conveys an intensified consciousness enabled by purification and spiritual baptism. The light emitted by the Star is healing as it comes from the astral plane of higher consciousness; it empowers the Hero with a feeling of confidence, and his self-esteem grows as he comes to the realization of his talents and life purpose. The Star symbolizes a crucial step of our active participation in the process of individuation, both individual and, significantly, collective, as will be addressed in chapter 9. The Hero is now in harmony with his environment; the four elements of air, earth, water and fire symbolize all four Jungian functions in balance, neither of them inferior.

But that is where the Hero must pay attention to the warning sign of The Moon, Arcanum XVIII. After the hopefulness, carried by The Star, the Hero is distracted by the cold light of the moon. Consumed by the underworld of confused emotions, he is unable to distinguish between truth and deception; he is full of illusions and sometimes even delusions. When The Moon Arcanum appears in the actual reading, in a certain context it may denote someone's dementia or Alzheimer's. The Hero's Ego is being taken over by what Freud designated as Id. Real or imaginary – but perceived as real by the psyche – enemies may be present. Obscurity is here like a fog between the Hero and his Self; he has to overcome emotional and mental pressure as The Moon distracts the Hero from following the path to individuation. This trump correlates with Jung's notion that the individuation process may become dangerous in case archetypes take over, possess individual psyche. Possession was offered by Jung as one of the fundamental concepts of psychopathology.

After having worked through confusion and self-deception, the Fool is welcomed by Arcanum IXX called The Sun, as though having been born again into the sunshine after the moonlit night. The Hero is now the Jungian archetype of the Divine Child. Each adult has an inner child, and Jung referred to its symbolism as a divine prerogative. The Divine child in the Tarot picture has found her place under the sun. This is a symbol for rebirth, an adult becoming a child again, a child always already having been born into the wholeness of the Self. Even as the archetypal journey was a challenge, it is the individuating and learning process that brought forth the healing of the psyche. The idea of rebirth, for Jung, was founded in worldwide multicultural myths "around Heracles, the Pharaohs, and Jesus: the rebirth ritual was used in medical healing at the dawn of civilization" (Ryce-Menuhin, 1992, p. 17).

The next Arcanum XX is Judgement, a symbol of resurrection when the sound of a trumpet from the higher plane of expanded consciousness can awaken the Hero's awareness. The Gospel song says that Gabriel blowing his trumpet calls us toward the New Jerusalem as a symbol of spiritual restoration, the end of the Fool's pilgrimage as we will soon see in the last Arcanum, The World. The figures in the picture are rising toward their true calling, true vocation. Even as the trumpet is blown by the Archangel Gabriel whose name in Hebrew means "the power of God", resurrection is not, as Mark Patrick Hederman comments, "some all-powerful divine act, but the visible and tangible effect of the meeting and union of divine love and human being" (2003, p. 200) or, as we said earlier, the mystical *coincidentia oppositorum* achieved by Eros and Psyche reuniting in the process of "biological life [becoming] resurrected life" (2003, p. 202).

The sounds of the trumpet leads to the soul's spiritual awakening, but also to the body's symbolic reincarnation into new experiences, that is, a person becoming free to act in a new way in real life, thus getting closer to becoming her authentic Self as the meaning of the subsequent Arcanum, The World. Noddings (1993a) addresses a symbolic meaning of resurrection in the context of liberation theology. As a form of religious humanism and critical theory of transformative, spiritual, education that gives the affirmative "yes" to life, the symbol of resurrection urges "human beings to take responsibility, to act, [and] to transform" (Noddings, 1993a,

p. 129) the symbolic death that we have already encountered in Arcanum XIII, Death, into an instrument of life.

This feeling of taking upon ourselves ethical responsibility *in* the world and *for* the world is embodied in the image of the final Arcanum XXI. The World, or The Universe as it is called in some other decks, represents the culmination of The Fool's archetypal journey. Liberation theology refers to the New Jerusalem as a symbol of a harmonious, peaceful world, a futuristic goal of all humanity. The circular *mandala* of The World conveys the meaning of having completed the search for identity and the existential meaning of life, but with a qualification.

The shape of the garland in The World picture represents a continuum, that is the idea that the real search for meanings is a never-ending process in the changing circumstances of experience. The ever-expanding and varying multitude of experiential situations and events always presents new challenges: the story of the Fool's journey describes, in symbolic form, the real-life journeys of us, human beings who learn in the school of life. The evolution of consciousness culminates in The World, the imagery of which represents the ideally individuated Self, that is, an integrated personality as inseparable from its life-world. As Jung said, our

> widened consciousness is no longer that...egotistical bundle of personal wishes, fears, hopes, ambitions which always have to be compensated or corrected by the unconscious counter-tendencies; instead it is a function of *relationship* to the world of objects, bringing the individual into absolute...and indissoluble communion with the world at large (Jung, CW 7, 5; italics mine).

The Fool that finally reached The World is the very symbol for the Self that finally overcomes the dualistic split between itself and the world at large and embodies a greater numinous, spiritual, dimension. For Jung, the Self is not simply the center of the personality like the conscious Ego, but the whole circumference – like the circular mandala in the picture of The World – in which conscious and unconscious aspects are integrated together, thus constituting psychic wholeness. The dancing female figure surrounded by a garland relates to the Dionysian mysteries, to joy and fulfillment, to soul or *anima* discovered in the rational, Apollonian, world. As Noddings (1993a) comments, dance is a soul-restorer, indeed. The totality of the psyche exceeds our mortal bodies and encompasses immortal souls blending into the ultimate archetype of the Self in unity with the world soul, *Anima Mundi*.

Still, in our actual lives, personal wholeness and oneness with the World may just be an ideal limit, and the archetypal Fool will continue on the road of discovery starting again from *zero,* as if from nothing, learning his moral and spiritual lessons anew when his widened consciousness brings him into better relationship with his subjective internal world and with the world of objects at large. The ever expanding and varying multitude of experiential situations and events always presents new challenges. The symbols may combine into ever new constellations; yet "[I]t is only possible to live the fullest life when we are in harmony with these symbols; wisdom is a return to them" (Jung, CW 8, 794) when their opaque meanings become clear and transparent in the process of Tarot hermeneutic.

When Rollo May advocated the importance of myths in human life, he concluded that solutions to the existential problems of being can be achieved through listening to myth. Using the Tarot looking glass, we are telling the mythic story ourselves through our participation in the Fool's symbolic journey via many life-lessons. An allegorical school of life presents us with pictorial symbolism as the search for meaning and identity. While the journey through Tarot pictures in this chapter was accompanied by an analysis of symbols from the perspective of the Jungian archetypes, chapter 5 will position Tarot in the context of other psychological theories.

PERSONALITY AND CONSCIOUSNESS

It seems that Tarot symbolism speaks to us clearly only when addressed from the perspective of the Jungian archetypes of the collective unconscious or viewed as the existential discovery of being through myths. Noddings (1993a) is adamant that existential questions are the central issues in life and "should form the organizing backbone" (1993a, p. 8) of education counter to the traditional curriculum with its "rigid boundaries between subject matters [that] makes learning fragmentary" (1993a, p. 8). There are many ways to address the existential problems pertaining to the meaning of life and human moral development; in fact Noddings comments on the Neoplatonic "principle of plentitude, espoused by many thinkers" (1993a, p. 9) not unlike the plentitude of experiences awaiting the Fool in his archetypal journey through the symbolism of Tarot pictures and images addressed in the previous chapter.

The universality of Tarot themes reflects the view of humanistic and transpersonal psychology that basic human values are cross-cultural. Cultural relativism surrenders under the fact that Tarot Arcana embody common values grounded in basic, yet universal, human experiences that include "the commonalities of birth, death, physical and emotional needs, and the longing to be cared for. This last – whether it is mani-fested as a need for love, physical care, respect or mere recognition – is the funda-mental starting point for the ethics of care" (Noddings, 1998, p. 188).

In the context of feminist moral philosophy and care theory in education, Noddings pointed to such common global human experiences as birth, marriage, motherhood, death, or separation, even while denying abstract moral universals when they are understood solely as some predestined rules for our actions. As we have seen in chapter 4, universal archetypal experiences are embodied in the imagery of Tarot Major Arcana. Importantly, the *abstract* universal principles as a theoretical construct acquire embodied reality as *concrete,* particular, real-life human experiences embedded in our practical lives, thereby transgressing the Cartesian dualism between body and soul.

The more one works with the Tarot the more highlighted become its correlations with many of the views on human nature up to the point of claiming, as Carl Sargent (1988) did, that "the Tarot is almost a 'super-theory' of personality. One can hardly find an original insight in personality psychology which is not foretold in the imagery of Tarot" (Sargent, 1988, p. vi). It should be noted however that all theories are only our human artifacts, our constructions in an attempt to explain human behavior. Jung himself was well aware about the danger of our attachment to a particular theory calling the psychological theories "the very devil. It is true that we need certain points of view for their...heuristic value; but they always should be regarded as mere auxiliary concepts" (Jung, CW 17, 7).

The references to a variety of personality theories in the context of Tarot are mainly to illuminate this or that important general aspect of our psychological template. In the context of personality theories, Sargent linked Tarot not only with Freudian and Jungian theories of the unconscious, but also with the key insights derived from the humanistic psychology of Abraham Maslow and George Kelly's theory of constructs.

In humanistic psychology, for example, there is a concept, introduced by Maslow, of the dominating drive in human beings as being an instinct to grow, develop, differentiate, and also to nurture our spiritual feelings.

Growth, development, differentiation, and spiritual aspirations go hand in hand, from one image of the Major Arcana to another as the symbolism of each picture tells us a story just like stories that "Jung and Maslow tell us about just how we can develop as people" (Sargent, 1988, p. 7). For Maslow, there is an endless dynamics to human drives, motivations, and the need to grow. The Fool's journey through the Major Arcana is a never-ending story, with the personality becoming ever more complex till it reaches the level of the authentic selfhood. It is at this level that Maslow's inner sense of one's own worth manifests itself.

Maslow referred to *esteem needs* as a set of our desires for strength, effectiveness, and recognition of ourselves as valued by others; yet not in the sense of attracting attention but as earning respect by virtue of a developed "internal moral agency" (Sargent, 1998, p. 44). Like Jung, Maslow emphasized being true to one's own nature as the highest level of self-actualization. In terms of Tarot dynamics, addressed in the previous chapter, the Fool achieves his full actualization in the archetype of the Self, symbolized by the Arcanum called The World.

The Fool then is pure potential for future self-actualization; he will go through the multiplicity of Maslow's peak experiences symbolized by the symbolism and the imagery on the subsequent pictures. The symbolism of The Empress as the Jungian archetype of the Great Mother points, in its positive aspects, to the symbolic representation of attending to what Maslow specified as basic needs. The Empress recognizes a basic human desire to be safe, protected and nurtured. The Empress is also the ultimate symbol for growth: as regards Tarot hermeneutic, her presence in a particular reading can often point to pregnancy and fertility.

The symbolism of Justice points to the inner sense of fairness in making a judge-ment. The Wheel of Fortune is the image of the very dynamics or developmental *process* pertaining to Jung's and Maslow's theories alike. A human figure, which is present in the majority of pictures but is absent in the imagery of the Wheel, indicates "not so much a part of personality, [but] a process governing [human] development" (Sargent, 1998, p. 86) *per se*.

It is commonly assumed that Carl Rodgers' person-centered psychological theory eliminates much of the unconscious in favor of classical conditions of congruence, positive regard, empathy and trust as applied in counseling situations. Still, Rogers was said to have discovered another characteristic precisely when being closer to his inner intuitive, as yet fully unknown at the conscious level, self. For Rogers, this slightly altered state of consciousness was what produced the healing effect. Working as a counselor, a genuine reader intuitively applies in practice the necessary qualities as articulated by Rogers: congruence, unconditional positive regard and empathy.

Without emphatic understanding it would be impossible to delve into the very depth of the psyche full of latent meanings implicit in the unconscious feelings, fears, hopes, desires, and the relationships with others (as we will see in chapter 8). As early as in 1940, Rogers described the dynamics of personal growth through a process of the expanding self-awareness focusing specifically on the recognition and acceptance of the self with all its components including childish, ambivalent, and even aggressive aspects.

These aspects can be recognized in the symbolism of The Fool, Strength, The Chariot, The Devil, and other images; depending on the experiential real-life contexts of a particular layout they are situated in. It is the Tarot hermeneutic that allows us to fully adopt the subjective field of perceptions, which constitutes the very basis for a genuine understanding of the other. By entering the internal world of the other's perceptions, feelings, desires, and anxieties, we move into a new, shared, area for understanding personality dynamics. Addressing "self-concept", Rogers emphasized the significance of the relationship of "I" to others even if it is "me" specifically who will be attaching a particular value to "my" subjective experience.

I personally found Rogers' nineteen basic propositions, embracing at once the humanistic, phenomenological and existential dimensions, invaluable both for the understanding of human nature and as a backbone for the hermeneutic process of Tarot readings. Habitually, individuals consider themselves to be in the centre of their phenomenal field comprising their subjective reality, even if their experience of it is incomplete because only part of it is capable of entering personal consciousness. Yet, the recommended persistent questioning – that is, trying to reach a person at the cognitive level – is insufficient for reaching the deep level of the psyche.

A Tarot layout presents what Rogers called the internal frame of reference of the individual herself, however it exceeds this person's conscious mind; and entering this frame of reference not through questioning but literally by sharing the phenomenal field is a prerequisite for understanding human behavior. Tarot hermeneutic thus helps a person achieve what Rogers called "optimal development"; and importantly as embedded in a dynamic *process* of fulfilling one's full potential rather than a static *state*. The three counseling qualities – congruence, unconditional positive regard and empathy –naturally take place during a genuine reading. To be able to read and interpret the symbolism of the pictures – to apply the Tarot hermeneutic method in practice and not simply discuss its advantage in theory – one must first of all free one's own mind from the baggage of any preconceived ideas, to address one's own complexes in the manner of "the wounded researcher", as we said in chapter 1; perhaps try to make one's own mind, as Eastern philosophy suggests, an empty vessel free of preconceived ideas and assumptions.

What can George Kelly's theory of personality with its model of a person as "a scientist" elucidate in the context of Tarot? It may seem that Tarot's spiritual, transpersonal, realm cannot be reduced to Kelly's notion of "personal constructs" that he introduced to psychology. Well, the value of Tarot is such that it can be interpreted at the level of, and applied to, all four planes of human existence: spiritual, emotional, mental and physical. In the framework of Kelly's conceptualizations, Tarot works in the constructivist manner: the physical world can be perceived through the construction of internal, mental patterns. These patterns or constructs can grow, and develop, and determine personal actions and behaviors.

For Kelly, we construct the world. Kelly's theory centers on human attempts to anticipate events and posits this as a fundamental characteristic of all human beings. Yet, human development still is a dynamic enterprise: an environing world is supposed to be tested just like a scientist investigating objects in the world by using the scientific method.

Personal constructs will have to be changed as a result of the number of tests so that a better prediction of future events may be achieved. It is the persistent human desire for prediction and control that constitutes Kelly's fundamental idea regarding human nature. And Kelly appears to have been right!

At the everyday level what does a person want, as a general rule, when she visits readers? Regretfully, only a small number would opt for a reading along the lines of Jung's *depth* analysis; notwithstanding a generic reader's capacity to be capable of putting in practice the genuine Tarot hermeneutic! The majority of people would prefer a quick fix along the lines "I want this to happen" followed by "How to make it happen". It appears that Kelly's wishful control as a persistent feature of human nature wins; as based on elementary binary dichotomy: this versus that. The mental health of an individual, for Kelly, depends on this desire and being able to predict the events in the world around us.

Harry Stack Sullivan's interpersonal psychology introduced the term "significant other" into psychotherapeutic discourse and addressed the individual as enmeshed in the network of relationships. While acknowledging the importance of the unconscious dimension, he strengthened the role of interactional, and not intra-psychic, dynamics. Pointing out the significance of the here-and-now in therapy, Sullivan emphasized developing *verbal* communication at the exclusion of two specific areas: "immutably private" feelings experienced by a person that she is unable to communicate, and the area of the unconscious process that was presumably taking place in a person's mind, to which there was no *direct* access either by a person herself or by her therapist. To have such access, for Sullivan, would require work that will have to be more than parlor magic (Sullivan, 1950).

Sullivan acknowledged the essential inaccessibility of the personality of "the other" due to "an ample residuum" that escapes analysis and communication, hence reducing our chances for understanding a personality other than one's own. Yet, expanding communication to encompass other modalities rather than the word alone, and to include the non-verbal pictorial means of communication of Tarot hermeneutic that can create a symbolic bridge to the archetypal depth of the internal world of "the other", helps us in accessing the other not only at the interpersonal level but also intra-psychically. Therefore we become capable of accessing the "unconscious... which cannot be experienced directly, [but] which fills all the gaps in the mental life" (Sullivan, 1953, p. 204).

A Tarot layout, as will be seen in chapters 7 and 8, provides significant insights into current situations; into helping or hindering factors that may affect them; into hidden issues or obscure themes; into significant others in a person's life that form (or do not) the support system. The pictures are the means to evaluate how functional (or dysfunctional) the system is and to weigh options embedded in the alternative behavioral patterns through addressing a person's anxieties, apprehensions, aspirations, wishes, hopes, fears, and motivations. In chapter 7 we will see that positions of the pictures in the layout have certain meanings; as for interpretation, it is never fixed and rigid, it is flexible and may mean different things to different individuals.

Among the fifty-six Minor Arcana there are those carrying messages of insecurity, anger, depression, frustration, anxiety, confusion, "pain in the neck", exhaustion, being overwhelmed, experiencing inability to carry on, or indecisiveness, etc; and Tarot hermeneutic brings those issues and affects into sharp focus and leads to the instant expression of the problem areas at a pre-verbal level by virtue of their projection into a layout (chapter 7). Predominance of any one suit (how many cups cards, or wands, or swords, or pentacles) in the spread may indicate the person's general mental and emotional status. What is her dominant affect? Is she emotional? Is she at her intellectual best or worst? Is she in touch with her feelings? What mood does she demonstrate? Does she have any insight? What bothers her most: an earthy practical matter or a heavy emotional burden?

Even if all the questions cannot be answered by a layout simultaneously, it nevertheless provides important supplementary material to work with. This knowledge helps a reader to tune into a person's typology, to level with her, to join her through a particular Jungian function or attitude projected in the layout. Each one of the personality theories is a valuable complement toward understanding some part of human nature. Each theory is far from being a grand meta-narrative but rather serves as a tool to be best used for performing certain specific tasks precisely because it was designed for the implementation of this or that particular task.

In the specific context of educational psychology, Bernie Neville (in press) posits Jungian archetypes as personifications of the multiple gods of the Greek Pantheon and argues that the Pantheon can provide educators with a *pluralist* language for talking about a wide range of distinct philosophies, value systems, dominant drives, energies, feeling states, habits of behavior and teaching styles. For example, the archetypal pattern personified in Zeus is the pattern of power that wants to maintain itself either brutally or benevolently and can both protect and punish. In the Tarot deck, The Emperor often plays such a role.

The archetype of Demeter suggests a "mothering" aspect to the teacher profession; this is a prerogative of The Empress. Hermes tends to subvert the conventionally accepted order of things, to disrupt our certainties, and to make changes possible. As the archetype of The Fool, Hermes encourages us to take chances and opportunities, to step into the abyss of uncertain experiences. Yet, Hermes demonstrates the often cunning and coercing qualities of the Trickster as the antipode, the opposite pole, of The Magician.

For Neville, each of the gods populating Olympus gives us a different meaning for our being, a different truth, which must be held in balance. We can interpret each archetype as a constellation of specific personality traits that constitutes this or that character. Each of the Greek gods represents a particular theoretical perspective and, as reflected in current debates on the aims of education, these immortal gods still demonstrate their eternal arguments. In the Tarot deck, each of the Major Arcana serves as a specific archetypal characteristic that itself may give rise to this or that theory of personality. As for the art of Tarot, though, Sargent qualifies it as "a toolbox containing almost all of the useful things" (1988, p. 58).

Tarot establishes a much sought-after synchronistic connection with the lived reality of "the other", thus filling the gaps in one's consciousness; those gaps where the unconscious resides. As Veronica Goodchild, a Jungian psychologist, says, "the conscious ego is thrust out of its isolated illusion that *its* world is all there is, and which stance is, for Jung, the source of neurotic suffering" (2001, p. 78). One may inquire who gives us permission to access the human mind, to intrude into unknown territory. But like any counseling session, a Tarot reading is a response to an implicit cry for help, a desire to communicate, to take away the six degrees of separation that produce a gap in the suffering psyche.

There is no intrusion: a person who wants a reading ultimately desires to become conscious of the unconscious material, this subtle erotic desire for wisdom having motivated her to seek the reading in the first place. She opens the gates to her psyche, thus allowing an epistemic access to the inner Gnostic self-knowledge that she strives to discover in herself, to perceive, to recognize, and to work through.

Similar to Jung's conceptualization of psychic energy permeating the field of the collective unconscious, Sullivan contends that "the ultimate reality in the universe is energy" (1953, p. 102) and presents life as dynamic continuous patterns of energy transformations. And it is Tarot that is the very embodiment of the transformations of psychic energy from one Arcanum to another as the archetypal patterns of behaviors, feelings and thoughts. And a particular type of energy is common to all human beings despite differences in individual personalities and despite the diverse theories that describe them:

> In every heart, in every mind,
> In every motion of every kind
> And in every verse, and in every life
> There is Light, there is Love, there is One.
> There is Light, there is Love,
> Far below, far above,
> There is Light, there is Love, there is One, only One.
> As without, so within,
> So it has always been,
> There is Light, there is Love, there is One, only One.

These words are from a song which is usually performed at the end of Jewish meditations that focus on the metaphorical return to the land of the soul. It is only when coupled with Love/Eros that Psyche can return to its transpersonal origins. This is what Wexler (1996), transgressing the disciplinary boundaries between education, social theory and religion, emphasized as the essence of the new age culture. Not merely mass-produced therapeutic recovery programs but a deeper recovery – the return of the soul; bringing the soul to life.

For Wexler, it is the language of the soul and the sacred that establishes the connection between the transcendental realm and the everyday cultural practices in which individual lives are embedded. The "cultivation of the soul in a new age will call out to a teaching for transcendence" (Wexler, 1996, p. 80); such teaching will have included the symbolic language of Tarot as a practice for the re-symbolization of ourselves, thereby becoming able to return to the land of the soul. To read and understand this language we need a developed intuition; reciprocally, to develop our intuitive capacities we need to immerse ourselves in the world of images and symbol embedded in Tarot that would trigger our imagination, insight and intuition. It is not only that "intuition contributes to learning, creating, expressing, and problem solving" (Noddings and Shore, 1984, p. 44) but that using Tarot as an educational aid will have reinforced and enhanced the human intuitive function.

All personality theories that focus on human *development* will have to address, by definition, both actual and potential "selves", hence implicitly recognizing the importance of all three aspects of time: past, present and future. As we will see in chapter 7, a typical Tarot layout such as the Celtic Cross used in my research, encompasses simultaneously all three aspects of time, and not only in theory but, importantly, in practice, thus explicitly demonstrating a paradoxical coexistence of the past, present and future time-dimensions in the developmental dynamics of a particular person. The hermeneutic method implies the emergence of new meanings as carrying the utmost significance thereby reflecting the future-oriented path to knowledge.

The collective unconscious encompasses future possibilities, and the pictures arranged in a certain pattern in a Tarot layout, analogous to the archetypal images that appear in dreams, perform a synthesizing symbolic, transcendent, function "seeking to characterize a definite goal with the help of the material at hand, or trace out a line of future psychological development" (Jung, CW 6, 720): Jung's transcendent function by definition bridges – transcends – the gap between past and future; both coexist in the present, in the hermeneutics of the here-and-now.

Indeed, in chapter 3 we addressed the Hermetic world view as going beyond the binary opposites of the modern discourse in terms of rigid *either/or* choices. Instead, it is a *both/and* relation that functions as a unit of analysis overcoming the many dualisms haunting us since the days of Descartes. Not only do mind and body become united via the symbolic function in the medium of Tarot pictures that *embody* the aspects of both conscious and unconscious *minds*; but also this medium demonstrates the unity between *both* subject *and* object; *both* past *and* future. The *subjective* experience is being *objectified*: the subject can literally look into herself as if herself becoming the object of her own thoughts, feelings, emotions, and habits.

Ultimately the "time" element tends to eternity: in chapter 4 the story of Eros and Psyche elucidated the mythic consciousness when Psyche re-united with Eros thus becoming able to partake of the gods' immortality: human Psyche became immortal, beloved by the gods, thus achieving what Jung, borrowing from alchemy, called the *mystical conjunction – coincidentia oppositorum* – between the human and the divine.

The material at hand – the spread of Tarot pictures – is used by a bricoleur-reader who understands that the "guiding and directing quality imputed to the unconscious, implies a prospective...aspect. The past determines the present to a large extent, but primarily our actions are geared with a view towards the future" (Kaufmann in Corsini and Wedding, 1989, p. 120). In other words, the "Tarot shows not just how, and who, we are, but also tells us something of what we have been and what we will become...This is part of the greater power of Tarot in helping us to understand ourselves" (Sargent, 1988, p. 6).

A note is due here. We should be aware that as any tool or instrument in the hands of people, Tarot can be used differently, both in constructive and destructive ways, depending on who is using it and how. Perhaps this is one of the reasons why Tarot has historically had such a dubious, occult, reputation and some have learned, in a negative sense, not to trust many unreliable "fortune-tellers" who, in my opinion, not only turned "sacred" into "profane" but may also have closed real opportunities that people would have taken if not for their "fortune" being already "told"!

As will be seen in chapter 8, the function of Tarot hermeneutic is – using Nel Noddings' phrase in the context of *excellence* in education – "to open opportunities – never to close them" (Noddings, 1993b, p. 13). Since the late 1970s, when Bergin and Lambert (1978) undertook a comprehensive examination of the available data for assessment in psychotherapy, it became clear how complex and enormous the task was and still is. In this respect I join Richard Roberts (1987) who was certain that the success or failure of any method depends on the level of consciousness of the practitioner using this method rather than on the method per se. Roberts' verbatim report of his Tarot reading for such an eminent personality as Joseph Campbell is a terrific example of an effective reading session, owing to the intelligence of both participants.

Let us see what other characteristics are symbolized by the Minor Arcana of the Tarot deck. Here are fifty-six pictures consisting of four suits – wands, cups, swords, and pentacles – with ten cards, from Ace to Ten in each suit, and also of the four so-called court cards in each suit (Fig. 5.1).

The symbolism of the four suits is related to the expression of the four Jungian functions: intuition is strongly present in cups, sensation is linked to pentacles, thinking is correlated with a sharp sword, and the idea of feeling is likely to manifest by wands. The forty numbered pictures, four in each suit, may demonstrate, within the frames of each suit, some typical behavioral patterns, emotional problems, mental concerns, physical sensations, logical considerations, intuitive guesses, strong feelings, the energy levels or the presence of ideas; in short the very characteristics of human nature in its multimodal aspect. Tarot hermeneutic in terms of the archetypal journey through Major Arcana gives way to the multiplicity of practical concerns embedded in the real life circumstances reflected in the Minor Arcana.

For Jung, there are as many archetypal images as there are typical situations in life. The pictures numbered from Ace to Ten in each suit indicate the never-ending dynamics; and the number of combinations and permutations produced by various archetypal constellations, although finite, is huge, seemingly tending to infinity. Yet there is *telos* inscribed in the developmental process; while for Jung it is "The Self [that] is our life's goal" (CW 7, 404) as we demonstrated in the journey through the Major Arcana, in terms of Kelly's theory of personality, a better mastery of a

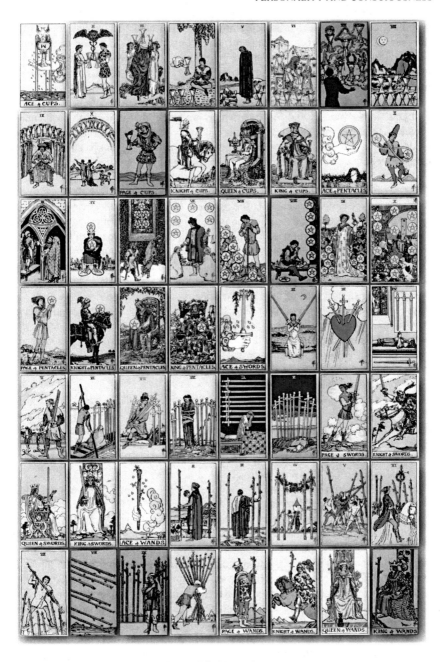

Figure 5.1. Minor Arcana.

specific problematic situation is being progressively established through travel from number 1 (or Ace) to Ten in each suit. Our consciousness expands in the sense of applying constructs more widely to the array of events, even if encountering a temporary defeat as a real-life lesson to be learned, as implied by some of the images of the Minor Arcana.

The numerical growth from 1 (or Ace) to 10 represents complex emotions, thoughts, ideas, moods, and feelings, which are embedded in real-life problematic situations. The pictures express the commonality of meanings similar to those that Nel Noddings, for example, finds "at the bottom of each suffering event [such as] pain that cries for relief, a threat of separation that triggers an increased need for connection, and a dread of helplessness that begs for empowerment" (Noddings, 1989, p. 129). Tarot hermeneutic as the reading and interpretation of many symbols leads to the discovery of meanings concealed at the *psychoid* level of the collective unconscious and creatively making them explicit, thus establishing "a metaphysical context and [providing] a human-to-human care process with spiritual dimension" (Noddings, 1989, p. 128, quoting from Jean Watson's work in the area of nursing).

In Martin Buber's approach to dialogue, the authentic relationship is being developed by means of "experiencing the other side" (Buber, 1971, p. 96). Buber also underlines the significance of Eros that constitutes "an inclusive power" (1971, p. 97) as the very *realization* of the other side. Importantly, Buber notices that a dialogical relation may continue even when self and other are separated in space and time due to "continual potential presence of the one to the other, as an unexpressed intercourse" (1971, p. 97). Buber comments on the important role of *imagining the real*, as though by grace, and on the limitations of us, human beings, the "creatures", as compared to the creator, God.

Still "each man...can expose himself to the creative Spirit" (Buber, 1971, p. 103). This intangible spiritual presence becomes tangible when embodied in the very process of interpreting images of the Tarot Arcana. In the context of Tarot hermeneutic, Buber's emphasis on imagining the real can be taken to the next power: it becomes our *realizing the imaginal*, which is made possible when Corbin's Imaginal world takes the form of visible reality.

It is by "cultivating the relation" (Noddings, 1991, p. 162) that we learn about the richness of the world pertaining to "the other side". This genuine relation is established in the course of caring occasions during actual readings that employ at once both interpersonal and intra-psychic modes of making inferences. Noddings (1991) lists several important components as characterizing what she calls interpersonal reasoning. They are an attitude of care, attention, flexibility, effort aimed at cultivating the relation, and a search for an appropriate response, also accompanied by a kind of metacognition. Such a meta-level is enabled by self-reflection.

Within Tarot hermeneutic, all of these characteristics are to be present with the addition of the intuitively present intra-psychic element. This element manifests itself because of the field of the collective unconscious *a priori* connecting both self and other, while self-reflexivity is achieved by means of the trigger-symbols that make us aware of implicit meanings of our experiences at the deep emotional level.

It is not only that a genuine reader experiences, even if vicariously, what the other is, or was, or will have been experiencing. In order to become such a real, authentic, reader, she will have to have indeed *lived through* these experiences, to go through her own school of life so that she has always already experienced the deep meanings embodied in each Arcanum, even if some of those pictures relate to quite traumatic experiences. For example, the image of the Five of Cups with its sad figure in a black cloak presents us with the feeling of loss, sorrow, or mourning. The three cups in front of the central figure are obviously empty, carrying the message of futility and wasted efforts. Yet, should he turn around, he would have seen two full cups standing erect and representing new knowledge, new fulfillment, new point of view or perspective.

The imagery of the Ten of Wands brings human endurance to the brink: the figure is struggling under the heavy load on his shoulders. The Nine of Wands depicts a figure with a bandaged head, a wound that still hurts, even if he is determined to protect his rights and defend his territory, especially because the threat appears to persist. The Three of Swords is one of the most dramatic pictures literally portraying a crying and broken heart, as a result of being pierced by three swords. It depicts separation, severance, divorce, and similar experiences. It may also indicate a surgical intervention, quiet often open-heart surgery. In either case, the experience is painful. The picture of the Five of Pentacles is a symbol for misfortune, poverty, either material or spiritual; or poor health alike.

Again, as I said in chapter 4, these would be just the general interpretations of the imagery depicted by Tarot pictures; in the actual readings the nuances embedded in the potential meanings depend on the context of a particular situation, on a specific position a particular picture is in, as well as on the proximity of other pictures that will affect the total feeling-tone or "sound" similar to different musical notes in a chord. The fifty-six pictures of Minor Arcana tell us multiple stories about feeling happy or being sad, making plans or breaking promises, winning or losing, experiencing financial difficulties or laying foundations for a marriage, falling in love or getting out of an abusive relationship, starting a new venture or experiencing separation anxiety.

The list is endless, and our real-life experience always presents new contexts and encounters that call for new evaluations, new meanings, and more education in practice. There is no doubt that human existence is

> locally conditioned by a multitude of biographical, cultural and historical factors, [however] subsuming all this at a deeper level [there are]…universal patterns or modes of experience, archetypal forms that constantly arranged the elements of human experience into typical configurations and gave to collective… psychology a dynamic continuity. These archetypes endured as basic a priori symbolic forms while taking on the costume of the moment in each individual life and each cultural era, permeating each experience, each cognition, and each world view (Tarnas, 1991, p. 385).

In other words, what takes place is our learning from experience and the progressive integration of the unconscious into consciousness in the symbolic process of growth embodied in the Tarot pictures. Considering that each layout would have combined the pictures in a new constellation, each time reflecting novel circumstances and presenting the perplexity of a novel problematic situation, the process of learning from the archetypal images embedded in the unconscious continues throughout a life-span.

Post-formal pedagogy as our learning in practical experiences abound in life, and in accord with personality theories focusing on the *dynamics* of adult development, brings to the fore the notion of individuation as our experiential "becoming" and specifically "becoming-other", which is the key concept in the philosophy of Gilles Deleuze (1925–1995) to be addressed in the next chapter.

CHAPTER 6

GILLES DELEUZE

Learning from the Unconscious

For the philosopher Gilles Deleuze, rational Cartesian consciousness as the sole constituent of thought is insufficient because what is yet "unthought" is equally capable of producing practical effects at the level of human experiences. Deleuze considers *"an unconscious of thought* [to be] just as profound as *the unknown of the body"* (Deleuze, 1988a, p. 19; italics Deleuze's). The quality of *profundity* is significant and relates Deleuze's particular mode of production of human subjectivity, that he together with social psychologist Felix Guattari called "schizoanalysis", to Jung's *depth* psychology. Kerslake (2007) notices that Deleuze's conception of the unconscious is closer to the Jungian rather than the Freudian. Jung's dynamic process of the individuation of the Self as the goal of analysis is akin to Deleuze's concept of *becoming,* and specifically *becoming-other* as a process of learning from the unconscious embedded in experience.

The Jungian collective unconscious is by definition *transpersonal,* thus exceeding the scope of traditional Freudian psychoanalytic conception as narrowly personal and simply repressed. Contrary to behaviorist psychology positing an individual as born in the state of a blank slate, *tabula rasa,* the Jungian unconscious is always already inhabited by archetypes. Analogously Deleuze is adamant that "one never has a *tabula rasa*; one slips in, enters in the middle" (Deleuze, 1988a, p. 123, italics Deleuze's). According to Deleuze, the world consists not of substantial "things" but of relational entities, or multiplicities, and the production of subjectivity is necessarily embedded amidst the relational, experimental and experiential, dynamics.

The dynamics of becoming, when any given multiplicity "changes in nature as it expands its connections" (Deleuze and Guattari, 1987, p. 8), is a distinctive feature of Deleuzian thought: becoming-animal, becoming-woman, becoming-world, becoming-child, and always becoming-other. This constant becoming-other constitutes the process of individuation, and "[i]ndividuation ...precedes matter and form, species and parts, and every other element of the constituted individual" (Deleuze, 1994, p. 38).

Deleuze posits the *virtual* field of becoming which is as real as the *actual* plane of manifested phenomena, and an object of experience is considered to be given only in its tendency to exist in its virtual, potential form. The realm of the virtual is reminiscent of, but not limited to, the Jungian archetype of the Shadow that hides in the collective unconscious or, at the plane of expression, for Deleuze, in the shadow around the words. This means that unconscious ideas need a means of expression other than words and sentences; they can take the form of legible images and symbols that we can read and interpret so as to makes sense of, and create meaning for, our experiences. For Deleuze, "Sense is essentially produced" (Deleuze, 1990a, p. 95).

The unconscious, which is over and above its personal dimension, is conceptualized by Deleuze and Guattari as Anti-Oedipal, that is, irreducible to Freud's master-signified. Similar to the Jungian collective unconscious, it always deals with social and collective frame and is "a productive machine...at once social and desiring" (Deleuze, 1995, 144). In contrast to solely theoretical knowledge, it is desire or affect that educates the human psyche by means of its active participation in life-experiences in the process of creative subject-formation. The process of becoming-other is embedded in the multiplicities of experiences and events, just like in the story of Eros and Psyche that we presented in chapter 2. The intensive capacity "to affect and be affected" (Deleuze and Guattari, 1987, p. xvi) is part and parcel of the dynamic subject's complex rules of formation. The production of subjectivity includes an encounter with pure affect analogous to Psyche encountering Eros and, from now on led by Love, necessarily engaging in Praxis.

Importantly, Deleuze's theoretical framework is inseparable from practice. Theory itself plays a practical, instrumental role – not unlike the theoretical step-stones that we have laid so far in the preceding chapters and especially as regards the "box of tools" quality of Tarot addressed in chapter 5 – and "must unsettle and disturb those who would use them [tools] in order to bring new objects and events within range of thought" (Murphy, 1998, p. 213).

Archetypes as virtual tendencies have the potential of becoming actual through the process of multiple differentiations of the transcendental and "initially undifferent-iated field" (Deleuze, 1993, p. 10) analogous to Jung's field of the collective un-conscious. We remember the undifferentiated abyss of freedom in The Fool picture (chapter 4) stepping into which the Fool begins to learn from his experiences, that is, he becomes able to differentiate between them, evaluating and re-valuating singular experiences along his long road towards becoming fully individuated in the image of The World, the archetypal Self.

In order to become one's authentic Self one has to engage with the world of experiences and become able to "to bring something to life, to free life from where it's trapped, to trace lines of flight" (Deleuze, 1995, p. 141). Indeed without the Fool taking a risk and leaping ahead into the abyss – tracing a line of flight – he would have forever remained a Fool, without the possibility of ever reaching the final Arcanum, The World. It is the lines of flight – the lines of becomings – that lead us into The World, or The Universe. As Deleuze says, "Each one of us has his own line of the universe to discover, but is only discovered through tracing it" (1986, p. 195), through living and learning as the means of acquiring Gnosis as we said in chapter 3, through becoming conscious of the unconscious embedded in the virtual space of the Deleuzian "outside".

For Deleuze,

The outside is...animated by peristaltic movements, folds and foldings that together make up an inside: they are not something other than the outside but precisely the inside *of* the outside. ... The inside is an operation of the outside: ... an inside ... is ... the fold of the outside (Deleuze, 1988b, pp. 96–97).

Like the Jungian *objective* psyche, the virtual space of the outside "possesses a full reality by itself [and] it is on the basis of its reality that [our human] existence is produced" (Deleuze, 1994, p. 211; brackets mine). Jung commented that Freud "was blind toward the paradox and ambiguity of the contents of the unconscious, and did not know that everything which arises out of the unconscious has ... an inside and an outside" (Jung, 1963, p. 153) – in accord with the critical thinking of Deleuze who conceptualized the relation between the inside and the outside as the *fold.*

The role of the Deleuzian "outside", as noticed by the educational researcher Elizabeth St. Pierre (1997b), is to "fold us into identity, and we can never control the forces of the outside" (St. Pierre, 1997b, p. 367), the archetypal forces that constitute the field of the collective unconscious. The relation between a rational conscious thought and an "unthought", unconscious dimension is also of the type of the fold, making the "unthought therefore not external to thought" (Deleuze, 1988b, p. 97) but folded into "its very heart" (Deleuze, 1988b, p. 97). To be able to reach to the very heart, to the very *depth* of the unconscious, we need to apply in practice the affective erotic method because (we repeat) it is Eros that animates Psyche.

This method is the hermeneutic of Tarot or, in Deleuzean terms, transcendental empiricism, which functions on the basis of what Deleuze called the transversal communication that establishes an intuitive access to the virtual reality of the archetypes akin to Jung's transcendent function enabled by a synchronistic connection of opposites. The prefix "trans" is significant: the unconscious dimension is *trans*cended by means of an indirect, transversal, link of a symbolic mediation via the archetypal images, thus establishing "the bond of a profound complicity between [unconscious] nature and [conscious] mind" (Deleuze, 1994, p. 165) leading to the conjunction and unification of opposites, the mystical *coincidentia oppositorum*, which determines the very threshold of consciousness.

It is the transcendent function performed by Tarot hermeneutic that establishes the mode of transversal communication in practice, and not only in theory: traversing the fold prevents the two realms of "inside" and "outside" remaining forever separated by the supposedly unbridgeable, indeed schizophrenic, gap of Cartesian dualism. Even if Deleuze is more often than not considered a radical materialist, there are strong connections in his philosophy with religion, spirituality and mysticism (Bryden, 2001). The recent special issue of the journal *SubStance* titled "Spiritual Politics after Deleuze" (Delpech-Ramey and Harris, 2010) brought to the front the esoteric currents in Deleuze's thought as bordering on the revival of the Neoplatonic Hermeticism during the Renaissance, the six pinnacles of which have indeed been addressed in chapter 3 of this book.

In his analysis of cinematic images, Deleuze (1989) posits mysticism in terms of the sudden actualization of potentialities, that is, an awakening of sense-perception, such as seeing and hearing, by raising them to a new power of enhanced perception as a future-oriented perception of *becoming*. However the most important feature of Deleuze's Hermetic philosophy is its value at the level of real-life cultural practices. This extends to the Tarot hermeneutic as an existing phenomenon at the level of popular culture.

Deleuze and Guattari relate mystical *participation in the reality of what is produced* to the figure of the schizopherenic, that is, a person who is considered abnormal in the context of the scientific medical discourse of modernity, yet the one who because of his intense connection to the unconscious lives within his very interface with nature, without however being capable of becoming conscious of this very predicament. It is schizoanalysis – such as the bricolage of Tarot – that would have enabled him to integrate the unconscious into consciousness; to heal his psyche, to become-other rather than stay on the margins of society, troubled by his present "fractured I of a dissolved Cogito" (Deleuze, 1994, p. 194). These fractured pieces comprise what Jung called complexes.

Derived from the common archetypal core as well as actual experiences, complexes act similarly to Deleuze's pure affects: they are autonomous and "behave like independent beings" (Jung, CW 8, p. 253) over and above the intentional conscious will of the Cartesian subject. Jung argues that "there are things in the psyche which I do not produce, but which produce themselves and have their own life…there is something in me that can say things that I do not know and do not intend" (1963, p. 183) because these "things in the psyche" act at the unconscious level over and above one's conscious will and voluntary control. Deleuze would have agreed; he says that the "intentionality of being is surpassed by the fold of Being, Being as fold" (1988b, p. 110). It is not the possibilities of our conscious mind but the multiple "things in the psyche" as parameters of the unconscious that continuously create novel relations in our real experience because as dynamic, archetypal, forces they are capable of *affecting* and *effecting* changes, thus contesting the very identity of subjects on the road to individuation and in accord with the unfolding dynamics of The Fool's journey addressed in chapter 4.

In this respect, the unconscious perceptions are implicated as subliminal, or micro-, perceptions (Deleuze, 1993); as such, they become part of the cartographic microanalysis – schizoanalysis – of establishing "an unconscious psychic mechanism that engenders the perceived in consciousness" (Deleuze, 1993, p. 95). Cartography, by definition, is a mode of graphic communication capable of transmitting messages. We will see in the next chapter the cartographic structure of a typical Tarot layout that serves as a means of graphic, albeit transversal, communication and embodies a rhizomatic network of uncertain self-other relations.

Sure enough, because the production of subjectivity includes the realm of the unconscious, "the cartographies of the unconscious would have to become indispensable complements to the current systems of rationality of…all …regions of knowledge and human activity" (Guattari, original French, in Bosteels, 1998, p. 155). This cartography of the collective unconscious is represented by the Tarot layout, and the hermeneutic method of Tarot readings and interpretation pertains to Deleuze's method of transcendental empiricism.

Deleuze's method for putting the fractured pieces of the dissolved "I" together, that is, integrating the unconscious into consciousness, is empirical as embedded in the multiple contexts, situations and events of human experiences; yet it is radically transcendental because the very foundations for the empirical principles are left outside our common faculties of perception so we have to transcend them in practice, hence ourselves becoming capable of perceiving the seemingly imperceptible, indeed becoming-other. Deleuze wants to achieve the means so as to be able to literally "show the imperceptible" (Deleuze, 1995, p. 45) that is, become capable of bridging the gap between the sensible and the intelligible, matter and mind.

Transcendental empiricism affirms "the double in the doubling process" (Deleuze, 1988b, p. 98). "Doubling" is taken in the sense of unfolding that presupposes a necessary existence of the extra – "outside" – dimension, without which the concept of fold is meaningless. This outside dimension becomes internalized, enfolded; hence doubling as "the internalisation of the outside [becomes] redoubling of the other [and] it is a self that lives in me as the double of the other: I do not encounter myself on the outside, I find the other in me" (Deleuze, 1988b, p. 98). "The other" is thus always implicit in the unconscious, the subtle language of which is to be made explicit so as to indeed effectuate the process of becoming-*other*.

The imperceptible affects can be shown – made visible, perceptible, sensible – rather than simply "thought" at the level of rational mind. Perceiving something essentially imperceptible – making the invisible visible – is made possible by means of laying down what Deleuze called the plane of immanence. That's how Deleuze and Guattari defined the plane of immanence which, for them, was not in any way reduced to reason alone:

> Precisely because the plane of immanence …does not immediately take effects with concepts, it implies a sort of groping experimentation and its layout resorts to measures that are not very respectable, rational, or reasonable. There measures belong to the order of dreams, of pathological processes, esoteric experiences, drunkenness, and excess. We head for the horizon, on the plane of immanence, and we return with bloodshot eyes, yet they are the eyes of the mind (Deleuze and Guattari, 1994, p. 41)

The construction of the plane of "immanence [which] is the unconscious itself" (Deleuze, 1988a, p. 29) implies the affective and erotic awakening of the inner eye (Noddings and Shore, 1984) as opposed to the cold, dispassionate and unblinking gaze of the rational *Cogito*. This awakening is a prerogative of "the genesis of intuition in intelligence" (Deleuze, 1991, p. 111) due to which we can perceive the imperceptible and become conscious of the unconscious.

The virtual and the actual are mutually enfolded, and "we go from fold to fold" (Deleuze, 1993, p. 17) within the unfolding experience – not unlike the archetypal travel from one Tarot Arcanum to another, from one fold to another. Says Deleuze, "I undo the folds ...that pass through every one of my thresholds...'the twenty-two folds' that surround me and separate me from the deep" (1993, p. 93). Citing Henri Michaux, he says that children are born with the twenty-two folds which are to be unfolded. Only then can human life become complete, fulfilled, individuated.

These twenty-two folds, implicated in subjectivity, correspond to the number of Major Arcana encountered, as we have shown in chapter 4, in the archetypal process of individuation as becoming-other. In Kabbalah, the twenty-two Paths on the Tree of Life represent the movement from one state of human condition to another and contain twenty-two letters of the Hebrew alphabet. The structure of the symbolic

Tree of Life, as well the structure of a typical Tarot layout, is what Deleuze would have called rhizomatic, that is, "more like grass than a tree" (Deleuze, 1995, p. 149) which means that the rhizome's growth – contrary to the growth of a tree – does not proceed from the root up, but is distributed among the multiple paths that trace our *becomings*.

Rhizome is a biological metaphor used by Deleuze and Guattari to describe a model of thinking irreducible to the single stable foundation represented by *Cogito*, as a principle for the certainty of theoretical knowledge. As embedded in Praxis, a rhizomatic network constitutes the *relational* dynamics that comprises multiple transversal lines leading to the creation of novel meanings for experience. Yet, because the rhizome's life proceeds underground, its growth appears imperceptible, invisible to the usual sense-perception. It is intuition or insight that reaches out "to the deepest things, the 'arcana', [hence making] man commensurate with God" (Deleuze, 1990b, p. 322).

The priority of relations prevalent in the Hermetic world-view is equally important for Deleuze: "A *and* B. The AND is ... the path of all relations" (Deleuze, 1987, p. 57). It is the conjunction "and" that enables a relation between opposites and connects them in a rhizomatic network in which the whole dualistic split of *either* sensible *or* intelligible, *either* rational thought *or* lived experience, *either* cognition *or* emotion, *either* material *or* spiritual, *either* human *or* divine is bridged, hence made "commensurate". The Tarot Arcana combined in the rhizomatic structure of a layout, as will be shortly demonstrated in chapters 7 and 8, are literally laid out on the plane of immanence, thereby mapping out the psyche and "suggest[ing] 'highs' or periods of depression" (Deleuze, 1983, p. 70) at the subtle, *affective,* level.

The process of becoming is impossible without the implicit presence of affect, of Eros guiding the Psyche. For Deleuze, affects are not just subjective feelings but "becomings that spill over beyond whoever lives through them (thereby becoming someone else)" (Deleuze, 1995, p. 127). Deleuze and Guattari say that "affects ... traverse [one's universe of being]... like the beam of light that draws a hidden universe out of the shadow" (1994, p. 66); this hidden, invisible, universe becoming known – visible – to us in the form of the inner, Gnostic, knowledge that we achieve by means of Tarot hermeneutic.

The Hermetic metaphors of light and holy sparks are used by Deleuze to elucidate the erotic presence of affect in the process of becoming as though pinpointing the attraction between Psyche and Eros, this Love eventually reuniting human Psyche with immortal Eros. Deleuze is concerned with the possibility of transcending toward "the divine part in us [and establishing] the spiritual relationship in which we are...with God as light" (Deleuze, 1986, p. 54). It is due to the Tarot hermeneutic that "the individual [becomes] able to transcend his form and his syntactical link with a world" (Deleuze, 1994, p. 178).

The syntactical link produced by verbal language that describes objects in the world does not include *Sens*, which in French means both meaning and direction, or our very *ethos* as the existential discovery of being that we addressed in the preceding chapters. This impoverished syntactic link is transformed into the meaningful, *synchronistic*, connection enabled not by verbal expressions of the conscious mind alone but by the pictorial language of Tarot images and symbols that express the depth of the unconscious.

Becoming-other is described as "an extreme contiguity within coupling of two sensations without resemblance or, on the contrary, in the distance of a light that captures both of them in a single reflection. ... It is a zone ... of indiscernibility... This is what is called an *affect*" (Deleuze and Guattari, 1994, p. 173). Deleuze purports to show the as-yet-imperceptible by laying down a visible "map" of the invisible "territory" by creating the conjunction "and" in our actual experience between what are customarily considered the dualistic opposites ("without resemblance") of matter and mind, *psyche* and *physis*. And now and then a holy "spark can flash ...to make us see and think what was lying in the shadow around the words, things we were hardly aware existed" (Deleuze, 1995, p. 141).

We can recollect the holy sparks in real-life practice: expanding on Deleuzian conceptualizations, we can actually *see* the aforementioned internalisation of the outside, which came about by redoubling, not in our mind as an abstract concept, but with our eyes as a concrete picture. Just so as to become able to be seen, it would have been *re-redoubled*; in a way, *transcended*, albeit in the seemingly primitive, savage, mode of spreading the Tarot pictures in a typical layout that functions as a transversal connection blending the plane of immanence and the transcendental field of the collective unconscious.

Indeed in chapter 2 we referred to Claude Lévi-Strauss who, in his work *The Savage Mind* was first to coin the word *bricolage*; and in chapter 3 we pointed out that making the invisible visible constitutes one of the principles of the Hermetic world view. It is laying out the plane of immanence that makes the invisible visible. The mode of transversal communication created by Tarot hermeneutic provides an epistemic access to the invisible transcendental field, never mind "in a mind of man or in the mind of god...when it is accorded a maximum of immanence by plunging it into the depth of Nature, or of the Unconscious" (Deleuze, 1987, p. 91).

Like an authentic bricoleur, Hermes establishes the transversal connection in-between the otherwise incommensurable realms. It is the Tarot hermeneutic that duly "upsets being" (Deleuze, 1995, p. 44), propelling a person towards her potential Self; yet along this very line "things come to pass and becomings evolve" (1995, p. 45). One is not consciously passing through the line of flight or becoming; just the opposite, Deleuze insists that "something [is] passing through you" (Deleuze, 1995, p. 141) at the as yet unconscious, subtle level.

Becoming-other is established via "diversity, multiplicity [and] the destruction of identity" (Deleuze, 1995, p. 44) so that a new identity can be created. Individuation presupposes breaking out of old habits and into new territories. Old habits die hard, and individuation depends on "the harshest exercise in depersonalization" (Deleuze, 1995, p. 6): the symbolic death of the old personality and (re)birth of the new one. In chapter 4 we addressed the meanings of the Major Arcana Death and The Sun, yet between death and rebirth there are Temperance and The Devil, followed by The Tower.

The symbolic death is a painful and lengthy process; time may appear to stand still (Temperance) especially if we remain unconscious of staying in the grip of our old habits (The Devil). So sometimes we have to be hit by symbolic lightning to break the ivory tower of the old outlived values we have imprisoned ourselves in (The Tower). Only then our symbolic rebirth (The Sun) and resurrection (Judgement) become possible so that we can become what in fact we were meant to be all along: our authentic Selves, even if so far only in the mind of God (as Deleuze says), outside our conscious awareness.

For Deleuze, the psychological crises that we may encounter in life are significant events that serve as the turning points or critical junctions formed by the folds that express the play of forces without which no transformation or change would have been possible. A Tarot layout embodies these significant events, and it is the Tarot hermeneutic that ultimately represents what Deleuze and Guattari call *transformational pragmatics* and we described in chapter 4 as the process when an individual Ego becomes transformed into the individuated Self. In chapter 8 we will see how the Tarot hermeneutic provides a real possibility for change in our habits, attitudes and value-systems.

The transformational pragmatics of Deleuze and Guattari originates "among a broken chain of affects" (Deleuze and Guattari, 1987, p. 9) enfolded in life experiences. Subtle affects and sensations inhabiting the unconscious have "the ir-reducibly synthetic character" (Deleuze, 2003, p. 33). Traditional Freudian psycho-analysis was considered reductive by Jung and Deleuze alike because of its sole orientation to the past marked by Oedipal conflict. Deleuze refers to the "levels of profundity" (Deleuze, 1991, p. 59) in the past. The synthetic, and not solely analytic, quality embedded in depth psychology and schizoanalysis alike is oriented to the creative emergence of new meanings, hence bringing in the dimension of the future.

Jung emphasized the prospective function of the unconscious or what Deleuze, following Henry Bergson, called the memory of the future that, together with all of the past, is enfolded in the cosmic "gigantic memory" (Deleuze, 2001, p. 212). We will see in chapter 7 how these three dimensions of time, past, present, and the potential coming-into-being, indeed *becoming*, future *coexist* in one and the same Tarot layout or spread.

It is only during esoteric experiences, for Deleuze, such as dreams, or déjà-vu – and of course, Tarot readings – that we are able to perceive the real virtual past enfolded in the grandiose time of coexistence capable of unfolding, or disclosing, the virtual. The synthetic method reflects the future-oriented productivity of affect or desire that – like Eros and Hermes inhabiting the *Imaginal* world, *Mundus Imaginalis* – is capable of transcending "spatial locations and temporal successions" (Deleuze, 1994, p. 83). We thus achieve an expanded perception of time and space, which therefore become "released from their human coordinates" (Deleuze, 1986, p. 122) that capture space merely in its three dimensions and time as chronological and linear.

The unfolding of the unconscious in the process of individuation presents "life as a work of art" (Deleuze, 1995, p. 94) that we actively create. What Deleuze calls thinking is "not just a theoretical matter. It [is] to do with vital problems. To do with life itself" (Deleuze, 1995, p. 105). This true, vitalistic and enduring, even if invisible and virtual, life is a life as pure immanence (Deleuze, 2001) concealed in the transcendental field of the collective unconscious. It thus needs to be *unfolded,* or revealed from its concealment, like the scroll held by The High Priestess (chapter 4) that hides in its folds the symbols of secret and esoteric, Gnostic, knowledge.

The mode of transversal communication is indirect, mediated by archetypal images, and operates in order "to bring this assemblage of the unconscious to the light of day, to select the whispering voices, to gather the tribes and secret idioms from which I extract something I call my Self (*Moi*)" (Deleuze and Guattari, 1987, p. 84); this very Self as the archetype of wholeness being the ultimate goal of Jungian individuation and the Deleuzian process of becoming-other alike.

The unfolding of archetypal dynamics proceeds not along the Freudian royal road to the unconscious but amidst "rough and uncommonly devious footpaths" (Jung, CW 8, 210) comprising what Deleuze calls the *nomadic* space of our growth in the process of *nomadic education* (Semetsky 2006, 2008). Nomad is a mobile, dynamic element; according to Deleuze, nomads are the very "becoming...they transmute and reappear" (Deleuze, 1995, p. 153) and would have eventually occupied the whole rhizomatic structure, not unlike The Fool becoming The World in the process of his archetypal, nomadic, journey.

Coincidentally, Jung uses the same metaphor of the rhizome as Deleuze:

> The life of a man is a dubious experiment. ...Individually, it is so fleeting ... Life has always seemed to me like a plant that lives on its rhizome. Its true life is invisible, hidden in the rhizome. The part that appears above ground lasts only a single summer. Then it withers away – an ephemeral apparition. ...Yet I have never lost a sense of something that lives and endures underneath the eternal flux. What we see is the blossom, which passes. The rhizome remains (Jung, 1963, p. 4).

Significantly, "in order for the virtual to become actual it must *create* its own terms of actualization" (Hardt, 1993, p. 18); and the condition for the actualization of the virtual in practice is the establishment of a transversal connection as the conjunction "and". We will see in chapters 7 and 8 how the Tarot hermeneutic is capable of actualizing the virtual so that we become conscious of the action of the unconscious archetypes through the images and symbols.

The integration of the unconscious into consciousness leads to the "intensification of life" (Deleuze and Guattari, 1994, p. 74). By means of interpreting Tarot images we immerse into this affective "experimentation on ourselves [that] is our only identity, our single chance for all the combinations which inhabit us" (Deleuze, 1987, p. 11); these multiple potential combinations expressed by the images of the Major and Minor Arcana. We become "filled with immanence" (Deleuze, 1997, p. 137), therefore necessarily fulfilled by *Sens* – meaning and direction – discovered by virtue of our learning from the unconscious dimension embedded in experience.

The explication of the meanings implicit in the multileveled rhizomatic network of the layout enables one to make sense out of the disparate bits and pieces of confusing issues, that is, to learn from experience, to become conscious of the unconscious. For Deleuze, learning is "infinite ... [and] of a different nature to knowledge" (Deleuze, 1994, p. 192); it is a creative process of assigning meaning and value to experience. Individuation cannot proceed without a means to both express and transform oneself, and Deleuze and Guattari (1987) referred to *metamorphosis* with regard to Jung's theory of the transformation of the libido as spiritual or psychic energy irreducible to Freud's limited definition of the libido as a sex drive.

Deleuze considered transformation, or change in nature, to be a precondition for becoming-other and it is the interpretation and re-valuation of experience by means of which "we rediscover singular processes of learning" (Deleuze, 1994, p. 25) capable of becoming creative and fruitful in our endeavors. We become able to bring novelty to life, to enrich life with Eros; only as such our life "reconquers an immanent power of creation" (Deleuze & Guattari, 1994, p. 140). It is along the lines of flight where novelty comes into being, or *becomes*. Novelty is created in experience when some potential, as yet "non-localizable connections" (Deleuze, 1994, p. 83) meet each other along the lines of rhizomatic *becomings*. The creative, transformative, and evaluative element embedded in learning enriches the reductive 3R approach to education (contrasted, in chapter 3, with Tarot's sympathetic approach by Mark Patrick Hederman) with its ethical, or values, dimension.

Experience is rendered meaningful, that is, it is capable of acquiring *value* in our symbolic journey through Tarot images, each of which is an "object of an encounter...a here-and-now [and] from which emerge inexhaustibly ever new, differently distributed 'heres' and 'nows'" (Deleuze, 1994, pp. xx–xxi) embodied in new experiences and reflected in novel archetypal constellations. The problematic situation embedded in a Tarot layout as the aforementioned *presentation of the unconscious* demands our learning from these subtle experiences. This unorthodox learning forms "an intrinsic genesis, not an extrinsic conditioning" (Deleuze, 1994, p. 154) pertaining to the formal mode of education based on direct instruction. As a genesis it proceeds from within the unconscious as the symbolic home for the archetypal images.

This type of education is genuinely ethical because it "does ... challenge deeply held beliefs or ways of life" (Noddings, 2006, p. 1) as our old and outlived habits of the mind. Yet, old habits can and should be transformed: a new mode of existence enabled by the Tarot hermeneutic would be characterized by "new percepts and new affects" (Deleuze, 1995, p. 164) as new ways of thinking, feeling, perceiving and acting, comprising our individuated Selves. Human life is not a straightforward affair but presents problems and obstacles, like Praxis imposing them on Psyche; it is how we might approach a particular real-life problem or resolve a moral dilemma that would give a particular value to our experience and enrich it with meaning.

The post-formal education embedded in real life will have had an ethical, what Deleuze called "clinical", dimension inscribed in it. Deleuze's "critical and clinical" (Deleuze, 1997) philosophy presents meanings and values as future-oriented and yet-to-become when we ourselves create them in the process of learning from experience, from the depths of the collective unconscious. It is not by accident that Tarot as the path to Gnosis combines both pedagogical and counseling elements. Our ideas are often so enveloped or enfolded "in the soul that we can't always unfold or develop them" (Deleuze, 1993, p. 49) by means of our cognitive tools alone, unless experience itself becomes saturated with affective, almost numinous, conditions for their unfolding, because this deep inner, Gnostic "knowledge is known only where it is folded" (Deleuze, 1993, p. 49).

The symbolism of The High Priestess affirms itself again and again! The experiential world itself is folded; only as such we are able to

> endure it, so that everything doesn't confront us at once...There's no subject, but a production of subjectivity: subjectivity has to be produced, when its time arrives, precisely because there is no subject. The time comes once we've worked through knowledge and power; it's that work that forces us to frame a new question, it couldn't have been framed before. ... Subjectification is an artistic activity (Deleuze, 1995, pp. 112–114).

Such artistic production of subjectivity is a function of time; it is not intentional or volitional but depends on our learning from unfolding experience so that we can "frame a new question" precisely because of our growth and the evolution of consciousness that brings to our awareness this or that question – a real-life problematic situation – that "couldn't have been framed before".

Jung's archetypal patterns that make us act unconsciously nevertheless lead us to learning because their "structure is part of objects themselves [hence] allowing its objectivity and its specificity to be grasped in the act of *learning*" (Deleuze, 1994, p. 64; italics Deleuze's). Learning from our very lives is the form of post-formal ethical education that takes us to future territories which are created from the virtual out of which we live. The actualization of virtual potentialities is "always a genuine creation" (Deleuze, 1994, p. 212).

We learn not by virtue of being instructed to do so, but because of our very engagement with, and our embodiment in, the objective world, so that learning is equated with creation, with creating new meanings for our experiences. Deleuze is adamant that "we learn nothing from those who say: 'Do as I do'" (Deleuze, 1994, p. 23); instead we learn by unfolding the experiential folds of the unconscious, represented by this or that Arcanum, thereby creating our Selves as whole persons, in the "artistic activity" of the production of subjectivity.

The process of discovering our real identity is a process of meaning-making and is a function of living and learning. Therefore our unconscious is the necessary– and quite often, as Deleuze would say, *dark*, especially when *projected* via the image of The Devil, or The Moon, or The Tower – precursor for learning, for individuation, for becoming-other. In the next chapter we will address Tarot specifically in the context of projective psychology.

TAROT AND PROJECTIVE HYPOTHESIS

For Deleuze, everything has "its cartography…What we call a 'map'…is a set of various interacting lines (thus the lines in hand are a map)" (Deleuze, 1995, p. 33). If, according to Deleuze, the lines in a hand form a map, so does Tarot bricolage in the rhizomatic structure implicated in a specific pictorial spread such as The Celtic Cross (Fig. 7.1) that I used in the course in this research to conduct readings for the study's participants.

By definition, "the projective hypothesis holds that an individual supplies structure to unstructured stimuli in a manner consistent with the individual's own unique pattern of conscious and unconscious needs, fears, desires, impulses, conflicts, and ways of perceiving and responding" (Cohen et al, 1992, p. 441). Thus a projective technique that externalizes a person's inner reality in some material medium is a means for organizing a person's unique experience as inseparable from her life-world.

The premise of the projective hypothesis is based on the dynamic approach to human development that runs counter to behaviorism (Abt & Bellak, 1959) and takes into consideration the relational aspects in the context of the *whole* person. The personality studied by means of projective procedures presents itself as a dynamic process incorporating past, present, and future aspects in the context of individual interactions and relationships as well as motivations and needs. It is a synchronistic, or transversal, connection, that we have addressed earlier, due to which projection actually manifests.

Jung's conception of projection is a particular case of relational dynamics when the archetype of the Shadow becomes activated and works behind the scenes, so to speak, implicitly affecting one's mind and explicitly influencing one to behave in a neurotic or compulsive manner. The Shadow can even posses the psyche completely and, importantly, the Shadow can often become *projected* onto others, and one may very well attribute to others those rather unsavoury qualities and traits that we, staying in the state of denial, are unable to recognize in ourselves.

In the framework of the projective hypothesis, we can see the invisible, intangible or virtual, reality of the archetypes actualized and made visible when projected onto the quite tangible and material medium of the pictures that embody powerful symbolic meanings. From this perspective Tarot comes close to the sandplay technique that has been called "the wonderful therapy" (Ryce-Menuhin, 1992). Similar to sand-play, Tarot uses non-verbal images as "a psychological guideline" (Ryce-Menuhin, 1992, p. 2). By projecting a person's life-world into pictures and images, Tarot symbolism stands for thoughts, emotions, feelings, level of awareness, current value-judgment, social adjustment, coping abilities, relationships with significant others, plus the whole world of repressions that may emerge and call for exploration during a session.

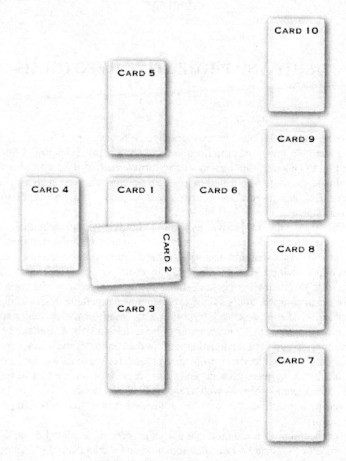

Figure 7.1. The Celtic cross spread.

Thus Tarot can be looked at as a supplementary source of valuable clinical material. In this respect it can parallel and even exceed the Rorschach test in terms of functioning not only as "an open and flexible arena for studying interpersonal transactions" (Cohen et al, 1992, p. 449) but also adding an extra, intra-psychic, dimension. From the standpoint of projective methods, Tarot goes into yet another direction: it is not only *what* the individual sees (as in an inkblot, for example) and *how* the individual perceives it, but also *why*.

At times when for various reasons it is difficult to understand the whole of the situation or attain an overview of seemingly disparate bits and pieces that do not make sense, a layout that symbolically represents the complicated and mixed aspects of one's life, further confused by the unique way the individual psyche perceives them, "connects the dots" and provides a chance to recognize how they all are interrelated. The Jungian transcendent function of bringing the unconscious into consciousness operates by projection of the archetypal images through the medium of the pictures, and a reader's task is the same as the analyst's, that is "according to Jung...to mediate the symbolic function for the patient...As the archetype per se is so deeply buried in the collective unconscious at its very bedrock level, we can never perceive it as such. It can be known only through its images...as portrayed in sandplays" (Ryce-Menuhin, 1992, pp. 20–22) and in Tarot layouts.

In the due course of the archetypal journey, many life situations and feelings associated with them are being externalized and provide an opportunity to literally look at them from the perspective of the Deleuzian "Outside", which is "more distant than any exterior, [and] is 'twisted', 'folded', and 'doubled' by an Inside that is deeper than any interior, and alone creates the possibility of the derived relation between the interior and exterior" (Deleuze, 1988b, p. 110).

The ten positions comprising the Celtic Cross carry certain connotations and constitute an important *context* within which each archetypal constellation is to be read and interpreted. Thus the Tarot hermeneutic is inseparable from the projective hypothesis. Different positions denote both external situations and internal mental or emotional states and thus provide a rich context within which each particular image is to be "read" and interpreted. While each position of the layout indicates a part of both the inner and outer world experienced by the subject of the reading, they however can be read only in the totality of the whole layout and only in the context of the subject's current, here-and-now, problematic situation.

Thoughts, emotions, hopes, fears, interpersonal relationships, intra-psychic conflicts, the immediate environment, desires and wishes – in short, the whole pheno-menology of a person's life-world, of which however the person might not yet be aware at a conscious level – is being projected into the layout, the symbolic representation of the said life-world. As Deleuze said, we "are never separable from the world: the interior is only a selected exterior, the exterior, a projected interior" (1988a, p. 125). The positions in Figure 7.1 comprise a network of relationships, a map or cartography that, as we said in the preceding chapter, functions as a visual communication channel capable of transmitting messages that can be summarized in brief as the following:

1. The card in the first position is the "presenting problem" at the core of a person's present concern, which may be either acknowledged or denied by this person when the reading unfolds. In this study, the participants' concerns covered mainly personal or professional problems. The questionnaire (see Appendix) included a "no problem at all" option so that the participants, if so willing, would have been able to exercise this particular option without giving me any information at all about their concern and what area of their life they would like to focus on. The symbolic *content* of a particular picture in the context of the person's presenting problem enables an expert reader to enrich and/or verify information that might have been indicated by this person.

2. The card in the second position represents a significant influence in the form of an impulse, or feeling, or trait, or behavioral pattern (not necessarily this person's own), or an event that may have strengthened or weakened the problem a person is concerned with. Under this influence the situation may grow and develop or, vice versa, development and progress may be hindered.

3. The card in the third position projects some important unconscious motivations affecting the current situation as it appears in the here-and-now of the reading. Perhaps a person is trying to solve her problem at the unconscious level; or maybe the roots of the matter are so deeply ingrained in her subconscious that they appear in her dreams, also something of a hidden variable that made an otherwise clear situation really confusing and problematic.

4. The forth position indicates what in Gestalt psychology is called "unfinished business" that might have led to the present situation becoming problematic. This is a position of the past in a temporal sense: an event that took place and the implications of which still persist. Depending on the number of pictures in this position and their symbolic content, the information they convey may be quite significant. Phenomenologically, it points to the essence of the person's past as it pertains to her problem to-date.

5. The card in the fifth position depicts future direction: where the situation is going depending on a person's conscious motivations. She may have been behaving in a certain manner or thinking in a particular way and in doing so has projected mental content into the future. This position reflects on a subject's potential future that might or might not come into being. At this point a reader may want to consider whether this behavior or thinking (as conveyed by the imagery of the particular card in this position) is to the person's best advantage. Is it productive or counter-productive to her wellbeing? How might it affect her mental and emotional health in the future?

6. The card in the sixth position represents the necessary development of the present situation. It is important to take into consideration the transpersonal perspective and to respect the fact that transpersonal psychologies recognize spiritual realities over and above our physical world. As Deleuze and Guattari stated, it is "[f]rom virtuals [that] we descend to actual states of affairs, and from states of affairs we ascend to virtuals, without being able to isolate one from the other" (1994, p. 160). Because of such *convergence* between the virtual and the actual we can say that the event – the state of affairs – described by the symbolic content of the picture (or pictures) in this position will take place in the near future.

7. The card in the seventh position is the person's mental, conscious, outlook. What is it that her mind is occupied with, sometimes to the point of fixation? The symbolic content implied by a particular picture (or pictures) in this position may indicate a thought/affect connection (or disconnection) for the person in her current state of mind.

8. The card in the eighth position indicates a person's immediate environment or people in her environment, such as significant others, family, friends, business associates, and the like. What is their attitude? In what context does the person have to deal with her problem? What is the level of interpersonal relationships? What is the role of "other"? The picture in this position may also point to a support system or the lack thereof.

9. The card in the ninth position projects a person's expectations, aspirations, hopes and ideals with regard to an important matter either directly or indirectly

related to the presenting problem. Often a person's hopes are connected with fear and anxiety. Is such a feeling justified by the collective unconscious? What is revealed by the person's reality checking?

10. The card in the final, tenth, position indicates a possible destination of the whole situation, which is highly dependent on the person's current level of awareness. However in the course of Tarot hermeneutics a developing dialogue with the back-and-forth of the person's free associations triggered by the symbolism of the pictures, as will be seen in chapter 8, contributes to intensifying a person's consciousness and expanding her awareness. This "outcome" card is to be read in conjunction with the rest of the layout and is by no means to be considered as an impending fate. This would be, as Roberts (1987) points out, "a most serious misconstruction...and ultimately spiritually debilitating to the one who holds to it" (p. 4). Rather, it contains information enriched by the dynamics that have unfolded in the course of the interpretation up to this point and the caring relationship that has surely been developing within a session. This may contribute to change, transformation and a probable change in attitude because of a person becoming-aware of the deep meaning of her experience as the sum total of all messages projected by the whole layout. The symbolic content of the image in this position, considered in the context of other pictures, is therapeutic material for personal transformation and "change, [for] conscious evolution [and] spiritual growth, all discovered inwardly" (Roberts, 1987, p. 4).

Functioning as a projection, the rhizomatic pattern laid down by the pictures presents itself as an expanded scope of space and time accessible to observations. It is because of projection that the virtual realm of the collective unconscious is spatialized and rendered visible. The *structure* of the layout is, sure enough, a projection, in the sense of projective geometry, or a static *snapshot* of a dynamic *process* that represents an unfolding of the archetypal dynamics. Still, the one-to-ten structure in the Celtic Cross spread is not as straightforward as it might seem. It does reflect real-life situations but in terms of trends and probabilities only, because human free will is a variable that cannot be written into any layout. However the "mood" carried by the archetypes comprising the field of the collective unconscious is "enveloping" (as we said earlier, citing Deleuze) one's actual reality even if as yet staying outside one's conscious awareness; and such affect is picked up in Tarot with amazing precision.

That is what gives Tarot its healing and educational quality, and not at all a dubious "fortune-telling" as a prediction of future events. If the layout transmits a feeling of anxiety, for example, it is a reflection of the potential warning function pertaining to the Tarot hermeneutic. Often our psychological problems start with an abundance of stressors and inability to recognize the presence of warning signs; this is a situation when the Tarot hermeneutic is invaluable by evaluating alternative options. Not at all does a reading act as a self-fulfilling prophecy, causing a person to act in a particular way due to a synchronistic precognition.

As a matter of fact, people tend to do what they were going to do all along if the unconscious habits still prevail. Tarot hermeneutic is a process towards awakening the person's awareness so that she is motivated toward the modification of behavioral or thought pattern. The awakening, the bit of insight lets a person see things in a new, meaningful, way, to explore and consider new possibilities in her life. Indeed intuition "that is intellectually oriented is characteristically directed toward understanding and insight" (Noddings and Shore, 1984, p. 80). By projecting her unconscious into a spread, a person discovers the means for expressing herself, for becoming capable of revealing something that sometimes she is unable, subconsciously – or is unwilling, consciously – to put into words. Both aspects provide a wealth of therapeutic material as, using the words of the man who coined the term 'projective technique', "the most important things about the individual are what he cannot or will not say" (Frank, 1939, p. 395).

A Tarot spread is an area with tangible boundaries determined by such "mundane" things as the size of the table the pictures are laid on. Similar to the bounded space of a sand tray, a Tarot spread becomes a container, in both the physical and metaphysical sense. The unconscious material, if not contained, may have a boomerang effect on a person, however the process of physically focusing eyes, attention, and mind on a layout, has a calming, centering, grounding effect. Plus the relief when the stuff with which a person has been overwhelmed is practically taken "out of her mind" and literally put, *projected*, onto the table.

A different type of boundary conditions is created by a reader who serves as a container for free-associations that may emerge during the hermeneutic process, as we will see in chapter 8. It is less threatening for a person with a high level of anxiety to communicate via the medium of a layout as a physical "bridge, a transversality" (Guattari, 1995, p. 23) between herself and the reader. Although resistance at the verbal level may be present, as in any traditional session, and may even contribute to character assessment, like for example in Rodney's case to be described in chapter 8, it has a tendency to be reduced because the bricolage of Tarot pictures triggers spontaneous associations for a person who thus tends to react equally spontaneously.

There is no persistent questioning that may be perceived by a person as threatening and only elevate her level of anxiety and accordingly resistance. As Roberts (1987) noticed, "Resistance never yields profound results" (p. 5). At the non-verbal level resistance is practically overcome. In contrast to such projective methods as, for example, the Thematic Apperception Test, any "intentional desire to fake good or to fake bad" (Cohen et al, 1992, p. 462) simply cannot take place: intentional means conscious, but a person is not choosing Tarot cards with pictures facing her, she simply shuffles the deck that the reader then lays down in the order shown in Figure 7.1.

While on the subject of resistance, a therapeutic technique called "story weaving" assigns to a counselor the role of a story weaver, a narrator who is making up various "threads" to put together the disparate elements permeating one's life, as well as infusing an emerging story with myths, hence facilitating a therapeutic change. Story weaving becomes a therapeutic intervention. Analogously, the Tarot hermeneutic creates a story told by life; and since a Tarot story is based on projections of how the psyche experiences physical facts because of the Jungian synchronistic connection, this is the person herself who metaphorically "weaves" her story. A reader, however, is weaving the "threads" together by translating the pictorial language into verbal and communicating to the person her own story while keeping in mind that "the psyche – naked – may need to be only observed at first, never interpreted irrevocably" (Ryce-Menuhin, 1992, p. 15). The person's psyche may be fragile and her ego immature, but it is her property, her territory, which is to be respected. The Tarot layout is a map and, as Gregory Bateson famously reminded us, "the map is not the territory" (1979, p. 30).

We will see in chapter 8 how the individual layouts provide insights to current situations, to helping or hindering factors, that may affect them, to hidden issues or obscure themes, to significant others in a person's life that form (or do not) the support system, they evaluate how functional (or dysfunctional) the system is and weigh probabilities ingrained in the person's behavioral patterns, addressing her anxieties, apprehensions, aspirations, wishes and motivations. It is the positions of the pictures embedded in the relational structure of the layout that produce correlations to allow for the creation of meanings in the hermeneutic process.

As for the interpretation, the meanings are created dynamically in the practice of the hermeneutic method *per se*. All three "variables", such as a person seeking the reading, the reader, and the symbolism of the pictures are embedded in a dynamic network of the "desiring-production", using Deleuze and Guattari's expression. In this respect the "situational variable" represented by a reader is of paramount importance and demands professional responsibility coupled with integrity, sensitivity and a developed intuition. The symbolic calling as per the imagery of the Judgement Arcanum will have had to be answered by a reader who is fully realizing her sense of vocation when performing the Tarot hermeneutic.

Jungian psychologist June Singer (1985) comments that the analyst must be seasoned and scorched in addition to being wise and compassionate. Only a genuine reader, whose own psyche reconnected with Eros in her journey through the tough life lessons, will be able to guide people seeking a Tarot counsel because one cannot take the other further than where she herself has already traveled. Years ago, when I was consulting with my Australian reader, he was immersed in his own archetypal journey; always an informal ethnographer, a nomad, as Deleuze would say. He has lived with Native American tribes, with Druids in Europe, with Hasidic groups in Israel, with Buddhist monks, in short, among worldwide spiritual traditions.

The reader must be individuated; her own unconscious must be integrated completely so that she presents to the world her authentic Self and not a Persona. To repeat, individuation is not individualism; the reader is always already embedded in a "double-pointed" relation at the level of the personal unconscious of the person seeking a reading and at the transpersonal level of the collective unconscious. It is at the very intersection of these multiple levels, including the spiritual as embedded in a rhizomatic network, that Martin Buber's ultimate *I-Thou* relation, the relation as much between men and God as "between man and man" (Buber, 1971), is being formed.

In fact human relationships meet in the eternal and timeless *Thou*. In the framework of Buber's Hasidic philosophy, a reader would have "fail[ed] the recipient [of Gnostic knowledge] when he presents [it] to him with a gesture of interference…

Interference divides the soul in his care into an obedient part and a rebellious part. But a hidden influence proceeding from his integrity has an integrating force" (Buber, 1971, p. 90). So in order to facilitate the integration of the other's unconscious into consciousness, the reader's unconscious *per se* should be fully integrated.

The continuous process of a genuine reader's *self-education,* that we addressed in chapter 2, becomes her very way of life that includes the symbolic lesson embodied in the archetype of The Chariot, which is closely linked, as we noticed in chapter 4, to the danger of her own ego getting inflated. The genuine *I-Thou* relation can be articulated only, as Buber emphasized, by the *whole* being. It transcends knowledge by word alone but includes what Buber called real imagining. It is the experiential *school of life* that includes many the archetypal lessons as learned, lived, and suffered-through that enables the reader, similar to Romanyshyn's wounded researcher that we referred to in chapter 1, to hold *all* Jungian psychological functions including feeling, thinking, sensing and – last but not least – intuition, in balance, leaving not one of them inferior.

It is intuition, sure enough, akin to Deleuze's method of transcendental empiricism as analyzed in the preceding chapter 6, that is central to the Tarot hermeneutic as reading and interpreting its archetypal, symbolic, messages and that succeeds in "bring[ing] into being that which does not yet exist" (Deleuze, 1994, p. 147) but still subsists in the realm of the virtual. In their book *Awakening the Inner eye: Intuition in Education* Noddings and Shore (1984) present intuition as a way of knowing and list four specific features to roughly distinguish intuition from the analytic, or conceptual, activity of the mind. The relation between the two remains complementary as "it is impossible to isolate the two meticulously and discretely" (Noddings and Shore, 1984, p. 69).

Developing one's intuition is a challenge for a reader especially if her role is what Noddings, in the context of the ethics of care in education, called "carer", or the one-caring, and who engages in a caring relation with the one "cared-for". In the hermeneutic process of Tarot readings intuition functions in accordance with its literal meaning as learning from within (*in-tuit*), from the very depth of the psyche enriched with the desire for Gnosis. Intuition always contains a spiritual, religious element especially if we read *re-ligio* etymologically as linking backward to the origin; the soul returning to its symbolic home in *Anima Mundi.*

Desire, Affect, Love, Eros! Whatever the name, this is what functions as an erotic "compulsion to think which passes through all sorts of bifurcations, spreading from the nerves and…communicated to the soul in order to arrive at thought" (Deleuze, 1994, p. 147), to achieve understanding, to make the unconscious conscious. Our cognitive faculties are inadequate to access the immaterial and virtual realm of the unconscious, if not for it being projected in the material form of the pictures that triggers intuition and raises "each faculty to the level of its transcendent exercise, … [when it] attempts to give birth to that second power which grasps that which can only be sensed" (Deleuze, 1994, p. 165).

The second, intensified, power of perception becomes a sixth sense, the "faculty" of love and compassion capable of "seeing" with Noddings' "inner eye", that is, grasping by virtue of "the unity of love and cognition" (Idel & McGinn, 1999, p. 22) the deep archetypal meanings projected in the Tarot pictures of our physical reality of space and time. What we usually consider our actual reality of three-dimensional space and linear time is only a projection of the virtual spiritual reality literally "outside" the confines of the physical, directly perceptible, visible world.

The invisible reality projects itself synchronistically on the material plane in the form of the Tarot layout, which is "neither one nor two [but] ...it is the in-between" (Deleuze and Guattari, 1987, p. 293), analogous to the in-between-ness of Buber's *I-Thou* relation in its immanent-transcendent "quality of conjoined opposites" (Jung, CW 8, 189). We thus understand that our habitual "space-time ceases to be a pure given in order to become...the nexus of differential relations in the subject, and the object itself ceases to be an empirical given in order to become the product of these relations" (Deleuze, 1993, p. 89). The object in question is the object of our knowledge, Gnosis, embodied in the structure of the layout where the pictures in specific positions relate to each other in the rhizomatic network; and time itself becomes "spread" or laid out in its three dimensions of the past, present and even future as indicated in the specific positions of the Celtic Cross.

A virtual event, for Deleuze, is always "already past and yet in the future, always the day before and the day after" (1990a, p. 77), coexisting on the plane of immanence when the unlimited becoming-other-as-becoming-the-authentic-Self unfolds in front of our eyes. The reason that certain pictures "fall out" in the precise positions and not in some other appears both rational and irrational at the same time. If synchronicity reflects "patterning in the universe...that could not be grasped intellectually" (Bolen, 1979, p. 13) solely, but requires the reversal of our beliefs and the habits of thinking, then the limits of the narrow deductive logic of explanation are to be transgressed and enriched with experiential and "spontaneous emotional response" (Bolen, 1979, p. 17) at the level of the body.

The infamous "verification" (as a prerogative of scientific method) comes about by what in esoteric literature is called "spirits talking" that can manifest itself as warmth or chill or related subtle *sensations* colored by what Jung called a feeling-tone. The Gnostic knowledge is to be *felt* in addition to being understood at the cognitive level; only as such can a harmonious re-symbolization of the Self be achieved. The very *depth* of the psyche is capable of making sense so that we can discover the deep meanings of our experiences only when it, as Deleuze says, "having been *spread out became width*. The becoming unlimited is maintained entirely within this inverted width" (Deleuze, 1990a, p. 9; italics mine) on the flat surface or plane by means of being projected on this very plane (a Tarot layout or spread) not unlike when we watch movies in the cinema in their dynamic unfolding projected onto a screen.

We perceive depth on the surface; the depth shines through the surface. The collective unconscious attracts our attention to specific problem areas. Or the person's individual unconscious demands attention reaching out toward consciousness; this is an important matter right now, otherwise this particular picture would not have appeared in the spread. "Why now?" we may want to ask, and thus begin an explicit dialogue with the person so valued by Buber.

Or some of the surrounding pictures may provide additional insight as past influences, present concerns, and future possibilities are all projected into the layout, offering a multiplicity of dimensions to be explored. The Tarot hermeneutic brings forth the *clinical* element in Deleuze's philosophy in terms of evaluating and outlining the structure of the layout: "which of [the rhizomatic lines] are dead-ended or blocked, which cross voids ... and most importantly the line of steepest gradient, how it draws in the rest, towards what destination" (Deleuze, 1987, p. 120).

The destination is not exactly destiny: by means of getting information on where our present line of thinking and acting may be taking us, we can literally change the direction we are taking. It is not only that the past affects the present, but the future appears to also affect the present. This most important and powerful relation is called by Deleuze "*a power to affect itself, an affect of self on self*" (Deleuze 1988b, p. 101; italics Deleuze's). In this relation there is yet another subtle "hidden variable": an affect of the Self on oneself. We remember that the archetype of the Self is always already implicated in the folds of the collective unconscious. The task is to find this line of becoming, that Deleuze calls the line of the steepest gradient, the synchronistic line of projection (in terms of projective geometry), and Tarot hermeneutic is the method that does exactly this: it helps us to bring the unconscious into consciousness and become aware of our potential, coming into being, future.

The pictures are aligned with the collective and personal unconscious, and the power of symbols transcends and moves through existing blocks and defenses. As themes emerge in the process of Tarot hermeneutic, therapeutic material is being created. An overview of the total spread may direct attention to a particular archetypal constellation, as will be seen in chapter 8; thus providing insight into a significant part of the whole. Both participants concentrate on shuffling the deck, the spread connects both people, becoming itself a virtually physical link. Metaphysically the connection is secured by the collective unconscious, therapeutically the connection is established via relation which is sustained, in turn, by the aforementioned physical and metaphysical means.

The layout in its symbolic content may manifest the presence of pathology, certainly not necessarily according to classifications of the clinical "bible", the Diagnostic and Statistical Manual, but rather indicating the areas of particular sensitivity: if you press on it, it will hurt. What, where, how and why it hurts, is projected into the pictures. This feeling of the *relatedness* of the reader brings congruence into the relationship, especially when in this interaction a person's unspoken view of herself becomes validated.

Rapport is thus being established, and from it grows trust; one cannot doubt one's mirror reflection. Or can she? This reminds me of a paradoxical though typical situation. I had a reading once for a woman whose main concern and disappointment were connected to the way her business was going. The session revealed that she lacked elementary training and the "know-how" of running her business. At a deeper level she projected an inflated ego and over-confidence well on the way "up" to the grandiosity complex.

Her reaction to a pictorial story, which indicated the desirability of opening a couple of books or attending a refresher course, was negative. She dismissed the suggestion, arguing that she knew better, thus explicitly confirming what the pictures have implied. When the archetypal patterns are projected into the cards, the reader's understanding of the current situation is assisted by the fact that, despite similar symptoms, a person might be presently affected by a completely different archetypal constellation, hence would be unable to avoid the repetition of past actions or mistakes.

Facilitating a person's awareness of such a possibility would eliminate or reduce guilt or shame, contribute to her self-esteem and the feeling of self-worth; in short, would promote psychological healing. In this respect Tarot functions in the manner of Jung's compensatory function, similar to dreams in the analytic process. The projection of the unconscious does compensate for whatever is missing, that is, as yet "outside" consciousness. The reading brings this material to awareness hence widening the boundaries of individual consciousness.

In addition to the dreams' compensatory mode, Jung "acknowledged that many dreams function in other ways, such as prospectively, that is anticipating a psychological direction or development extrasensorily, affording one information about an occurrence outside of the awareness of one's five senses; and prophetically, predicting a future occurrence" (Hopcke, 1992, p. 26). We said earlier that the sixth position in the layout in Figure 7.1. is the one of immediate future, while the fifth shows a probable destination, and the tenth is the overall development.

I find myself in a peculiar situation: attempting to present in a logical linear form, using a sequential structure of propositional language, something that is apparently non-linear and appears to defy logic or rational explanation. Both intuitively and empirically I know what I am writing about, but any verbal and linear analog of this seems to paradoxically reflect "the apparently insurmountable difficulties of breaking away from our ingrained habits of thinking in terms of cause and effect" (Koestler, 1972, p. 97). There is a logical paradox, almost a trap, in an effort to apply explanatory, *causal* terms to the phenomenon that manifests itself due to the *a-causal* principle of Jungian synchronicity.

Nevertheless the effort is being made. The next chapter focuses on the practical art of the Tarot hermeneutic method. It is their real-life stories as embedded in the actual readings for the fifteen participants that constitute the core of my research and have motivated me to write this book in the first place.

STORIES LIVES TELL

As noted by Maxine Greene in her Foreword to the remarkable book *Stories Lives tell: Narrative and Dialogue in Education* (Witherell and Noddings, 1991), from which the title of this chapter is taken, we can hear "the sounds of storytelling... everywhere today. Narratives of many kinds are being opened and explored. Journal keeping goes on apace on all levels of learning: people write autobiographies, shape family histories, become authors of their own lives" (p. ix). Relating narratives specifically to "women's ways of knowing" (Belenky, Clinchy, Goldberger, & Tarule, 1986), Greene situates them in classrooms and counseling centers alike.

It is whenever the gap between cognitive, moral and emotional dimensions in education is bridged that learning becomes associated with the holistic "sense of seeking, struggling to name, striving to find language for what was repressed and suppressed over the years... [and giving] shape and expression to what would otherwise be untold" (Witherell and Noddings, 1991, p. x). To bridge this gap means to release one's imagination (Greene, 2000). For Green, imagination is intimately connected with the *healing* arts; the release of imagination is equivalent to releasing the power of empathy; but also to breaking with something that we habitually take for granted, thus breaking into possibilities that may lie ahead. Imagination pushes the Ego from its position in the center of the personality where it can comfortably focus on "self-regard [and] into a space where we can come face to face with others" (Greene, 2000, p. 31).

This coming face to face with Other takes place during Tarot hermeneutic that unfolds real-life stories of human experiences embodied in symbols and images. It is a story that unites a teacher in a classroom with a "counselor or analyst...in the therapeutic dialogue, and the pastor, priest, or rabbi, in narratives of faith and loss" (Witherell and Noddings, 1991, p. 1). Tarot images talk to us "in a different voice" that brings forth the subtleties of Carol Gilligan's views on moral development and Nel Noddings' relational ethics (Noddings, 2002). Noddings (1993a) argues that our modern liberal education, devoid of feeling and caring dimensions, does not enrich the human mind and spirit but tends to narrow its scope.

Presenting feminist spirituality as an alternative to traditional patriarchal religion, Noddings acknowledges that women have long suffered inferiority under the prevailing theological and philosophical theories. She suggests that students should be exposed to both the story of the Fall and to its feminist critique with an emphasis on the Goddess religions, in which the biblical serpent is not evil but instead educates humans in Gnosis and brings healing. Such Gnostic knowledge that, as I argued in the preceding chapters, embodies the ancient Socratic "Know Thyself" dictum is available to us by means of the Tarot hermeneutic method when, in the course of Tarot readings, the images and symbols become narrated and interpreted, thereby articulating the individual and collective experiences in the school of life as many of humanity's ethical, intellectual, and spiritual lessons.

In chapter 2 I addressed the bricolage of Tarot in the context of my study as a mix-method of phenomenology, hermeneutics and narrative knowledge; also assisted by methodologies within projective psychology, as per chapter 7. To satisfy Pacific Oaks College's requirements of collecting behavioral data via human subjects I proceeded with performing readings for the self-selected sample of participants. Each participant signed a consent form in agreement with research ethics guidelines. Each session was of fifty minutes duration, similar to a standard counseling session. In lieu of free readings my participants were asked to complete a questionnaire (as per Appendix) on which they indicated the area of their concern or "presenting problem" as it is usually called in the intake form during conventional counseling and therapy sessions; and they also indicated the purpose of the reading analogous to the usual counseling practice of asking clients during the very first session what are this person's expectations from her therapy.

The reason that I selected only fifteen cases for detailed description in my research is a simple one. I simply stopped collecting data because those fifteen sessions when described almost verbatim amounted to a number of pages exceeding the requirements of my research. The sample happened to cover a diverse adult population of males and females across different ethnic groups. No more specific questions in the form of how they usually appear in conventional intake forms, concerning past history, family members, etc., were asked. All relevant information was assumed to will have been projected (as per chapter 7) into the participants' respective layouts. However I anticipated that a situation might arise when, due to sheer curiosity or the opportunity to get a free reading, I would have encountered someone who under other circumstances would not even considered counseling. Irrespectively, their layouts would still contain significant material to work with, as we will indeed see in some cases further below.

The narratives as described below derived from the audio tapes and copies of the layouts I made during each reading; each individual case reflecting the unique personality of a particular research participant while retaining the universality of the archetypal dynamics actualized in the here-and-now of each reading. It is the archetypal meanings rising from the depth of the unconscious that provoke our "wide-awakeness...imaginative action, and...renewed consciousness of possibility" (Greene, 2000, p. 43) which is becoming actuality as a particular story unfolds. All participants have signed a consent form allowing me to publish this material for educational and research purposes. All names have been changed.

CASE 1. MICHAEL

Michael, a white professional man in his early forties, stated a relationship problem as his main reason for this reading. He specified it in the questionnaire as a hope for a romantic relationship, free of past obstacles. The purpose of this reading for him was to gain insight into future and significant others; to interpret behavior and to focus on solutions. Michael's layout is shown in Figure 8.1.

Figure 8.1. Michael's layout.

The picture in the first position, Five of Pentacles, indicated the feeling of disappointment and loss. The reason for such deep emotions was Michael's experience of himself as having missed out on something. Apparently when facing a choice, he

87

selected to "pass-by" his possible "reward" therefore experiencing, as the consequence of his passivity, the feeling of defeat, rejection and "being left out in the cold". Michael interjected, saying at this point that he, sure enough, walked out of his last relationship because he felt unable to make a commitment, and he still felt affected by those upsetting emotions. The picture in the second position represented the obstacles that presented a challenge for Michael in the context of his present situation. The Four of Pentacles demonstrated that subconsciously he was desperately trying to hold onto something and not let go of it. Was it his habitual pattern of behavior? The imagery of the Four of Pentacles conveys miserliness, when one clings to her few possessions, either monetary or emotional, without sharing them with people in her environing world. Apparently Michael was unable to share his emotions and feelings with anyone who could potentially become his significant other because his clinging to a habitual pattern of behavior was providing him with a rather paradoxical feeling of security, at least in avoiding a risk. Still this feeling was doomed to turn into loss as per the Five of Pentacles in the first position as the core of Michael's problem.

The Major Arcanum in the fourth, "past", position indicated that issues of power and control had at some point become dominant and continued to influence Michael's present behavior and his state of mind. The image of The Emperor as the strong archetypal animus had taken over Michael's unconscious and was, "in the name of the Father", still governing his psyche. Of course Michael's anima was over-compensating by making him behave in a manner of a stereotypical, even if metaphorical, submissive "woman" who prefers to stay subject to male dominance. Perhaps the unconscious motives for Michael to choose not to be committed to the relationship were based on his erroneous ideation of giving in or losing his ability to be in control if staying in any relationship.

What happened in the past that made Michael so sensitive to the issues of power and control? Was it his real-life past relationship, I asked. Michael said that he had the most traumatic experience nearly twenty years ago when he was in love but the other person did not accept him. But under the archetypal influence of The Emperor, as if intoxicated by him, Michael – by not choosing to be in a relationship, that is, making negative but still his own choices – could maintain his perverse feeling of authority so as to prevent his own victimization, yet end up as a victim nonetheless. His feeling of being rejected had been internalized and continued to be projected onto the relationships Michael had since; his subconscious desire not to be rejected again caused Michael, who was in fact insecure, to become controlling in defense of his insecurity and to make choices to end relationships so as not to find himself in a reenactment of the situation that had been engraved in his mind, repressed and so far never dealt with at the conscious level.

The picture in the third position, the Three of Pentacles, as the root of the matter, told me that although Michael appeared to miss being in a relationship, there was no romance in his attitude. It was more like a social consideration or strong pressure from family members acting in tandem as an institution. The Emperor indicated that his family may have had old fashioned, patriarchal values and was putting pressure on Michael, quite likely using the words "you have to" or "you must", in the manner of The Emperor often using law and order to maintain the status quo. The Emperor archetype affecting Michael's psyche led to the idea of upgrading his social position or status if and when he succeeds in getting involved in a personal relationship. There was no notion of any emotional involvement, though, in this pattern, in the line of development from the initial Three of Pentacles, through the Four of Pentacles that "crossed over" the issue that presented the problem in the first place, and toward the picture in the fifth position, as a probable development of this situation, the Ten of Swords.

This image of a human figure lying motionless on the ground as if nailed in the back by ten swords at once, in the position of the likely "destination", demonstrated that if Michael continues in his present behavior, driven by the motivations that were not based on his ownership of his real feelings, not only might each relationship be ruined, but he himself might become affected by major depression. In the feminist interpretation by Gearhart and Rennie (1981), the imagery of the Ten of Swords points to putting a significant part of one's life on the patriarchal altar as a symbolic sacrificial lamb.

However the Ten of Swords, as the last tenth card in the suit, simultaneously indicates the end of the situation as it presents itself here and now, as though the worst has already happened. Thus for Michael the possibility of modifying his behavioral pattern and changing his habits was already "in the air" (with the "severance" card in the fifth position) and confirmed by the sixth card, the Six of Swords, in the position of the immediate future, that indicated a sure move from a destructive pattern of behavior to a constructive one, even if the details were still unknown. The human figure in the picture of the Six of Swords does not yet look into the future; she is simply happy just to get out of the present situation, without yet making plans for the future, simply retreating from a failure which happened to be only temporary. And peace of mind will have followed as the result of changing habitual patterns of behavior.

At this point Michael said that he had felt paralyzed in the past, but now has a clear understanding that he has to do something about it. To me, though, the whole constellation of the pictures showed that Michael's *rational* decision to get in a new relationship and subsequently get more involved, were bound to failure *a priori*. In the past Michael was affected at an emotional level, his "unfinished business" as represented by The Emperor and "stamped" on with the Four of Pentacles was still "alive and well" in his present situation. So in order to be avoided in the future it is necessary for Michael to work through it not at the mental level of the rational thoughts but at the more subtle level of feelings. But how to do it? The duration of each session within this study was only 50 minutes, in accordance with any standard counseling sessions, so we could only explore a few options. Gestalt therapy would be beneficial for Michael's character and his personality type as Michael's rational mind, Logos, appeared to work so powerfully (in the image of The Emperor), that it "succeeded" in the suppression of emotions Michael had long been experiencing. Also, the guided imagery would be helpful to work at the deeper "psychoid" level of the psyche, where Michael's issues of power and control were buried together with his insecurity in a paradoxical and most unfortunate mix.

The imagery of the Major Arcanum Justice in the seventh position, as a powerful fixation in Michael's mind, indicated that Michael was preoccupied with the issues of fairness. He was deeply hurt by the thought that he had been treated unjustly, and his apprehension grew from that. His mind became a slave to this constant mental outlook that might have even grown into a world view. Michael needed to work now on distinguishing between his subjective values and the objective, socio-cultural, world and to not transfer his personal apprehension onto the world. At this point Michael interjected, saying that he was concerned more with societal injustice rather than with his own problem; his comment confirmed how deeply the Justice archetype has affected him. Was an anticipation of unfairness becoming a type of a self-fulfilling prophecy wrecking his personal life and interpersonal relationships?

The picture indicating Michael's immediate environment in the eighth position was the Two of Pentacles. Apparently Michael did not enjoy his job as much as he could. He was performing his duties, but more because he had to rather than wanted to. He had to please his co-workers and to make an effort to present a pleasant disposition. It appeared that he could be easily manipulated at his workplace. It did take away his energy as a matter of course, and the imagery of the Two of Pentacles warned Michael to pay attention to how he applies himself, as his habit of making an effort to accommodate others might cause him to eventually become unable to cope and drop his duties at once if he becomes stressed. The Two of Pentacles in this position may have also indicated a custom of sexual one-night stands rather than a permanent romantic relationship (and we remember that the absence of the latter was stated by Michael on the questionnaire as his presenting problem).

Three pictures that fell out in the ninth position highlighted the fact that Michael's main concern was the hope for, and anxiety about, future relationship. The ninth position is the one of hopes and fears. Three images, of the Queen of Cups, The Fool and the Page of Cups, strongly suggested that a possible realization of Michael's hopes would be in making a choice of creating a stable relationship, perhaps even planning a family (as the queen and the page of the same suit in the same position "told" me). This would be a totally new stage in Michael's life, symbolized by The Fool as a lucky chance, fresh beginning, and a start of a new life cycle, where his old attitude would not fit. Alternatively, and quite likely, Michael may meet a woman with a young child in the future. So Michael will have to be prepared to make a step, to take a risk and face the unknown if he wanted personal relationship to manifest. Michael said at this stage that although he has taken himself off the mainstream of social life on purpose, he recently started to socialize again.

The tenth card, the Ace of Wands in the position of the outcome, indicated that the beginning stage had good potential to blossom and that the idea of a relationship might very well materialize and become a reality in Michael's life. Three supplementary images in the 11th, 12th and 13th positions indicated that some of Michael's wishes were coming true, as per the Nine of Cups; stagnation and inactivity turning into stability. The Knight of Pentacles suggested a stable employment. The Ten of Cups suggested the possibility of new commitments at the level of interpersonal relations; especially now that Michael appeared to be financially secure. Michael said at this point that he felt more self-confident, especially with regard to his career (as the practicality of the Knight of Pentacles indeed indicated), but still often finding himself unable even to approach somebody he finds attractive, even if simply to say hello.

Yet, the fact that he was becoming consciously aware of his behavioral patterns was a means to take him out of hopelessness, out of passivity and into new endeavors (the Ace of Wands).

The outcome card, being the Ace, encouraged Michael to allow himself new beginnings and to look forward to reaping the possible fruits, even if now they were only little buds; this imagery also was a strong antidote to the dark depressive mood of the Ten of Swords in the fifth position. The overall card was the Queen of Wands as an actual woman among Michael's acquaintances, but not at the level of a romantic relationship. Still it was because of her (the Queen of Wands) that Michael's situation was taking a turn for the better. The Queen of Wands appeared likely to be a work associate who assisted Michael with his career development.

At this point, approaching the end of the counseling session (50 minutes) I asked Michael if there was anything he wished to clarify. The most important concern for Michael, during the course of a reading, became how to deal with the issues of control and power, how to conquer the archetypal Emperor in his psyche. Michael's question indicated that, in the course of this counseling session, he was indeed able to get to the roots of what really constituted his presenting problem. He picked up the card from the remainder of the deck thus letting the collective unconscious communicate and clarify his concern; when he turned it over, we saw the Four of Wands. Even before I started to interpret the imagery, Michael began to laugh spontaneously; apparently free-associating with the image of the happy, triumphant figures carrying floral wreaths, on this picture. This image carried the message of a positive relationship, very beneficial for Michael, perhaps even the foundation for marriage.

Thus for Michael, becoming open to the possibility of a committed relationship would simultaneously contribute to eliminating the obstacles and struggles with issues of power and control. Then we summarized what we had read; Michael said he realized that nobody would come knocking in his door, he had to go out and look for a person, but the manner in which he said it, the tone of voice and the facial expression indicated no bitterness, no fear, those affects having been replaced by awareness. Michael said that all was "very, very true." He stated in the questionnaire: "I was able to better understand the reasons for past behaviors and self-defeating actions; and how to enable more self-fulfilling actions." He answered "yes" to the question weather this reading contributed to achieving his purpose and explained that "the reading was focused on positive outcomes through positive actions." Michael expressed a desire to have a follow-up session stating that "the explanations discussed helped me to better understand how to solve questions or problems in an interpretive way." He indicated that this reading was very significant and meaningful "in helping to work on solutions. Also to help me understand how to 'let go' and to be confident that everything will work out, as long as I am willing to take even small risks, knowing that failure is only temporary."

CASE 2. LOLA

Lola, a young white professional woman, not yet thirty years old, specified a professional problem as her main reason for the reading. She was involved in creating her own project in her professional field. The purpose of the reading was for her to gain insight into herself, into the present development of the project and into its future outcome. She wanted to clarify issues, to focus on solutions and "to find out what is making me resist and keeping from manifesting this project." Lola's layout is shown in Figure 8.2.

The Major Arcanum Strength in the first position was crossed by the Ten of Pentacles in the second position. This indicated that, as pertaining to her project,

Figure 8.2. Lola's layout.

Lola's main concern was satisfying her ambitions and exercising her willpower for the purpose of establishing herself in the professional world. The inability to relate to people and distancing herself may have also been the case. The crossing position of the Ten of Pentacles, a positive card by itself in its image of stability and security, carried the message, though, of a hindering influence: perhaps an unconscious goal of Lola was not the creation of the project but the creation of a safety net for herself by means of the said project, by meeting a certain standard in her professional life. It appeared from the imagery that the demands that Lola imposed on herself were rather overwhelming. Indeed, the feeling of incompleteness and solitude, manifested by the card in the third position, the Nine of Pentacles, and also well-controlled thought process, was the motivation behind Lola's inquiry into the current status of her enterprise. Although in the past she went through internal struggle with herself, perhaps through a period of self-doubt, as suggested by the Five of Wands in the fourth position, her endurance and determination had so far carried her towards achieving her goal, but determination in fact beginning to border on self-indulgence.

Self-mastery was suggested by the vertical line that showed the evolution from the Nine of Pentacles, via Strength, toward the Two of Wands in the fifth position. The imagery of this card suggested a potential fulfillment of purpose, providing more research will have been done. Apparently nothing was actively happening presently, despite Lola's determination, and Lola was becoming restless. Despite her being goal-oriented and strong, the results of the project did not seem to manifest in the near future. A period of at least seven weeks spent on further researching the project would be to Lola's best advantage.

The imagery of the card in the position of the immediate future, the Seven of Cups, carried the symbolic message of "castles built in the air", so Lola needed to focus on further analyzing data for her project because if nothing were to change in the energy field surrounding the project its outcome would be quite questionable. The project appeared to be vague and more the product of Lola's wishful thinking rather than practical reality. Apparently Lola's talents, skills and imagination worked over-time and have clouded the clear design of her study with the almost innumerable options. Focusing on a single goal would definitely contribute to her becoming clear about what exactly she wanted to achieve versus an excessive obsession with the multiple and diverse details of her project that appeared to pull her in too many directions simultaneously, as per the Seven of Cups imagery. Still the potential presence of the Two of Wands provided the necessary balance. At this point Lola inter-jected, saying that she was in therapy and was having weekly counseling sessions.

So what was keeping her from manifesting results? Is it because her mind is else-where? Lola seemed busy focusing on her private life and evaluating her personal relationships rather than concentrating on the particularities and subtleties of her professional life. Three additional cards (the positions added to the standard ten positions of the Celtic Cross), the King of Cups, the Wheel of Fortune and The Hierophant, suggested a continuous stable relationship with a man, who responded to Lola at the emotional level and seemed to be quite serious in his intentions, even wanting to take the relationship to the next level; making it official by virtue of traditional wedding. Lola was lucky to have such a "karmic" man nearby. Lola said that the man was good and, yes, oriented towards a conventional steady relationship. However the constellation of three cards in the seventh position clearly demonstrated that Lola's mind was preoccupied with thoughts about another man, with whom she was hoping for a love relationship even if presently facing a dilemma (The Lovers). This other man, the King of Swords, symbolized quite an authoritative and independent personality, and perhaps those qualities both attracted Lola and kept her apprehensive about getting involved with him. Lola was becoming obsessed with the thoughts about the King of Swords; her confusing personal life distracted Lola from concentrating on her project and devoting time and effort to her professional aspirations and obligations. The overall card, the Seven of Pentacles, demonstrated Lola's anxiety concerning the fact that she has invested in the project, and since no results had yet come to pass, there was a feeling of wasted efforts, some doubts about seeing the results and perhaps some financial loss too. Lola said that, yes, she put her own money into the project. The symbolism of this card, however, carried a message for Lola not to stop but be consistent in her efforts, perhaps reassessing what she has achieved so far and what still needed to be done, including reevaluating her own attitude and motivations.

Since the whole layout suggested that Lola was strongly motivated to get the project moving, her subconscious driving forces needed to be addressed in detail to find out what has been keeping this project from being realized. The picture in the eighth position, the Eight of Swords, indicated that Lola's environment was quite oppressive. But since her project was an individual one and of solitary nature (the Nine of Pentacles), there were no factors coming from somebody else, like administrative or paperwork obstacles that might have hindered the development of any idea. In Lola's case the restrictions came upon her through her own confusion, symbolic blindness and suppressed emotions. This card further emphasized the necessity for re-evaluating her own motives. Teamwork and cooperation was suggested by the Three of Wands in the ninth position. Perhaps Lola wanted all rewards for herself only, considering that solitary creativity was at the heart of her problem, but at this stage should she not cooperate with others the project would not move ahead from its present stage, there would not be any hope for progress. The Major Arcanum in the "outcome", tenth, position indicated Lola's willpower symbolized by The Chariot. In order to lead her project to successful completion, Lola must get out of the conflict she has created within herself, torn apart by the confusing issues of personal ambitions versus the ideals of her creative goal. What was the original purpose? There seemed to be a danger of the project becoming secondary to Lola's primary concern with establishing herself professionally in her field. The Chariot indicated a high probability for Lola exercising self-discipline, providing she would learn to control those opposing driving forces that were splitting her apart. The Chariot has assured Lola that her self-control should carry her on. Perhaps a period of waiting, aligned through the Two of Wands with The Chariot, would need to be spent in further counseling. working on those issues that surfaced during this reading and also learning to distinguish between her subconscious personal urges and the conscious choice of common sense. Lola said at this point that self-discovery was a significant part of her project. The pictures, however, carried a strong reminder to not lose the main original idea or turn it into a vanity exercise that might happen to be lost in the clouds of the Seven of Cups. Lola wanted to further clarify this sixth card and on my suggestion she picked up the supplementary card for this position out of the deck. When she turned it over, she discovered the Major Arcanum The Devil.

Associations that this image usually brings forth are frightening. On the other hand, if and when the collective unconscious directs someone to subconsciously choose this particular card (all the pictures are face down), it means it is extremely important that this archetype must be addressed here and now. No wonder the total layout kept pointing towards further counseling, as The Devil, one's very Shadow, needs a lengthy exploration by itself. The time span of this reading session, fifty minutes, made a focused inquiry into this major card quite limited, but nonetheless very insightful for Lola. She exclaimed, "How frightening it is to pick up the Devil card!" I asked her what was so frightening (an associative process thus begun). Lola mentioned darkness, then paused and added the word fear.

At the unconscious level Lola's psyche was overwhelmed by the dark underworld of fear and constrictive emotions. She fantasized about the project and eventually became enslaved by the idea she herself gave birth to. It was not she anymore who controlled the course of events with regard to her project; instead the archetype took over and possessed her. She became obsessed with the idea and was now governed and controlled by it. The idea, instead of empowering Lola, became overpowering, the difference, however, being very subtle. Lola picked up one more card, to find out what, that she was not aware of, might keep her "imprisoned" (her expression) by the Devil. The card turned out to be the Three of Pentacles, very positive by itself, but in conjunction with the Devil, carrying a message of the inflated ego, and a strong desire to improve one's own social status and to earn approval from people in positions of authority. Lola said at this stage, "Yes, I want recognition!"

So why was her project not manifesting? A further challenge for Lola would be to work on her motivations, on the relation between fantasy and reality, on ability to concentrate on a single goal, in general on making herself more of a whole person in order to achieve wholeness in her enterprises. Several times during this reading Lola repeated, "This is the story of my life..." On my suggestion Lola picked up the last card to find out what else might be helpful in addressing all the issues that emerged in this session. The imagery of the Six of Cups indicated the idea of an honest open conversation and sharing the deepest concerns with somebody Lola could trust, perhaps continuing the therapeutic process that would bring healing.

Lola said that this reading contributed to achieving her purpose, stating that she "gained insight in what is restricting [me] in achieving [my] goal, namely fear and confusion in [my] specific intentions within the project." She indicated that she would like to have a follow-up session, explaining her answer as a desire "to find out more". She said that the reading was significant and meaningful to her and provided the following comment: "I gained some clarity on where I need to focus my attention in seeing my project through as of today. I understood how Tarot works as a tool in self-discovery along psychology, allowing for more personal issues to come out and be pin-pointed for future discoveries."

CASE 3. OMAR

Omar, a black professional man in his late thirties, did not have any particular problem that he wanted to address through the reading. His main reason for the reading was based on his being "always interested in the science of Tarot...and curious about personal reading." The purpose of the reading for him was to gain insight into all of the listed items: past, present, future, himself, significant others, and to find out more about Tarot. Omar's layout is shown in Figure 8.3.

Figure 8.3. Omar's layout.

Both the first and second positions were taken by the images of the Major Arcana, The Hierophant and The Fool. Since Omar did not state any concerns as his presenting problem, I have associated card number one, The Hierophant with Omar's quest for spiritual meaning in his life. Mid-way in his life journey, he might have found himself in a dark wood and searching for a straight way out, as Dante said once in *The Divine Comedy*. It appeared that Omar has accomplished certain goals in the material world and perhaps now had a fresh opportunity, represented by The Fool, of starting a new life cycle. Omar said at that point that he always wanted to make a difference and felt ready now to start some enterprise of his own. The Hierophant indicated that Omar sensed the blessing within himself and the readiness to go out in the world and to test his beliefs and values for himself, to apply them now at the level of physical reality. For that he must take a new path, provided by The Fool, and face the multiplicity of new unknown experiences.

Apparently he had made some preliminary inquiries in the recent past, as indicated by the Eight of Wands in the fourth position, his mind traveled freely and no obstacles or hindrances interfered with Omar's search. The time was ripe for new initiatives and actions, and at the present moment Omar appeared to be at the threshold of a new beginning.

The Three of Cups in the third position provided some information with regard to what motivated Omar in his search. He achieved happiness and abundance in his personal life, and he felt that to maintain the joy and bring further happiness into his life and the life of his significant others he needed to commit himself to further achievements. But were his glorious dreams justified by the collective unconscious? The answer appeared to be yes and no! The Ten of Wands in the fifth position warned Omar that although he was a man who was accustomed to taking full responsibility for his actions and carrying a load on his own shoulders, this new goal, a new choice that he was about to make, might become a heavy, almost unbearable burden. The load was definitely self-imposed. It appeared to be a matter of an attitude, and the lesson of another Major Arcanum, Temperance, in the sixth position would be to slow down, to reevaluate past achievements and perhaps be open to compromise regarding the issue of priorities in Omar's life. Moderation will be to Omar's benefit; he should stop rushing himself and needs to treat himself with more forgiveness.

At this point Omar, free-associating with the reading, made some comments that confirmed the pictures' messages. His mother was divorced, and evidently Omar accepted the responsibility of being a husband-substitute figure to make his mother's circumstances easier. His first marriage ended in divorce too, and in his present relationship Omar worked hard emotionally, mentally and physically to make a seemingly perfect marriage. The Knight of Cups in the overall position depicted Omar as a gentle and sensitive, while idealistic and romantic, man with high hopes of filling the cup he holds with good deeds and offering it to those in need. His principles were of high standards and he was a seeker of perfection. Like the knights in search of the Holy Grail, Omar shared their quest for what he considered to be the only Truth.

The image of Temperance thus became valuable, timely and necessary advice for Omar, especially in view of his being preoccupied with thoughts of some upcoming financial investment in order to provide security for his family. All Omar's wishes were focused on a desire contained in his family being secure and safe, as suggested by the Ace of Pentacles and the Nine of Cups in the seventh position. In his mind he was prepared to often fight for his family, and the Seven of Wands in the seventh position carried the message of the deep purpose and valor. However the fact that the three cards fell out in the seventh position indicated that Omar's rational mind was overstretched thus again confirming the need to follow the lesson of the Temperance and allow himself a temporary stop-over. The Three of Wands in the eighth position indicated that Omar's significant others provided the necessary support and would have gladly accepted a part of his load if only Omar allowed it. Omar said that, yes, his wife was a support and assisted him in many tasks, however my notion that the emotional load was carried solely by him – even if at the unconscious level only because Omar made a habit of it – made him think. I repeated the warning of the Ten of Wands, saying that the emotional and mental load, if continued to be carried exclusively by Omar only, might become the last straw on his back.

Omar said that he just wanted his family to be happy, and his children from the first marriage to be happy. Was there a presence of a feeling of guilt? The card in the ninth position, the Seven of Swords, pointed to anxiety connected to some action that seemed to cause in him a feeling of unease and escapism. Omar said that he had brought up his children himself. The mood of the Seven of Swords with the figure on the picture obviously involved in an unethical action, especially in the position of hopes and fears, carried the message that Omar felt that there was nothing he could do for them that would be enough. This idea permeated his unconscious mind and appeared to have brought in a subtle – but nevertheless picked up by the spread – notion of guilt combined with an accentuated feeling of responsibility and loyalty, perhaps because Omar subconsciously expected the possibility of betrayal as at some point trust may have been lost.

Still, the Six of Swords in the tenth position indicated that energy surrounding Omar's new venture was moving towards content, victory and peace of mind. This card denoted the release of tension and encouraged Omar to new endeavors. The tension was apparently associated with Omar's vivid recollection of getting into arguments (apparently with his wife, according to the Five of Swords next to the Six of Cups in the supplementary position) when justifying his desire for new ventures (the Three of Pentacles in the same position). Omar asked me to clarify the meaning of Temperance; he wanted to get concrete information. He picked up another card; when he turned it over he discovered it was the Four of Swords. This image high-lighted and also was complementary to the meaning carried partially by Temperance: the necessity to accept a temporary truce, to take some time off and retreat quietly for thinking things through. This card promised more clarity after some meditation on issues that came up in the reading.

Omar also stated that his main concern was for his family to stay happy, safe and together. He picked up the Hanged Man as advice from the collective unconscious in this respect. As it was a Major Arcanum, I wanted to get more "everyday" infor-mation too, if possible, and asked Omar to pick up two more cards. They happened to be the King of Swords and the Nine of Swords.

The associations carried by the constellation of these three pictures in the context of Omar's query about his family were of the necessity to give in, to sacrifice something for the sake of the family. Was Omar becoming too dogmatic, obsessive, and even aggressive with his fixation on the issues of safety and security? The Hanged Man clearly said that we all live in a rather unsafe world, and the more Omar were to focus on that, the more sleepless nights he would guarantee for himself, as suggested by the Nine of Swords. Staying in the image of the King of Swords may contribute to the changes in Omar's character that would only interfere with and be counterproductive to the family's homeostasis. The balance in the family may be hanging by a thread. To this Omar commented that he wanted to get a gun for protection and had to get in a quarrel with his wife who was strongly against it (sure enough, the theme of the argument was picked up by the Five of Wands). The Hanged Man thus advised to accept the situation as it existed in today's social reality and stop creating conflicts in the family based on issues that were beyond Omar's control.

Omar then answered the questionnaire, stating that this reading contributed to achieving his purpose and explaining his answer by the following: "Gave me some insight on my attitude and ways of thinking on certain issues that are important to me." He wanted to have a follow-up session, indicating that "accuracy of statements just increased my curiosity." The reading was significant and meaningful to him because he "got much out of it." His overall comment was: "Great session. Got some good feedback that will allow me to take a clearer path to things."

CASE 4. SAM

Sam was a white professional man, forty years old, whose main reason for this reading was a professional problem. The purpose of the reading for him was to gain insight into the future regarding his career pursuits, to focus on solutions and to find out more about Tarot. Sam's layout is shown in Figure 8.4.

The Knight of Cups in the first position indicated that things in Sam's life were not progressing as quickly as he would like them to be; in fact Sam's ideals and aspirations may have been missing their target. Sam's profession was likely to be connected with the field of arts, poetry, or similar means of emotional self-expressions. To that Sam commented that he was an actor, however earning his living by means of various unrelated jobs and occupations. The Major Arcanum Judgement in the third position suggested that Sam had completed the previous life cycle and heard the call of the trumpet depicted in this card's imagery. The voice of the unconscious was trying to wake Sam up, to open his psyche to a new level of awareness. It appeared from the layout that Sam felt that the time for stepping on the right path had come. If Sam were to continue in his present occupation, the feeling of being buried alive, as further transmitted by the Judgement imagery would prevail. He had to acknowledge his true calling. Sam needed to move in the direction where his abilities and talents, presented by another Major Arcanum, The Magician in the fifth position, would be recognized and rewarded.

It did not appear, though, that the past energies were supportive. The Seven of Swords in the fourth, past, position indicated that Sam's present stagnation had

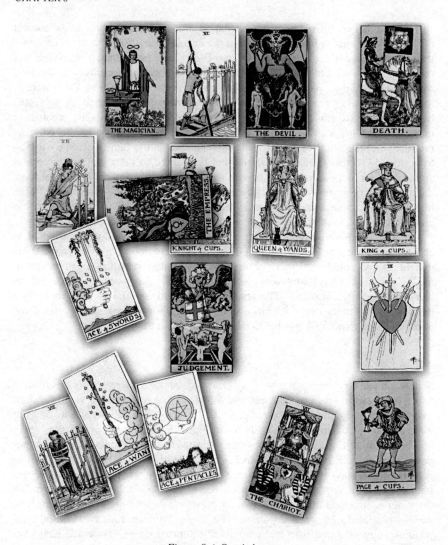

Figure 8.4. Sam's layout.

been influenced by his deep feeling of defeat or even deception. Sam said at this point that yes, he felt cheated because somebody did not keep his promise to Sam regarding a career offer or contract, and it happened quite recently. Were there any psychological reasons for Sam not having been able to get the promised contract besides circumstantial ones? His mental outlook, according to the Page of Cups in the seventh position, was a centre of concentration on the wellbeing of his child or children, represented by the Page of Cups, at the expense of Sam devoting sufficient time, effort and emotional investment to pursuing his career. A lot of Sam's ideas and projects had not come true by now due to the longstanding trait in his personality pointed to by the Eight of Swords in the supplementary position combined with two more images, the Ace of Wands and the Ace of Pentacles: creative ideas and career rewards. According to the Eight of Swords, Sam was quite unaware how his creative power has long been suppressed whenever a new professional opportunity arose. So far Sam has been walking blindfolded, stepping on his repressed feelings and unspoken emotions and not allowing them to manifest. Furthermore, the Major Arcanum of The Empress in the second position told me that at the deepest level Sam's psyche was taken over by the powerful Mother archetype. The crossing position of the Empress indicated that, instead of being a positive, helping factor, it became a hindering one, affecting Sam's personality and changing it to the extent of becoming counterproductive to Sam's personal and professional development. The idealistic Knight of Cups as Sam's present persona had been overpowered by the Mother archetype. Although by itself Sam's loving and motherly nature was a terrific quality, it had not helped him so far in accomplishing his goals. The over-protective mother – part of Sam's personality – was working overtime and not getting paid for that. The imbalance between conflicting, conscious and unconscious, forces had led Sam to an impasse represented by the Eight of Swords. The impasse that he reached, however, was also an indication that he could now finally cut through the cord. The time came for him to become more clear-sighted regarding the constricting issues especially in view of someone having taken advantage of Sam's naiveté and indecisiveness (the Knight of Cups) and given the contract, promised to Sam, to somebody else – likely to a person with lesser talent but greater assertiveness. Yes, Sam was capable enough to quite probably accomplish his goals in a chosen field (The Magician in the fifth position) but if he continued in his present Self of making choice that resulted in his taking excellent care of others and poor care of himself, he would remain only halfway towards achieving success in his favorite field.

The cluster of three pictures in the fifth position – the Magician, the Six of Swords and the Devil – indicated a high probability of Sam having a tendency to fluctuate between the calling of his real talents and aspirations and the Shadow part of his nature making him a dependent personality, progressively sinking deeper and deeper into the underworld of the unconscious, to the point of becoming chained to it. The shadowy chains of The Devil appeared to outweigh the tools in front of The Magician, even if they were potentially available to Sam in the form of his own versatile abilities and talents. Sam said at this point that I was wrong: he did not consider himself being dependent at all; as a matter of fact, he said, he was working at a job that he would rather give up because he was supporting his wife through law school. Sam was rationally justifying his opinion that it was not he but his wife who depended on him financially. Such was the unconscious Shadow projection! Significantly, the Three of Swords as one of the most dramatic images in the deck in the eighth position of the immediate environment indicated that Sam definitely lacked any support system at home.

Before narrating the meaning of this card to Sam, since it was such a sensitive issue, I asked him if he felt supported at home. Sam answered that he never felt supported but he accepted it and learned to live with it. Such was the Devil in the action: this image took away Sam's self-esteem; it imprisoned Sam and made him repress his real emotions and exist in a state of strong denial of the actual state of affairs. As Jung was saying, the archetype of the Shadow can easily possess one's psyche, reinforcing the phenomenon of projection. The Three of Swords provided further insight into the affects and effects of The Empress. Sam, who was governed by the activated Mother archetype into the behavioral pattern of giving love, attention and support to significant others, either at home or at work, was not getting the reciprocal qualities in return, his energy thus being depleted and subsequently his being unable to achieve his desired goal in the professional field. Sam was a slave to emotional or even, quite possibly, sexual dependency, in the guise of The Devil; he was immobile and blindfolded as if chained by his feelings towards his wife. His wife, however, was not giving him any love in return (as per the Three of Swords, she may have even been threatening a trial separation that would have broken Sam's heart...) so as to keep his psyche in balance. The Devil indicated that although Sam was convinced that he has made a conscious choice of having learned "to live with this", that is, with the total lack of emotional support or love, he was in fact driven by the shadowy instincts and co-dependent character traits. The issues of co-dependency, as depicted by The Devil, called for further exploration and counseling.

The King of Cups in the position of hopes recommended Sam to get truly in touch with this aspect of his personality, to get out of the sate of denial of his true feelings and acknowledge the fact that he was in denial. On a positive note, The Chariot in the overall position and Death in the tenth "outcome" position, both indicated that the transformative process was about to begin and Sam would develop from being the Knight of Cups to becoming the equally noble and kind, but now wise, King of Cups. The Chariot signified that Sam definitely had a potential energy he needed to fight for a desired goal and to control his unconscious traits by means of first becoming consciously aware of them. From the inertia, idealism and immaturity of the Knight of Cups, Sam would be carried by The Chariot into the new life cycle, represented by the change and transformation as depicted by Death. Of course the parallel influence of The Devil may interfere with the transformative process of growth and adult development, and Death was confirming that the path to individuation was not going to be painless: Sam was to actively break the chains and face changes in his whole psychic template to enable him to achieve success he deserved. Indeed, on the everyday level, the Queen of Wands in the sixth position of Sam's immediate future indicated supportive energies provided by a woman, perhaps Sam's business associate, who would definitely reciprocate Sam's positive qualities and help him enthusiastically in his professional affaires. Sam said at this point that he wanted to contact an agent and expected to be assisted by her in his pursuits.

Sam then asked a question regarding the state of his health (in line with the message from the collective unconscious that his energy has been over-expended). He picked up a card that happened to be the Ace of Swords. Sam's physical health had been damaged to the point where it needed to be watched continuously and to be protected, his life thus being a constant battle to overcome obstacles pertaining to his health. Assisted by determination, though, the upright sword promised to win over the illness, especially since Sam's emotional and mental health were about to improve as a result of the insights provided by this reading. The issues as depicted by this reading came out as being very sensitive for Sam, and his answers to the questionnaire reflected this point. He mentioned that the reading partially contributed to achieving his purpose and did not write anything in order to explain his answer. Indeed, the final picture of Death indicated a process rather than an instant answer as a particular solution to Sam's problems and it was only natural and appropriate for Sam to feel somewhat puzzled, especially in view of ending an old life cycle and being just about to start a new one. Sam wanted to have a follow-up session, however he again did not explain why. He stated that this reading was significant and meaningful to him as "it pinpointed several issues" in his life. He made the following overall comment: "I really enjoyed the reading. It made me nervous when it hit emotional nerves." Well, the archetypal influences of The Devil and Death together in one spread may be overwhelming: the breaking of old habits represented by the Devil's chains and the stripping of old outgrown feelings and thoughts that were about to be discarded in the transition to begin a process of adult development aligned with the growth of Sam's character.

CASE 5. LINA

Lina, a young black professional woman, not yet thirty years old, came for the reading for the reason of a career choice. She specified her problem as the following: "I am not satisfied with the job that I am being asked to do. Not enough clarity in my responsibilities and position." She wanted to get insight into the future to find out if she would be successful in her endeavors, and to clarify whether she had made good decisions with respect to her professional life. Lina's layout is shown in Figure 8.5.

The overall mood carried by the layout with the Major Arcana of The Sun and The Magician standing out was that of wholeness and harmony. It presented Lina as a person free of inner conflicts, at least at the time of the reading. Everything seemed to be in harmony in her life and psyche, and to this Lina commented that yes, she considered herself blessed, perhaps due to having had a happy childhood and a blessed family. The Page of Cups and the Ace of Cups in the first and second positions suggested an emotional involvement, which had quite a fragile beginning but reached now a new, deeper level in a love relationship, one of mutual understanding and support. Perhaps Lina was not sure about her own feelings at first, because until now she had been rather careful and cautious in allowing herself to get into new relationships.

The Nine of Wands in the fourth "past" position carried a message of Lina being on guard against possibly being wounded again, as an old wound still hurt. Yet Lina had enough strength in reserve. Lina then said that some time ago she had been about to get married but the engagement had broken. No wonder that she was examining her new relationship carefully, taking into consideration the issues of maturity, sincerity of purpose, and security, as was depicted by the Ace of Pentacles in the third position, representing the roots of the matter in question.

The Sun in the fifth position indicated a happy and prosperous development in Lina's affairs, and when Lina asked at this point a supplementary question whether

Figure 8.5. Lina's layout.

she had made a right decision with regard to her emotional life, she pulled out from the deck the picture of the Queen of Cups, confirming her choice based primarily on sincere feelings and on her partner being really emotionally involved with her. Lina, in the image of the Queen of Cups, demonstrated a person who has reached a certain degree of understanding of her own emotional depth and became the object of the love of her partner, attracting admiration for her qualities of gentleness and sensitivity, yet remaining self-contained.

In view of her upcoming responsibilities Lina wanted to feel self-contained at work too; and The Magician in the sixth position definitely promised the accomplishment of her goals. Not only did Lina have abilities, determination and a clear purpose, the image of The Magician embodied the idea of assistance from above, as if Lina's guardian angel was always here for her. At this point Lina interjected, saying that since her father passed away, she had felt his presence and perceived his guiding powers in listening to his advice as it has been when he was alive. This statement was quite emotional for Lina but even her tears were light and clear, as if reflecting her pure soul.

Lina's mind was busy assessing her working situation. She felt that she had not been treated fairly (the image of Justice in the seventh position), that her position did not allow her to demonstrate any initiative (the Page of Wands), that she was rather underpaid (the Knight of Pentacles) and promotion prospects seemed to be vague. The Five of Swords in the eighth position of her environment and support system pointed toward the turmoil connected to her work situation; however Lina was choosing the correct way of action of retreating and keeping away from arguments. This mode of acting might have given her fellow workers the erroneous idea of Lina as a person unable to assert herself, but Lina's best choice would be indeed being adaptable and flexible (the Two of Pentacles in the ninth position), precisely the way she behaved at her job.

Instead of getting into unnecessary arguments, Lina, while still lacking the power necessary for moving ahead, has chosen the correct option of becoming eligible for promotion through obtaining some sort of diploma or certification that would enable her to get out of restrictions at her work place (the Eight of Swords and the Page of Pentacles in the supplementary position). This choice promised to be a victory for Lina as she was definitely to achieve success as depicted by the adjacent picture of the Six of Wands. Lina confirmed the pictures' message by saying that she had taken an exam and was waiting for the results of her teacher certification.

The Queen of Wands in the tenth position indicated that Lina's promotion would be determined by the woman who assigns her duties. The Ten of Wands that fell out as a complement to the court card, The Queen, in the final outcome position that, as a court card in the final position, needed additional information as the next card in the deck indicated that Lina should be careful and on alert and not let herself accept responsibilities that would be out of her area because the Queen of Wands tends to exploit her "court" to the maximum. The Three of Pentacles in the overall position, however, indicated that Lina's professional growth and achievements were taken into consideration by her employer and regarded very positively.

After the reading was over, Lina stated on the questionnaire that it did contribute to achieving her purpose. She provided the following explanation: "I believe that the reading supported my beliefs." She was not sure if she wanted to have a follow-up session as she felt satisfied with this reading and said that she "may want to see if anything has changed." The reading was significant and meaningful to Lina because, as she wrote, "quite a bit of the information that I got from the reading I can agree with and it gives me a clearer picture of myself." Her overall comment was the following: "The reading was very informative and it gave me a new appreciation for this type of talent."

CASE 6. MARINA

Marina, a white professional woman, about thirty years old, was a graduate from Pacific Oaks College and picked up my flyer there. Indicating a relationship problem as a main reason for the reading, she felt unable to move forward and wanted to gain insight into present, future, herself and significant others. She also wanted to clarify issues and to gain self-understanding, specifying it by saying that she wanted to mark this period "with the structure and validation of Tarot." Marina's layout is shown in Figure 8.6.

The card in the first position indicating Marina's presenting problem, the Ten of Cups, was crossed by the Ten of Swords in the second position, both Tens indicating that at the present time happy and committed relationship was coming to an end, making Marina feel that everything was ruined in her life and bringing her to the threshold of depression, as her emotional endurance appeared to have reached its limit. Marina interjected saying that this relationship lasted three years and she had married her spouse just a few months ago.

The grim-looking Ten of Swords, however, signified not just a possible end to the relationship, but also the cut-off of an erroneous or false way of Marina's own perception of this situation. Perhaps the relationship lasted relatively long because Marina had taken a point of view that let her stay in the situation of *status quo* during this period. Three cards (instead of one) as a numerological reinforcement of the third position indicated a strong urge to become aware of the unconscious motivations and issues Marina was overwhelmed with. The prevailed suit in Marina's spread was that of swords. Was it Marina's own typology? Not exactly. But the multiplicity of swords indicated a number of Jungian complexes and fragmented or "splinter psyches", little part-subjects that were tormenting Marina and destroying her integrity and the sense of self.

The King of Swords in the fourth position depicted the character of her spouse, Marina's own personality being to a certain extent dissolved in her husband's, thus making co-dependency issues (The Devil as the long-standing, even if "underground", archetypal presence in the supplementary, eleventh, position) the central theme of this reading.

The Devil had confirmed the presence of the Jungian archetype of the Shadow as a defining factor in Marina's situation. An authoritative and controlling person (The King of Swords), Marina's spouse had influenced her life and psyche in the past to such an extent that it still persisted in the present. The immediate future however, indicated the collapse of a structure as it had existed so far, as represented by the image of The Tower, an archetypal *temenos*, in the sixth position. The original meaning of temenos in Greek is a sacred precinct like a temple; a synonym for it is a hermetically sealed vessel or, for that matter, The Tower that was sealed at the top before being struck by symbolic lightning from above. Temenos, as employed in Jungian analysis, has acquired psychological connotations as the psychically charged area surrounding a complex that can be experienced through the symbolism of any closed container such as a womb, a prison, or for that matter, The Tower.

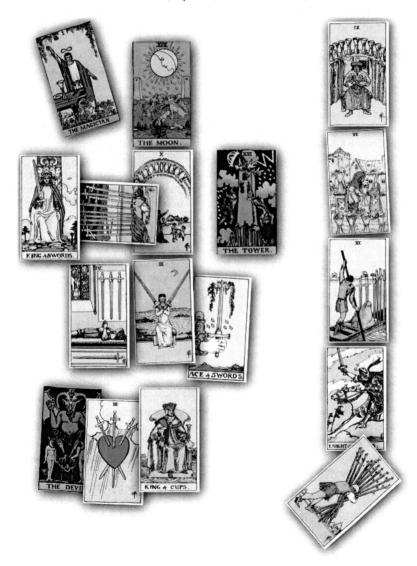

Figure 8.6. Marina's layout.

Until now, Marina had been procrastinating, at an impasse, and unable to decide for herself where to turn and in which way to move (the Four of Swords and the Two of Swords in the third position). She was so frightened, or lacked confidence to such an extent that her actions and confrontations (the Ace of Swords) appeared to be self-defeating, leading to the creation of further confusion and fogginess around her. This message was reinforced by The Moon in the fifth position carrying the information that if Marina continued the course of action she currently pursued, believing that by not confronting the issues at hand they might go away by themselves, it would become a road to self-deception. The probability of the archetypal influence of The Moon with its deceptive mood-lit world of ghosts was a warning sign that Marina's distress might grow into a clinical depression or another major affective disorder if not addressed.

At this point, Marina stated that she had been confronting her husband, but that he did not seem to understand her point. But of course. He *chose* not to understand, and Marina accepted the situation, the conflict thus having reached an impasse (the Two of Swords). Marina was overwhelmed with stress and felt helpless, the emotional burden having come to the limit of what she could bear (the Ten of Wands in the overall position) as she was embedded in conflicting emotions and contradictory thoughts. She hardly coped with the load of contradictions that were contributing to her symbolic imprisonment in The Tower, this image connoting the meaning of the breakdown. Jung, non-incidentally, used the notion of contradiction with regard to the meaning of the tower which he, at a symbolic level, identified with the Tower of Babel, that is, a symbol of false omnipotence and mistaken certainty, *a priori* condemned to destruction during the most powerful and confusing instance of the persisting contradiction. But the position of The Tower in Marina's immediate future suggested that the weight on her shoulders would soon be lifted, and the reason for that should be Marina's sudden awareness and the intensification of consciousness precisely as a result of breaking out of an old habitual mode of thinking and behaving.

This moment became the turning point of the session. Although at the time of laying down the cards Marina's thoughts were centering on wanting her husband to reach for her, to approach her (the Knight of Swords in the seventh position) while both hoping for and being anxious to implement the nostalgic fantasy of being sweethearts in a sharing and trustful relationship (the Six of Cups in the ninth position) – the resolution of this contradiction was about to occur! In fact, the supplementary constellation of the images – The Three of Swords between The Devil and the King of Cups – was an index of a particular behavioral pattern in the past that had a tendency to replicate itself in the present. Marina's unresolved complex of co-dependency or attachment-separation issues (The Devil) had led to a painful separation (the Three of Swords) with a person who in fact deserved her full trust and unconditional love (the King of Cups). This event caused Marina her bleeding broken heart (literally, the Three of Swords). Yet the dreams of a happy relationship will indeed become a reality for Marina, but only after her understanding that it is she who must make a decisive step. Such was the message of The Tower in the position of the immediate future as a symbol of "breaking" turning into "making" – the making of Marina's "Self" as "self-making", the unconscious becoming conscious in the individuation process.

Indeed, each Jungian archetype has both dark and light aspects, and the symbolism of The Tower is particularly poignant in this regard. Symbolic thunder and lightning from above, by breaking the order of things and so negating the stasis of one's identity within the existing order, simultaneously illuminates the way to the new order and new identity, thus not only breaking the old but also creating the new: Marina as her-Self! At this point, Marina, unable anymore to contain the torment of her bleeding heart (the Three of Swords in the eleventh position), burst out in word associations, thus manifesting the catharsis (The Tower) promised by the spread by the position of her immediate future. Her psyche was freeing herself from the chains of The Devil; her weak ego was getting out of the Shadow of fear and dependency toward the individuation of her Self.

Engaging in a dialogue, Marina mentioned that in discussing birth control methods, she and her spouse came to the mutual decision of using condoms. But was it really a mutual decision, or only apparently mutual? Marina admitted it was his decision that was accepted passively by her. Marina said, however, that she was a fertility specialist; the conflict was thus based on her being fully aware of her cycle, but having been enslaved by The Devil – under the influence of the Shadow-projection from her husband – she felt immobilized (the Two of Swords) and unable to persist in her attempts to communicate her preference to her husband. He, being in the archetypal image of the King of Swords, was likely a personality not in touch with his feelings. Had he ever demonstrated his feelings, I asked. Marina said that only once and he could not cope and broke down in sobs. Indeed! The King of Swords is a personality that has its own projections at a deeper archetypal level, such as Jungian Persona. The time allotted for the reading (50 minutes) did not allow for a further exploration of this issue, but the fact that Marina's husband was insisting on condoms carried the message of a person who was scared of intimacy, like the King of Swords can often be. The body and bodily contacts (as the symbolism of the earth element) are not something that the King of Swords (swords reflecting the element of air) would prefer. So Marina's husband could have easily projected his own inferior part onto her, and although she was seeking counseling, his preference, even if unconscious, would be to just stay in the image of the King of Swords!

The Six of Swords in the eighth position indicated that there was a tendency to get out of the troubled waters of a stormy relationship toward achieving a sense of harmony. This card denoted a sense of reconciliation and a release of tension and anxiety after a period of strain in Marina's immediate environment, further reinforced by the reassurance of the Nine of Cups in the tenth position. This "outcome" card conveyed the meaning of emotional security and the feeling of contentment, wishes fulfilled and desires coming true – provided of course Marina is to become aware of her unconscious! And in order to become aware, she is to go through the realization of the actualized Tower with its rapid and sudden cognitive, emotional and spiritual awakening – a process that started to take place in the here-and-now of the reading. Marina was going through the process of realization with obvious pain (the presence of the Three of Swords!) but also being newly empowered by this insight. Associating with the images on the cards in front of her, she said that she would like to go to a conference, to be away for four days, and that her spouse was against it, telling her not to go and that he would miss her. It sounded rather manipulative, but very much in the framework of the King of Swords with his inquisitive mind and controlling attitude. On her side Marina feared, she said, that he might find somebody else. In four days!? Well, thus spoke The Devil, manifesting Marina's deep anxiety and co-dependency, and the time came to break away from his bondage.

Interpreting the symbolism of The Devil to Marina led to new themes emerging from the spread, like Marina's low self-esteem, lack of confidence and the deeply hidden fear of abandonment and separation anxiety (supported, sure enough, by the unfinished business as per imagery of the three cards in the supplementary, eleventh, twelfth and thirteenth positions). Marina said afterwards that she made a decision and would go. This dynamics was also visible in the Six of Swords: the symbolic movement towards calmer waters was to be actualized in the real travel Marina was about to undertake, the latter in turn "causing" the relationship with her husband to move forward and improve. On my suggestion, Marina picked up one card from the remainder of the deck so as to probe the "attitude" and get possible advice from the collective unconscious. When she turned it over, it was the Major Arcanum, The Magician. The Magician, the teacher-guide, the very antithesis of The Devil was thus communicating the message of a lesson that Marina was to learn in the school of life. The Magician at a deeper level is a figure of Hermes, the god of communication and quick action that revealed to Marina her real potential and encouraged her in pursuit of goals and the ability to take initiative in her hands. He also encouraged her to talk to her husband, reassuring her that she will find the right words and this time around her husband will be ready to listen. The archetypal energy now available for Marina was one of action, purpose and will. Her consciousness was literally rising from the unconscious "hell" of The Devil to the heights and "heaven" of The Magician.

Marina answered yes to the question of whether this reading had contributed to achieving her purpose, stating in writing: "It allowed me to conceptualize the polarities in a way that I can use to help myself grow and gain heart...and go to the next cycle." She wanted to have a follow-up session and explained it by stating, "to continue the Tarot clarification as I move into the new cycle." The reading was significant and meaningful to Marina and she wrote, "Very helpful! It redeemed me from a state of shock and promoted my strength." She provided the following overall comment: "Important and skilled work! A much needed type of guidance and counseling that is multifaceted engagement of the psyche."

CASE 7. RENATA

Renata was a white professional woman, in her forties, and a graduate student at Pacific Oaks. She met me with a baby on her lap, and another little girl was playing nearby. She expressed her main reason for this reading as a professional problem, saying that she wanted to organize her life. The purpose of the reading for her was to gain insight into present, future, herself and into the best choices for her. She also wanted to clarify issues, to focus on solutions and to become aware of, as she stated, "road signs – see deeper into that which is in front of me." Renata's layout is shown in Figure 8.7.

Figure 8.7. Renata's layout.

The predominance of the Major Arcana indicated that Renata was likely a highly spiritual person, able to perceive the directions her unconscious was guiding her.

Renata responded to my interpretation that her spiritual beliefs are those of Buddhism and she often meditates. The image of Temperance in the first position, crossed by the another Major card, The Hermit, indicated that in the current life cycle Renata reached a level of acceptance and moderation and already stepped on the path to the Jungian individuation of the Self. The Jungian archetype of the Old Wise Man (The Hermit as Buddha) had been guiding her in her search; she acquired wisdom on the road of self-discovery and learned to apply the karmic laws to her everyday life without conflicts or confrontations.

The foundation for her life philosophy and world view was the activated Mother archetype, which governed and underlined Renata's quest, The Empress in the third position deeply engrained in Renata's psyche. In her heart Renata was a nurturing person, capable of giving and receiving love, yet her mind complementing her heart by means of the actualized Father archetype – The Emperor in the seventh position. Perfect balance existed in Renata's psychic template, and this manifested at the everyday level by her having a perfect partner. Renata interjected here and said that they met late in life and she had been rewarded with a blessed husband. The Knight of Cups in the eighth position depicted her spouse as a sensitive and noble person with spiritual aspirations and, still quite young at heart; he was feeling the same romantic emotions towards Renata as when he proposed to her. The High Priestess in the fifth position pointed to the likelihood of Renata achieving an even higher level of spiritual awareness. She did have the potential to be filled with grace, providing the lessons of moderation and necessary compromise are learned, limits accepted and respect for the power of spiritual forces lived through in her practical everyday experience.

In the past, as per the Major Arcanum The Chariot in the fourth, past, position Renata learned a lesson of controlling and monitoring the conflicting traits in her character and overcoming obstacles by maintaining loyalty to her spirit. In return, the power of knowledge was at hand whenever necessary. This interpretation triggered Renata's free-associating with the reading and her mentioning the Los Angeles earthquake, when she intuitively decided to travel the day before, and at the night of the Northridge earthquake her family was away from the San Fernando Valley where her house was located and subsequently destroyed! The picture in the sixth position of Renata's immediate future, the Four of Cups, brought us back from the spiritual realm to the physical world. It suggested to Renata to meditate before accepting any offer, and think through before making any decision. Free-associating with the card's imagery, Renata said that there was an option for her to start some training soon in her professional capacity: the Four of Cups, though, recommended not to rush (very much in the mood of Temperance), as another opportunity might follow and contemplating the offer would be to Renata's advantage.

In the eighth position of hopes and fears there were three cards reinforcing the significance of this specific position for Renata. I interpreted the constellation of the Page of Cups, the Five of Cups and the Eight of Wands by intuitively asking Renata if it was the case that she has lost a baby before, was in mourning, and yet was trying to have another one. It was a very sensitive issue, and outside of the format of the reading I perhaps would not even pose that question. Renata responded that yes, she miscarried twice and, even if blessed with two children, she and her husband wanted another one as soon as she stopped nursing. The Ten of Wands as the possible outcome card warned Renata to gain more strength, though, before taking upon herself yet another responsibility. She needed to improve her health as she was working hard and, despite her spirit being high, was coming close to the limits of her physical endurance. This message was closely linked to the suggestion of the Four of Cups to contemplate the ideas and meditate before implementing them, in any case in line with Renata's philosophy of Buddhist meditation and mindfulness. This image was the warning sign that, aligned with The High Priestess in the fifth position, invited Renata to really listen to the messages embodied in the layout very carefully! The supplementary pictures of the Ace of Wands, the Three of Wands and the Seven of Swords demonstrated that not all ideas that Renata put into practice were to her best advantage and she may have ended up being ripped off.

At this point Renata wanted to ask some supplementary questions. Her earthquake-wrecked house was being renovated and she wondered how professional her contractors were. She pulled out of the deck the two cards that, when she turned them over, happened to be the Page of Swords and the Seven of Cups. This constellation manifested quite a ruthless attitude, not deliberately malicious, perhaps, but unconcerned with the feelings of others, rather cold and rushed. Simple matters may have been purposefully fogged and made confusing, and Renata was thus getting information from the contractors which could not be fully trusted. This message was indeed supported by the cluster of three supplementary pictures. When Renata asked a practical question about the mode of payment, the collective unconscious, via the Six of Wands that she picked up, confirmed that Renata's idea of how to pay them looked like her best choice to lead to the successful outcome of the matter in question.

Renata also wondered about the possibility of a new job, especially in view of not rushing to accept the current offer as the only opportunity that was available. She picked up the cards that happened to be the Major Arcanum Wheel of Fortune and the Two of Wands. A turn of events was about to manifest, a new chapter in life was about to start, a new run of good opportunities to commence. Some waiting period better spent on researching the job market was to pass until Renata's aspirations materialize. She asked about the probability of her speedy graduation from the graduate school. The cards she pulled out, the Queen of Swords and the Eight of Swords, demonstrated obstacles and constrictions, connected perhaps with the friction between Renata and some woman in a position of authority and power, perhaps her thesis advisor. As the whole layout pointed towards not taking on extra responsibilities at the expense of Renata's health, the images once again warned her not to rush as a matter of course, but to accept the situation – indeed, as Buddha would have advised – and try to mediate it as best as possible as well as focus on research necessary for the completion of her studies, even if it meant that her sense of freedom and decision-making ability were somewhat compromised during this study period.

Then Renata completed the questionnaire. She answered yes to whether this reading contributed to achieving her purpose and commented that she "got information about approaching life at this time – involving meditation and accept that which comes." She wanted to have a follow-up session and wrote, "Inna is an incredibly perceptive person. I enjoy her insights." This reading was significant and meaningful for Renata because she "got clear answers, actions to take." Her overall comment was the following: "What a wonderful opportunity. Please stay in touch!"

CASE 8. PAM

Pam, a white professional woman in her forties, invited me to her house for two readings, for her and her husband (see case 9 for Ross). She specified her main reason for this reading as a professional problem, stating that she was about to make a choice between several career options, and to further advance in her pursuits. The purpose of this reading for Pam was to gain insight into the future, herself and significant others, to focus on solutions, to feel empowered and to gain self-understanding. Pam's layout is shown in Figure 8.8.

The first position happened to be occupied by the Major Arcanum Judgement. It indicated that at the spiritual level Pam had outgrown her current profession and in the deep "psychoid" substratum of the collective unconscious she felt the urge to evaluate herself and her previous accomplishments. To stay in the present state would have been spiritually degrading or, at the mundane level, selling herself short. Not in the material sense, though. Regarding her personal development, Pam felt that her present occupation had become too narrow for her, so the time had come to transgress the boundaries and rise towards new beginnings. The sounds of the trumpet were very much active in Pam's psychic template and she was ready to be symbolically "reborn". The Arcanum of Judgement often indicates a vocation or calling in contrast to just earning a living. A process of self-appraisal was going on, and Pam was getting the message from the collective unconscious that either over- or underestimating herself would be erroneous.

At this point Pam interjected, saying that she felt ready to make a choice about a career change from teaching to either law school, or a Ph.D. program, or art school. The Knight of Cups in the second position suggested that the field of arts was a possibility, but may be rather a hindering influence to Pam's main desire to maintain the wellbeing of the family (the Ten of Cups in the fourth position). Another Major Arcanum, The Hierophant in the fifth position represented a somewhat conservative, rather than artistic, influence, and being a major card, its influence was stronger than the one represented by the image of the Knight of Cups. It apeared that a conventional career like law school, represented by the institutionalized rules, laws and regulations symbolized by The Hierophant, would be a better choice and one aligned with Pam's deepest desires on the spiritual level. On the physical plane, such a choice was also linked to the high probability of stability and security for the whole family as represented by the "outcome" card in the tenth position, the Ten of Pentacles.

Was there a woman in Pam's life, perhaps a relative, who was particularly sensitive and supportive to Pam's desires and able to understand her to such a degree so as to communicate with her at a subtle level? The Queen of Cups in the third position represented a female energy that guided Pam in her search, perhaps appearing in her dreams too. Pam said at this point that she often sees in her dreams her grandmother who has passed away, and yes, they do communicate. The unconscious realm,

Figure 8.8. Pam's layout.

inhabited by the Queen of Cups, thus represented a strong and positive influence, and the unconscious messages which Pam perceived in dreams were to be listened to carefully as they guided Pam in the direction which was to her best advantage. The constellation of three cards that fell out in the supplementary, eleventh, twelfth, and thirteenth positions represented the energy that accompanied Pam in her day-to-day life. (I noticed that the pair of the Page of Cups and the Five of Cups was the same as in the reading for Renata in case 7.) After initial hesitation I asked if Pam was concerned with the loss of a child (the Five of Cups strongly suggested that she was still mourning the loss of somebody she holds dear). Yes, said Pam, she had miscarried four years ago. The grief and bereavement, though, as transmitted by the positions of the cards, were as acute as ever and the emotions were raw. Pam still was looking back to the past (the Two of Wands), contemplating her loss. But the future promised new alternatives after the initial waiting period. Pam was definitely developing a new outlook, and the Two of Wands suggested perseverance, as new initiative could overcome old obstacles, this card's imagery depicting some, as yet unfulfilled, potential. Pam told me at this point that she has been thinking about adoption.

The sixth position of the immediate future with the cluster of three cards was the one that presented the most concern for Pam. It was the strong possibility of a confrontation – perhaps unspoken but nevertheless strongly felt through – with a woman, represented by the image of the Queen of Wands and connected with Pam through a likely change of residence (the Five of Wands and the Knight of Wands). The whole event would have been initiated not by Pam but by this woman. Pam responded to this interpretation that a friend visited from Thailand and was staying in Pam's house, and the whole day had been spent by Pam going through an internal struggle with herself due to the presence of this woman under her roof. When Pam asked for this issue to be clarified, she pulled out the card that, when turned over, happened to be The Hanged Man. It looked like the situation with Pam's friend was a testing period in Pam's life, perhaps a lesson to be learned. This Major trump carried connotations of a certain duration thus accentuating the sixth position and advising Pam to be prepared to go through The Hanged Man's challenge. It would be a sacrifice she would have to make, perhaps for her friend's benefit. The Eight of Pentacles in the seventh position of Pam's mental outlook indicated that whatever choice Pam would make, she should be prepared to work diligently and in sequential steps during the process. Pam was slightly apprehensive at the idea of starting her education all over again but nevertheless highly motivated under the influence of Judgement.

At a time of the new beginnings one would appreciate support from significant others. The Ten of Swords in the eighth position was, however, in sharp contrast with the otherwise overall positive and encouraging mood of the layout. This picture indicated that Pam was surrounded by quite a negative energy in her immediate environment and for some reason was not supported in her pursuits. This looked strange, especially in view of the Ten of Cups depicting a lasting, happy, and committed relationship. It seemed to be an issue, and the collective unconscious was attracting our attention to the specific imagery of the Ten of Swords with the power-less figure pierced by the ten swords in her back. Yet this image was making it explicit that possible ruin had already reached its peak and nothing would make it worse, even if Pam buried this issue deep in her subconscious and was unlikely to articulate it. Her personality reflected the Nine of Pentacles in the ninth position, which suggested that on many occasions Pam used to rely on herself and was quite self-sufficient even in her quest for becoming ever more self-sufficient. Finally, the reward of a settled way of life was a highly probable outcome of Pam's achievements as depicted by the tenth card, the Ten of Pentacles.

Pam wanted to consult the collective unconscious regarding her three career options, so she pulled out three cards for each of her options. The Nine of Cups for the query with regard to law school suggested the attainment and assurance of both material and emotional security and also that this course of study should not be too great a challenge. (Was "Hierophant" pointing in this direction? It seemed so.) The card for the choice of a Ph.D. program happened to be The Chariot. With determination, control and willpower Pam would succeed on this path too, but real self-assertion would be required and the process of obtaining this degree would be of a greater duration than attending law school. She picked up the Three of Cups for the choice of an art school. This suggested a hobby rather than profession, and recommended to Pam not to leave the idea altogether but enjoy it with friends, during weekends or vacations or on some other joyful occasions. Her options were thus discussed and the collective unconscious provided the information but the choice was left for Pam to make.

Pam then filled out the questionnaire. She wrote that the reading contributed to achieving her purpose and explained her answer by the following statement: "I feel validated in my concerns, and supported in other areas where I questioned my perceptions. Though I am a strong person according to both my friends and co-workers observations, I know that my 'style' is to constantly 'bounce off' other people and present reality. I am always checking where my opinions, feelings, perceptions are in relation to my reality." She wanted to have a follow-up session. She wrote, "I feel the reading was VERY relevant to me today, and included several things that I have been dealing with in the last twenty four hours!" This reading was significant and meaningful to Pam, and she explained her answer as follows: "Yes – the information about: concern for the lost child (miscarriage four years ago); interaction with female (argument); female guiding me (my grandmother); whichever course I choose will be attainable, though need to be step-by-step; final success is to be!" Pam made the following overall comment: "I loved it! Inna – you are very insightful in your readings of the cards. Thank you. I hope you will 'do me' again."

CASE 9. ROSS

After the session with Pam, I conducted a reading for her husband, Ross. He was a graduate student at Pacific Oaks College and picked up my flyer there. He indicated his age in the over-forty category. His main reason for this reading was a professional problem specified as seeking assistance in the Master's Thesis process. The purpose of this reading for him was to gain insight into future and to gain self-understanding. Ross's layout is shown in Figure 8.9.

The picture that stood out in the layout was the card in the second crossing position, the Ten of Swords, which instantly depicted the general mood of the layout or the main affect projected by Ross, depression and desolation and the feeling of misfortune;

Figure 8.9. Ross's layout.

possibly with regard to the issues of material security. But not only that: it was the same card that in Pam's reading occupied the eighth position, the one which indicated her immediate environment, significant others, and the presence (or absence) of a support system. It became clear that the atmosphere at home was permeated with the depressive mood projected by Ross, although at the time of the reading for Pam the reason for the Ten of Swords having appeared in the position of Pam's support system was yet unknown. Not only could Ross not provide any emotional support to his wife, but he was hardly capable of coping with his own stressors. The timely guidance of the collective unconscious thus became of paramount importance.

The card in the first position of Ross's presenting problem was the Major Arcanum Death. Its appearance shifted the focus from what had been stated by Ross as a professional problem to a much deeper archetypal level. Ross's psyche had been affected by the archetype of change, renewal and transformation. His unconscious was protesting against any *status quo,* perceiving it as stagnation. Ross was going through a process of transition which started quite abruptly with the collapse of the existing structure of Ross's life as depicted by The Tower. In fact, a symbolic death often means clearing the way for a really big change and The Tower often destroys what is outdated, superfluous and counterproductive to the development and growth of personality. The Tower in the fourth position of the recent past carried the connotations of destiny itself that had to interfere into Ross's life by means of a shock. The lightning-struck Tower had destroyed everything that he did not need for the journey ahead, even if that Tower had been constructed and built by Ross himself in the course of his life. However the time came when this lightning, this new vision, empowered Ross with the freedom to choose, to break down the existing form in order to make way for a new one. Spiritual meaning aside, it was not totally clear from the layout what happened at the actual physical plane. Did Ross lose his job (as The Tower may have suggested) and as a result was feeling confused and depressed? Ross responded that he himself chose to leave his job of many years and to start a new career, for which he needed a Master's degree, which meant again going back to study. His answer supported the idea carried by The Tower of the defeat of the old world view and breaking down old habits. However if it was Ross's free will, why was this change so painful for him, as implied by the Ten of Swords, as to bring him to the verge of depression? The Death card carried the message that his sudden decision was the starting point of the whole transition period in the course of which Ross's ego was transforming into the individuated Self, with all its growing pains, and at the moment of the reading Ross was at the point of no return on this road to individuation. In this respect the Ten of Swords manifested the end of a cycle which meant that the worst was behind and from now on, with a newly acquired awareness, Ross's mental state would only improve. Ross's ego was lost halfway between his "Id" (in Freudian terms), represented by the King of Pentacles in the third position, and the superego depicted by the Knight of Cups in the seventh position of his mental outlook. This current split in Ross's personality caused an intra-psychic conflict and led to him feeling ruined, in doubt and desolation, as per the Ten of Swords.

While consciously Ross was pursuing a noble goal of being of service to others, with all good intentions and inspired by spiritual ideation and idealistic aspirations (the Knight of Cups), his subconscious (in the image of the King of Pentacles with all his practicality) in the third position representing the root of the matter, was pulling him back. Ross commented at this point that his purpose contained in fact a certain altruism. In the meantime unconsciously he resented the fact that his income had to stop when he went back to study, as he has been working hard and honestly during many years to create a safety net.

Was money an issue? Had Ross's apprehension grown from the necessity to make tuition payments while he was not earning anything? Ross confirmed that he was concerned with this. The Seven of Pentacles in the eighth position indicated that an investment has been made and Ross confirmed that his moneys were tied up now. Well, the Ace of Pentacles in the sixth position of Ross's immediate future suggested to Ross not to worry about the financial side, as money (perhaps some return on investment, or maybe a grant or a stipend) was to be given to him and he would be able to make a tuition payment. A helping hand would extend itself, advised the Ace of Pentacles, and this correlated with the overall message, depicted by the Nine of Cups, that Ross's wishes were coming true. So should financial matters be the least of his worries, asked Ross. It looked that way from the layout.

However the spread contained a warning for Ross: if his old self – the King of Pentacles – remained unrecognized and not dealt with, the probability of Ross's depression turning into an ailment at the level of the physical body (the Three of Swords in the fifth position) may well manifest. Thus the whole layout was attracting our attention to the appropriateness of the intervention by the collective unconscious right here and now. During the archetypal transition of such depth as in the imagery of Death, Ross's total personality was changing. His old world view was slowly and not painlessly being erased from his psychic template so as to make room for a new set of values to be created and nourished. The pain suffered by Ross under the influence of the archetypal Death was related to the part of him being unwilling or unable to surrender to the inevitability of evolution and transformation. The ninth position of hopes and fears was emphasized with three cards: the Ace of Cups, the Queen of Wands and the Eight of Swords. This indicated much anxiety: while Ross's relationship with his wife (Pam, case 8) was in fact at the level of a loving and emotional union, his own perception and an unconscious fear (especially under the effect of the Death card) was a feeling that his wife, being a very strong inde-pendent woman, was overpowering him in some respect or capacity. Ross's perception, in the midst of his existential crisis, was far away from reality; and the collective un-conscious, while acknowledging and respecting Ross's feelings, was nevertheless bringing to his awareness the fact that there was no foundation for such anxiety. Just the opposite, his whole existence was permeated with the activated Temperance and The Empress together with the Ten of Cups, as depicted by the supplementary position of the eleventh, twelfth and thirteenth cards. This constellation of images suggested that the marriage was bringing into his life a much needed balance and compassion and was a calming influence on his psyche at a time when his personality was in danger of becoming fragmented.

Pam was prepared to support and cooperate with him during the process of transition and even compromise if necessary. She had completed her life tasks in the current cycle and, in the image of The Empress was projecting the energies of the protective Mother archetype into Ross's being, making his own transition easier. The Empress was bringing to Ross's awareness the lesson that each age of man has its phase, and each phase must end when it is lived out. This lesson was being learned by Ross within the process itself, which was certainly creating an extra stress on his state of mind. I made a suggestion at this point that although so far Ross was going through this difficult period in his life by himself, he may need weekly counseling sessions to monitor the individuation process.

The tenth card, the Six of Wands, was a terrific and timely encouragement for Ross. It suggested the high probability of a successful outcome in Ross's pursuits. The previous phase has cleared the ground (the Ten of Swords) for the current transition, and a reward for Ross's efforts was soon to follow. The Six of Wands indicated a sense of achievement in the near future, precisely what Ross, being depressed, was lacking presently. Thus the future was very promising.

Ross then filled out the questionnaire, answering yes to the question if this reading contributed to achieving his purpose and explaining his answer by the following statement: "My feelings have been positively reinforced that I am making a correct choice in my life change." He was not sure if a follow-up session was needed as he "was still sifting [his] thoughts and reactions." This reading was significant and meaningful for Ross as it was "specific enough to align itself with [his] thoughts and concerns." His overall comment was: "I feel comfortable with this reading and the personality which I feel manifests itself. And I do not feel that there is a search for earthy reward, it is not easily explained." This last sentence was a confirmation how deeply Ross's old self was engraved in his unconscious. It *was* a search for earthly reward before (the King of Pentacles usually gives earthy practical values their dues), and in Ross's psyche this issue presented a conflict, a sort of personality clash with the emerging Knight of Cups with his highly romantic, idealistic values. Never would the Knight of Cups admit in himself the existence of something he would not consider to be refined and high-principled!

CASE 10. DONNA

Donna, a white professional woman, in the over-forty age category, indicated as the main reason for the reading a professional problem, specifying it as a choice of a direction in her profession. She wanted to gain insight into the future and to feel empowered. Donna's layout is shown in Figure 8.10.

The central card in the first position was the Page of Pentacles, indicating that Donna was at the very beginning of her professional career and quite possibly was concerned with getting a certificate or a degree. She has been working hard and diligently towards achieving her purpose. Donna commented at this point that she had applied for her teaching certification. The Five of Pentacles in the second, crossing, position suggested that Donna experienced a feeling of anxiety about the matter in question and also felt that time was passing her by. The imagery suggested that Donna felt she might have missed an opportunity and might end up feeling deprived and not being recognized professionally. Even if at the subconscious level, Donna was strongly motivated by the image of The Hierophant, the Major Arcanum in the third position representing the roots of the matter. The Hierophant symbolized the establishment and Donna's implicit desire to become "a part of the system". The Hierophant is a symbol of the established order and law in the society, the rule of logic, patriarchal politics, dogmatic religion (this card is also called The Pope in some other decks) and/or masculine rationality. However, with the Three of Swords in the fifth position (as a linear, even if not certain, progression from The Hierophant) the question of making such a choice in Donna's career directions did not look as being to her advantage.

In the past Donna managed to apply her willpower and had the quality of energy needed to fight for a desired goal, as represented by The Chariot in the fourth position. She learned to be self-assertive, but her purpose of establishing a career for herself

Figure 8.10. Donna's layout.

was manifesting at the expense of some other values, which so far had not been considered as being a priority by Donna. Was the goal she was so diligently pursuing to her best advantage? The Three of Swords in the fifth position suggested the possibility of this being a wrong direction, as having achieved the goal was unlikely to bring Donna any satisfaction or contentment. Just the opposite, the Three of Swords with its images of a bleeding heart carried a symbolic message of a self-inflicted wound. This message from the collective unconscious was reinforced by The Tower in the sixth position of Donna's immediate future. Perhaps what was so far considered by Donna as a highly desirable goal may have soon very likely lost its sense of importance and value. Her whole present belief system was about to suddenly crash and be replaced by a new awareness.

The imagery of The Tower conveys the meaning of a sudden collapse of the *status quo:* the two figures in the picture have built the Tower and sealed it at the top; they appear to have imprisoned themselves in their own creation – the rigid, phallic, mental structure of "false consciousness" – and the only way out is through the agency of a violent breaking force bringing along a traumatic, but a consciousness-raising and awakening, experience. The creative force looking for its way out will ultimately be felt as if acting from within, as though *giving birth* to new beliefs, new consciousness, like the goddess Athena in Greek mythology who springs to life from the head of Zeus. For Donna, it may very well have been that her whole set of beliefs so far and her attempting to structure her life and work according to convention (symbolized by The Hierophant) was based on the erroneous (for her personally!) philosophy of life, and a new one was about to manifest. At this point Donna commented that all her life her attempts to settle down or to have a steady job had been in vain.

But could it be that Donna's present dilemma and her desire to settle down was too narrow a choice for her? The walls of her field of vision were soon to be expanded by the rather sudden and abrupt shake-up of The Tower. The governing archetype for her right now was one that Jung called the Wise Old Man. His counsel was symbolically represented in the image of The Hermit in the overall, fourteenth, position. He was inspiring Donna for a further search, and *to seek within, not without.* The imagery of The Hermit brings forth the message that s/he who seeks shall find. The Hermit holds a lantern symbolizing the light of inner knowledge, or Gnosis as a spiritual guidance, assisting Donna in her dilemma. The Hermit traditionally embodies the ancient "Know Thyself" principle as the call for self-knowledge, self-discovery, and reflexive awareness that can enrich our existence with meaning and authentic values. Donna was guided by the Hermit's lantern to reflect on herself in order to individuate, to discover in the *embodied experience* her authentic Self capable of choosing between alternatives. The road of self-discovery is always paved with many dilemmas and therefore demands our learning from experience in the school of life.

Donna learned many life lessons through her experiences and gained enough wisdom to decide for herself whether she should continue looking for "establishment" as a sole criterion equivalent to happiness and authenticity. The time had come to re-evaluate and accept the validity of soul-searching. This necessity to weigh up the possible options and life-choices was further highlighted by the Major Arcanum

Justice in the supplementary position. In the past Donna was going through stiff competition and had to apply much strength and determination to overcome obstacles represented by the imagery of the Ace of Swords. I inquired whether she had already applied for a teaching position. Yes, was Donna's reply; and it appeared from the imagery that she went through the interview with perseverance and courage. Donna's endurance and determination was further reflected by the imagery of another Major Arcanum, called Strength, that transmitted the meaning of self-mastery and control. Strength promised to overcome her doubts and distractions and to support Donna in her present quest for her real strengths, and her real values, while learning new skills and overcoming limitations in this process.

Donna's mind was very much focused on the idea of moving, as reflected by the Six of Swords in the seventh position. Was it moving away from difficulties to a more peaceful state of mind, or was it that Donna contemplated a literal journey? Or both? When I asked this question, Donna confirmed that she was indeed thinking about moving and had practically made up her mind. This idea was also reflected in the ninth position (of hopes and fears) that was especially significant for Donna. The constellation of three pictures, the Eight of Wands, the Seven of Cups and the King of Pentacles, has suggested that perhaps Donna was going to move closer to a male friend, and – even if other options were still being discussed – Donna was indeed about to go ahead. Donna commented at this point that she was about to move in with her boyfriend, whom the imagery depicted as a well-established person, perhaps a home-owner.

With all his positive qualities why there was a sense of confusion over Donna's decision to move in with him? The Seven of Cups carried the connotations of possible illusions and even "castles built in the air" in relation to her male friend. Donna's motivations to move and the circumstances surrounding the issue were best further explored even if a single 50-minutes session could not provide enough time for this. Yet it was clear that the outcome of Donna's pursuits depended to some extent on the decision made by the King of Cups. Indeed, the "outcome" picture – the Seven of Swords in the tenth position – carried the message of Donna depriving herself of other choices, so this was a warning sign for Donna to once again evaluate her options, especially since Strength in her immediate environment encouraged her to be courageous and let spiritual forces in her psychic template (the female figure in the picture) to overcome materialistic concerns (symbolized by the lion in the picture).

At this point Donna wanted to ask for spiritual guidance regarding her artistic pursuits that had so far been her hobby, existing solely outside of her job-search and main career aspirations. Focusing on her question, she pulled out a card. When she turned it over, it was The Star. The Star is a remarkable image in the deck: it connotes a field of meanings which include hope, healing, inspiration, creativity, and the realization of our spiritual dreams. As the first figure in the sequence of the Major Arcana – importantly, feminine – without any clothes on, The Star is a symbol of being stripped of the heavy load of exclusively patriarchal rationality, strict moral duties taken out of context, and dogmatic imperatives. The vessels are red, this color representing the fully flesh-and-blood body in unity with the spiritual essence symbolized by water and the color blue. The Star is often called The Star of Hope: the hope for new understanding! This imagery carried a happy message for Donna, inspiring her to go in the direction of developing her talents which, guided by the Star of Hope, would enrich her with a sense of purpose, fulfillment, and striving towards an authentic goal instead of pursuing the illusion of imaginary stability and conformity. The realization of Donna's talent would be to her best advantage. As a matter of fact the sky would be the limit in this area of Donna's life, as the imagery of The Star suggested.

The reading had ended. I asked Donna to fill out the questionnaire. Donna answered "yes" to the question whether this reading contributed to achieving her purpose, explaining it by the following statement: "I understood that I need to go toward my talents." She did not want to have a follow-up session, explaining that "it won't be necessary because whatever is within me will come through." This reading was significant and meaningful for Donna as it "validated [her] belief in [her] art." Her overall comment was "It was a great reading."

CASE 11. TESS

Tess was completing her Master's Thesis and wanted this reading for the reason of a personal problem. She specified it as the lack of a relationship. Tess indicated her age group as between twenty and thirty. She wanted to gain insight into the past, present, future, and herself, to focus on solutions and to gain self-understanding. Tess's layout is shown in Figure 8.11.

The card in the first position was the Three of Pentacles which indicated that the core of Tess's problem of not being in a relationship was, as a matter of fact, in her being elsewhere, namely investing time and effort into upgrading her social status and earning recognition and approval from people in her environment. This attitude, very positive by itself, was nevertheless taking away Tess's energy that could have otherwise been devoted to exploring relationships and finding a boyfriend. At this point Tess interjected, saying that her dad always encouraged her to grow, to achieve a certain status in both a professional and social sense. Were her parents still helping her financially too? The Ace of Pentacles in the fourth position depicted a helping hand, extending itself in order to maintain the present status quo (the Three of Pentacles). To this Tess responded that her parents were supporting her and paying for her tuition. It was making her life quite comfortable, wasn't it? The Seven of Swords in the "crossing" second position, however, indicated tendencies for escapism and self-defeating actions. Tess's desire to grow socially seemed to be at the expense of some other priorities in her life, Tess thus to a certain extent being involved in impoverishing herself, as if scheming against her own self and unfortunately thus performing a rather dishonorable act upon herself.

Why did Tess subconsciously want to escape, to run away, and created the whole moonlit deceptive fantasy world (The Moon in the third position) to justify, even if unconsciously, for herself her present way of life? The Moon symbolized that at the archetypal level the unconscious realm took over and manifested itself in all its unpredictable and uncontrollable aspects. The collective unconscious called for Tess's attention to make her aware that the uncertain and delusional world of the Moon

Figure 8.11. Tess's layout.

was to be addressed so that those aspects could be brought to the level of cognitive awareness. If archetypal influence of the Moon persists, there was a probability for Tess to stay where she was or, as suggested by the fifth card, the Queen of Wands, to remain a single woman, though very well positioned socially. By being seemingly safe and secure, with the financial support of her family and social support of her fellow students, Tess appeared to be a self-contained woman who did not let any man into her life, there being simply no room in her life for a relationship. The imagery of the Seven of Swords as being one's own worst enemy, especially when grounded in the moonlit illusionary world of ghosts and apparitions versus real people in actual life, thus spoke with a clear voice.

Why now? What was happening in Tess's life and accordingly affecting her state of mind, as represented in the here-and-now of this layout by the constellation of three cards in the supplementary positions of the eleventh, twelfth and thirteenth pictures? The Four of Wands, Four of Cups and Five of Wands were here together so that the importance of their message was not to be missed. It looked like there has existed a relationship, even a foundation for marriage, and Tess had either not accepted a proposal or ignored and let it go, or contemplated an offer as if caught between the worlds of thought and action. The opportunity offered had not been taken, and discontent caused emotions to turn inwards, creating the constant internal battle (the Five of Wands) and struggle of opposing emotions in Tess's psyche. At this point Tess asked if I was talking about the past or of what was happening now. This information was not available from the layout but, either in the past or in the present, Tess's feelings hurt, and an affect regarding the matter in question seemed to be as fresh as if it has happened today, even if the supplementary positions more often than not describe past experiences whose significance is so strong that the consequences still persist in the present. Tess broke into tears and, re-enacting the reading, said that she had a relationship, could not make up her mind, and later this young man died.

Loss and bereavement had never before been addressed by Tess, she had suppressed her feelings and, instead of the closure of this loss in her life, she closed herself to the world of happy emotions and intimate relationships. Did she have a child? Why was the presence of the child (the Page of Cups in the overall position) a central idea governing Tess's psyche? Tess said that she had a nephew and loved him as her own, spending as much time with him as possible. Well, ironically and sadly, Tess's world looked complete: she was getting an advanced degree, her parents were taking care of her being well financially supported, and she even replaced the need for a child of her own with being able to relate to an external object of love, affection and care. There did not seem to exist room for anything or anybody else in the closed circuit of her world.

Tess's mind was preoccupied (three cards in the seventh position) with blocks and inhibitions that she imposed on herself, such as her inability and apprehension of moving forward with determination and clear purpose (The Chariot), or taking upon herself the additional responsibilities that any relationship would bring into her life (the Ten of Wands and the Three of Wands). Being daddy's little girl had so far been a defense mechanism Tess successfully exercised.

To get out of the sealed world of self-imposed restrictions, Tess needed to move along the road of self-discovery as was suggested by the Knight of Cups in the sixth position. To recognize and acknowledge the existence of spiritual aspirations rather than materialistic ideals would be to Tess's advantage. She must seek truth for herself and be prepared for nothing to distract her from her quest.

The Star as the Major Arcanum in the eighth position prompted me to ask Tess if she had any special talent that she might consider developing. Tess responded that she likes to write poetry. The Star thus recommended for Tess to continue in this creative field as expressing herself through poetry would become a real support system on her road to individuation and self-discovery. Inspired by The Star, Tess would acquire a sense of purpose (rather than having that of her parents imposed on her) and would be able to heal the wound of her loss. Two more Major Arcana in the ninth and tenth positions indicated that spiritual guidance would be available for Tess the moment she moves on. The Hierophant promised the presence of a helpful teacher, maybe a priest as a spiritual counselor, or the school, or those philosophical values that Tess may discover and recognize as her spiritual meaning in life. The Hermit, the Old Wise Man himself, was even more determined in his message for Tess. He clearly stated that the time had come to clear Tess's mind of external distractions and concentrate instead on soul-searching. Temporary solitude might be the price to pay for self-knowledge because, until Tess herself discovers her Self, no one else would be able to see her Self, to recognize its presence and develop a meaningful relationship with her.

Tess then filled out the questionnaire. She answered yes to whether this reading contributed to achieving her purpose. She explained her answer by the following: "The reading was very ON. It talked about how some passed [past] issues plus social climbing have interfered with allowing men to enter into my life." She wanted to have a follow-up session but not before six months to one year's time (the lesson of The Hermit was manifesting). She stated that this reading was significant and meaningful because, she said, "It gave me insight and made me look at some powerful issues that I have been avoiding." Tess's overall comment was "I really enjoyed the reading. I hope I will be able to grow spiritually from this experience."

CASE 12. CATHY

Cathy, a white professional woman in her forties, told me she had just been enrolled in the Master's program at Pacific Oaks. She wanted to have a reading because of personal and professional problems. Cathy hoped to gain insight into herself as well as into the past, present, and future. She further wanted to analyze feelings, to clarify issues and to simply find out more about Tarot. Prior to the reading she mentioned that she was curious as she "heard about Tarot and wanted to try." Such was the only information provided by Cathy. Cathy's layout is shown in Figure 8.12.

The first picture representing the core of Cathy's problem in the centre of the Celtic Cross spread was the King of Swords. It described male energy that had a negative effect on Cathy's psyche. The imagery indicated the presence of an aggressive and controlling person in her life that could be either a boyfriend, or father, or both. Compassion happened to be an affect unknown to such a personality and, accordingly, absent for Cathy. Was there anybody in her life who had ever said that he was there for her? It did not appear so from the spread of the images on the pictures, and Cathy said at that point, "True".

The card in the second position, however, with its image of the Knight of Wands crossing over the first card, provided a positive counterpart to the negative influence of the King of Swords. Symbolizing a creative energy, this Knight indicated that Cathy was about to move out, to seek a new place of residence for herself. When I asked Cathy if this indeed was the case, she said she was constantly thinking about moving out and changing her living situation.

Figure 8.12. Cathy's layout.

Still, the unconscious motivation of maintaining the *status quo* (the Four of Pentacles in the third position) was an anchor pulling Cathy back versus the driving, pushing force of the Knight of Wands. At the subconscious level Cathy desperately tried to keep what was her only family with its shallow stability and security (the Ten of Pentacles in the fifth position). Cathy's deeply engraved belief in her inability to take even the slightest risk enmeshed with the feeling that it is better to have than have not.

She did not realize, though, that the family's fragile homeostasis was based on such a precarious foundation as her being the victim in this situation, quite possibly the victim of abuse. Cathy interjected here, saying that she had indeed been in therapy for the last four years.

I wondered if in the past she did try to leave, to walk off – as the Eight of Cups in the fourth position unequivocally suggested. Cathy answered yes. According to the imagery of the Eight of Cups, she had tried to leave her situation behind, because the feeling that it was not right persisted. However the feeling of what *is* right was not there either, and Cathy remained confused, her confusion leading to the vicious circle of feeling more and more depressed up to the point of immersing herself in the dark night of the soul (the Ten of Swords).

The cycle of depression, though, was just about to end, as depicted by this very image of the Ten of Swords in the sixth position, the Ten of Swords indicating that very soon Cathy will start seeing her situation in a new light. However this would be conditional on Cathy, as influenced by the positive constructive energy of the Knight of Wands, making a decision to move out and on with her life. At this point Cathy said that her therapist kept telling her exactly the same thing.

Well, perhaps she was not ready before, but right now the collective unconscious identified Cathy with the Page of Wands (in the overall, extra, position), who carried a message of optimism and vitality. The image of the Page of Wands was encouraging Cathy that she had those qualities within herself, even if not yet actually but potentially.

Cathy's state of mind, though, as per the constellation of the three cards in the seventh position, reflected the severity of mental blocks and the presence of inhibitions. The Major Arcanum Judgement was of particular significance. In a Tarot deck this Arcanum immediately follows The Sun, the symbol of Rebirth as a precondition for Wholeness. Judgement is a symbol that brings into being the possibility for self-renewal, vivification of life, and integration into the world. Symbolically, integration is always related to resurrection, or, as famous Jungian psychologist Marie-Louise von Franz put it, one's waking up from Hades and standing up from the grave. Even though von Franz was not making any reference to this particular Arcanum, the symbolic meaning and poetic language of the image appear the same. The imagery of Judgement conveys a call to action. Although Judgement indicated that Cathy has "heard the call of the trumpet", aiming to wake her consciousness from a state of deep sleep akin to being buried alive, her desire to finally have peace of mind and to achieve emotional stability and security (the Nine of Cups) was sabotaged by the presence of the Six of Cups in the same position. Unconsciously, Cathy was fighting her own development and her own growth by resisting the possibility of re-entry into an authentic existence as per the Judgement imagery. Importantly, the image of the Six of Cups "located" in the seventh position in the context of mental fixation carried the message that Cathy has been blocking her childhood memories. That is, to get rid of self-recrimination and low self-esteem, to gain confidence in herself in order to be able to get "up and going" was only possible through the recovery of Cathy's memories.

When Cathy heard the interpretation of the images at this point, she said that she went to hypnotherapy, engaged in workshops, but she did not have any childhood memories at all, neither good or bad. So Cathy knew that she needed to recover her memory, didn't she? How then had Cathy become aware of the importance of recovering her memories, I asked. Cathy said that her therapist, after *four years* in therapy, told her that she had all the symptoms of having been sexually abused as a child, and Cathy's lack of childhood memories was an issue of concern and indeed discussed in her therapy. That is why the collective unconscious was persistently attracting our attention to this theme: even as specifically sexual abuse was not explicit in the layout, the issues of overall emotional abuse and persistent neglect were overwhelming in the images. The image of Judgement was invoking the Jungian "inferior" function of *feeling* as a complement to the superior rational *thinking;* the latter perhaps the only function available to Cathy in her traditional – quite likely, of cognitive-behavioral orientation – therapy! No wonder that four years spent in therapy did not bring in the desired results. The activated archetype of Judgement, however, was making it impossible for Cathy to continue in her present state. Nichols associated the Judgement Arcanum with "a very precise value judgement based on how one feels…rather than what he might think about it" (1980, p. 340).

The reality of physical or emotional abuse and neglect in the past as well as, quite likely, in the present, was reflected in the constellation of eleventh, twelfth and thirteenth supplementary cards (added to the usual ten for the purpose of gaining some insight into events of extremely high impact). The Chariot indicated that whenever Cathy had the quality of energy and determination to be able to fight for a desired goal and was prepared to direct her actions for self-assertion, not only she did not have any support in her pursuits, but she was punished, scolded, felt abandoned and was constantly reminded about how bad, useless, and destructive she was (the Five of Cups). Worse, her mother practically turned her back on her (as symbolized by The Queen of Swords as a spouse to the very first picture of the King of Swords in the position of Cathy's presenting problem).

At this point Cathy said that her parents always call her names, call her crazy, tell her she did not earn enough money, etc. This was a clear case of continuous emotional abuse. The past had been repeating itself in the present as Cathy's psyche made an enormous effort to suppress her memories. Therefore having subconsciously jeopardized her own personal development was the only possible survival mechanism for her in her immediate environment. The Nine of Wands, however, in the position of hopes, suggested that despite Cathy feeling as though she had come to the end of her ability to protect her interests, there was still strength and determination in reserve. The old wound hurt, but victory would be achieved through endurance.

The Three of Pentacles as the "outcome" card in the tenth position suggested a strong likelihood for Cathy to take the first step towards her growth and personal/ spiritual development. A long-awaited feeling of self-worth, being respected and achieving recognition from others would be Cathy's reward, provided she stepped up and out of the oppressive environment. She would not be without a support system either. The Page of Pentacles in the eighth position indicated not only Cathy getting a degree, but her college environment becoming a supportive environment for her, where she would gain all due respect in accordance with her being hard-working and diligent. Once again, the major influence of the imagery of Judgement as a calling, "a vocation" (Nichols, 1980, p. 341), was obvious.

At this point Cathy said that she realized the necessity of moving out, but how to recover her memories? She wanted the guidance of the collective unconscious and pulled out the card that happened to be The Fool. A new, happy life cycle would begin should Cathy choose to make a fresh start. Cathy commented that her therapist also kept telling her that she was the one to make a decision in this respect. Surrounded by the same walls, so to speak, Cathy would be unable to re-collect the past as it would be too painful for her. Moving out, though, and expanding the world of experiences around her (as conveyed by The Fool imagery) would allow Cathy to feel safe – something she lacked in her family. It would be safe to remember, and *the inner child* in Cathy would be born again, this time feeling happy, safe and secure.

I handed over a questionnaire to Cathy after we finished this reading session. Cathy answered yes to the question of whether this reading contributed to achieving her individual purpose and explained her answer as "I was a little skeptical but now I believe more because it was true for me. My situation was in the cards." She added, "I live with my parents and my boyfriend. My father and boyfriend are verbally abusive and my mom usually agrees with them. She does not do anything except what my dad wants her to do." Cathy was not sure if she needed a consequent session as she "just did not know what it would entail." She said that this reading was significant and meaningful and added that "it verified what I had been told by my therapist."

CASE 13. RODNEY

Rodney was a graduate student in the middle of studying for his MA Degree. He wanted to have a reading for him and his girlfriend Gordana (case 14). He indicated he was in the above-forty age group. His main reason for this reading was a personal problem. *After the reading* Rodney added more specific information: "I would like more insight into my style of relating and connecting with others." He then added his purpose of this reading in terms of gaining insight into future and specifying it as "to learn more about my expectations of others in response to my needs and myself in response to their needs." He also wanted to gain self-understanding. He wrote: "Ideally I would like a meaningful clue as to why so many of my daily personal inter-actions are full of an irrational sense of tension – that each transaction may be either glorious or disastrous." Rodney's layout is shown in Figure 8.13.

My first feeling when I glanced at the layout was of a certain dissonance. At the moment of spreading the cards, *the only information* provided by Rodney was that he wanted to address a personal problem. *All specific information, as listed above, was included in the questionnaire by Rodney only after we had completed the reading and after I reminded him that he had agreed on his consent form to answer the questionnaire in the format of this study.* The feeling that something does not add up stemmed from the very first card, the core of the problem. It was the Six of Wands, which signified a sense of achievement, great satisfaction, victory and success. The imagery of this card suggested that Rodney was surrounded by an audience who admired him and applauded his success.

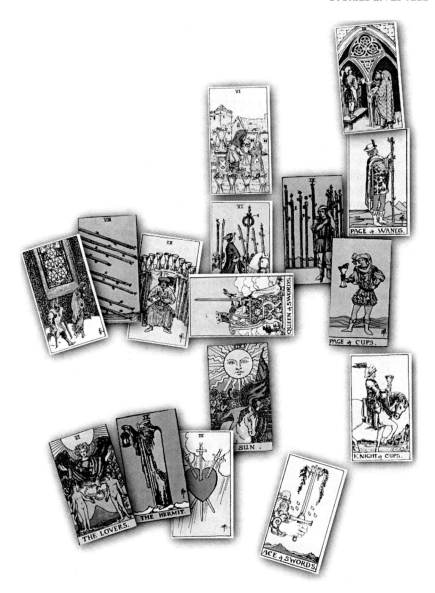

Figure 8.13. Rodney's layout.

Such a great card – and positioned in the spread in the position that, according to the collective unconscious, was Rodney's presenting problem?! It couldn't be, unless... unless... the problem was the very nature of Rodney's character, his having wanted glory more than anything else, eager to overcome difficulties and obstacles in making his wishes come true (as per the Nine of Cups in the fourth, past, position of some "unfinished business", which was also preceded by the Eight of Wands pointing to the fact that Rodney was used to taking initiative into his own hands). Yet both the Eight of Wands and the Nine of Cups were preceded by the Five of Pentacles. Rodney's past, reflected in three pictures rather than in only one, his whole unfinished business, was accentuated by the collective unconscious as an issue of great importance. What was the actual situation that Rodney, according to the Five of Pentacles, chose to pass by, even if subconsciously? What did he leave behind? Rodney said that he had been previously married. Currently he was living with his girlfriend in her condo.

The Ace of Swords in the overall fourteenth position carried the message of showing strength in adversity, or that out of evil something good was nevertheless appearing. Gearhart and Rennie (1981) also interpret this image as the ability to win in verbal games. Perhaps all Rodney's efforts to achieve success were just for the purpose of satisfying his Ego. Maybe that is where my feeling of a strange dissonance was coming from: Rodney being, paradoxically and unconsciously, in need of this adversity around his persona as well as of the aura of admiration from whoever was next to him even among the adversaries.

Several apparently contradictory images thus started to make sense the moment it became intuitively clear to me that Rodney's layout suggested narcissistic and rather passive-aggressive personality traits. Such a personality may need to identify with the Jungian Persona to present it to the world and, sure enough, here it was: the Knight of Cups in the seventh position.

Rodney's mental outlook was strongly fixated on the idea of making a conscious effort to be a noble, altruistic and high-principled person. At this point Rodney quite timely interjected, saying, "That's the image I want to project; yes, it is a fixation." Well, this idea was well thought over and based upon a solid foundation (The Major Arcanum The Sun in the third position, representing the roots of the problem) of trying to structure and regulate feelings according to pure rational thought, logic, and calculation. The paradox of passive-aggressiveness was such that Rodney's driving force, represented by The Sun, which provoked such behavioral traits and his "Apollonian" attitude of over-rationality, was totally unconscious (the layout's third position). The imagery of The Sun, which usually embodies the Jungian archetype of Rebirth with the figure of a naked child warming in the full sunshine, demonstrated its dual nature in Rodney's case, as indeed does each one of the Jungian archetypes having both light and dark aspects. Rodney was obviously resisting the possibility of being symbolically reborn. The Sun, with both its straight and serpentine rays, transmitted the dual nature of its archetypal essence.

The Sun thus, despite its brightness, in relation to Rodney, manifested its dark negative aspects, indicating that its lesson has not been learned and Rodney was prone to repeating his habitual patterns of thoughts and actions in each life cycle. Rodney said at this point that he tends to get into arguments with fellow workers because he provokes them; and it happens as if by itself. Sure enough, the motivation was totally outside Rodney's conscious awareness, as if Rodney was blinded by the bright sun that was making him paradoxically over-rational. The Sun as a Major trump had exerted a strong influence, almost possessing, as Jung would say, Rodney's psyche.

What about Rodney's home situation? What was his relationship with his girl-friend, who was signified by the collective unconscious as the Queen of Swords, in the second "crossing" position? As the Queen of Swords, Gordana appeared to be an intelligent independent woman, who too seemed to be connected with Rodney through the world of thought and intellect rather than affect or emotion. Rodney said that they were very happy together. Free-associating with the images, he started to describe his girlfriend to me as an intellectual woman, holding a doctoral degree and a university position. Apparently, these qualities in Gordana attracted him in the first place, though at the unconscious level he was manifesting a desire for an intimate relation-ship and to share the most intimate thoughts, not unlike a couple of innocent children who, according to the Bible, can re-enter the Kingdom of God as depicted by the Six of Cups in the fifth position.

In the meantime, the constellation of the eleventh, twelfth and thirteenth cards in the supplementary position strongly suggested that his choice of partner was based on duality involving logical considerations and perhaps with some sort of trial involved (The Lovers). This position also pointed out the break-up in his previous relationship in the image of the Three of Swords, even if Rodney subconsciously chose to turn away from the heartache associated with the previous relationship. Still, solitude (The Hermit) that could have been devoted to soul-searching frightened him. However ultimately his new girlfriend Gordana seemed to be very positive and beneficial for Rodney, and their relationship was to Rodney's best advantage, at least in the here-and-now of this reading, as had been suggested by the Wise Old Man, the archetype of which in the guise of The Hermit, not unlike Jung's own Old Wise Man, Philemon, had been guiding Rodney in his choices.

The last card in this constellation, the Three of Swords, considering that Rodney was repeating a cycle as per the image of The Sun hiding in his unconscious, mani-fested difficulties in this relationship. I asked Rodney if quarrels with Gordana were taking place. He answered quite emotionally, saying that they quarreled terribly, however less often than earlier in their relationship. The collective unconscious was thus attracting our attention to the unstable and rather neurotic behavioral patterns at home. Apparently all the intelligence of Rodney's girlfriend could not penetrate into his passive-aggressiveness (more details about Gordana's own peculiar situation in the context of her relationship with Rodney will be addressed in case 14, through my reading for Gordana).

I asked if Rodney had considered counseling. He said that both he and his girlfriend were in long-term psychoanalytically oriented therapy. Intuitively I felt (and three cards, rather than one, in the "past" position emphasized this feeling) that perhaps Rodney, with his deeply hidden passive-aggressive traits, had chosen this type of therapy, psychoanalysis, because at the deep "psychoid" level he preferred to stay in the past rather than face the present and work through it in order to change the future by modifying his attitude and behavior. My feeling was further reinforced by the Nine of Wands in the sixth position of the immediate future, the imagery of which depicted Rodney being very much on guard of his intra-psychic world. And despite him being burned in his previous relationship, he would ironically "succeed"; indeed the lesson had not been learned, it did not hurt enough, his defense mechanism remained in charge and he was cautious and careful not to surrender his heavily protected territory.

What was the image of a child as depicted by the Page of Cups doing in the eighth position of Rodney's immediate environment? Rodney said that his children from the previous marriage were going to be in town. (As I found out later, when reading for Rodney's girlfriend Gordana, the reason was much deeper and presented a real issue at home.) The Page of Wands in the ninth position confirmed the good news of Rodney planning on spending time with children. At the subconscious level they were the source of vitality for Rodney, even if he expressed some anxiety on the news of their visit as a possible disruption to his usual routine. The total layout focused on the symbolic message that Rodney needed people to reciprocate upon them, to engage in some sort of projective counter identification, his own mask of a Persona being just a false pretense.

The possible outcome card, the Three of Pentacles in the tenth position, suggested that his major goal had a good chance of materializing; that is, he will likely succeed in achieving his dream of appearing "bigger and better" in the eyes of those with whom he interacts. Yes, they will continue looking "up" at him, but it will have cost him: his emotional body was not going to be healed while his rational one was taking over. The activated defenses of the Nine of Wands seemed to prevail, and Rodney said at that point that yes, he was aware of himself being defensive.

He did not have any supplementary questions, so I asked him to please fill out the questionnaire. When he handed it back to me I found that he merely checked boxes without giving any explanations, which was very much in the spirit of any passive-aggressive personality. Was he provoking or testing me, trying to make me angry, similar to his other interpersonal relationships? The 50-minute format of the reading did not allow me to explore all those issues, so I merely asked Rodney to kindly complete the questionnaire according to the previously discussed conditions of participating in this study and signing the consent form. He then filled out all the answers as specified above. He also answered "not sure" to the question whether this reading contributed to achieving his purpose. He explained his answer as the following: "I don't think I got any new information or insights, but some previously identified issues may have been framed in a usefully different perspective. I want to see how I feel about the reading in a day or two." He did not want to have a follow-up session. "Right now my sense is that nothing said in the reading resonated power-fully enough to justify further explorations in this direction." Rodney also answered "not sure" to the question if this reading was significant and meaningful to him. When I pointed out that the form asked "Please, explain your answer," he then provided an elaborate explanation, perhaps – and in the framework of a narcissistic personality – trying to compensate by being seductive for what his psyche perceived as an up-coming danger. Very much in accordance with his reason for this reading, he seemed to demonstrate tension and anxiety in our "transaction" as well. Well, the layout indicated, sure enough, that his defenses for the time being would remain in full force. Rodney wrote, "If tomorrow something meaningful stirs in me as a result of this reading, it will have been meaningful. But my sense is that a perceptive, intelligent, psychologically sophisticated person with a high level of confidence in their intuitive skills (as you clearly are) who used any of many different available techniques for stirring up psychological issues (i.e. crystal ball, palmistry, word association tests etc.) would very likely have covered similar issues. In other words the issues discussed were more dependent on my openness and your perceptivity than on the cards." Rodney's overall comment was the following: "Thought provoking, but I am still skeptical about its validity. I have recently finished a class on psychological testing. One thing I learned is that though many of the tests are seriously flawed, they still have value in bringing out otherwise hidden issues. Tarot cards, whatever their objective validity may be, certainly seem to have the potential of bringing out or stirring up otherwise hidden issues." As a matter of fact, Rodney's allusion to Tarot as a potential means of psychological testing was a compliment, indeed, even if Rodney, over-rationalizing in his usual manner, had completely missed the paradox!

CASE 14. GORDANA

Gordana, Rodney's girlfriend, was a Latina woman, who lived and worked in Los Angeles. She had a Ph.D. in physics and held an academic position. Her main reason for this reading was a personal or relationship problem that she specified as a "wish to have a family with children". And a child as an issue had just come out in the position of Rodney's immediate environment and significant others, so he was either in denial of the importance of the matter in question, or choosing to distract my attention by being evasive. Could it be that Gordana's desire for a family had never been discussed with Rodney, or if it had, could it be that Rodney buried the issue in his subconscious? Or simply pretended that the issue was non-existent, therefore not an issue after all? The purpose of this reading for Gordana was to gain insight into the present and future that she explained in the following way: "If I gain insight into my present situation my future will be better." She also wanted to gain self-understanding, to get counseling and to find out more about Tarot. Gordana's layout is shown in Figure 8.14.

The first card, the Nine of Swords, carried the message by the collective unconscious of Gordana being in despair. She seemed to be overwhelmed by a lot of duties that she chose to impose on herself, and the weight of taking upon herself the responsibility of planning a family and having a child was turning into an overwhelming burden that was about to break Gordana's endurance (the Ten of Wands in the second, "crossing", position). The imagery of the Nine of Swords motivated me to ask Gordana if she wakes up in the early hours or even suffers from insomnia, whether she has crying spells ("sometimes," was the reluctant reply), and if she finds it difficult to get up and going. According to this image, Gordana was suffering from depression; indeed Gordana instantly free-associated with the imagery of the Nine of Swords by saying "she is in pain" with regard to the sad sleepless figure in the picture who does not want to face yet another day.

Gordana's depression was the direct outcome (as based on the third position underneath) of the attitude projected by the King of Pentacles, the man in Gordana's life, who had been substantially affecting her psyche. The pictures in the first,

137

Figure 8.14. Gordana's layout.

second and third positions depicted Gordana as if having no choice but to bear the burden that this King casually, however with all his earthy practicality (represented by the suit of Pentacles), put on her shoulders. Let her carry the load, if she so desperately wants it – such was the message transmitted by the images of those cards. But the image of the Nine of Swords often carries spiritual connotations as well, as the Holy Spirit, an apparition or ghost, that we are unable to directly interact with in our regular waking life, but that may visit us in the "transition zones" between being asleep and just waking up so as to make us aware of her existence. For the Holy Spirit is yet another name of Shekhinah, a feminine counterpart to God, who dwells in between the celestial and terrestrial realms, longing to find her beloved. (And sure enough, Shekhinah was to manifest her presence in the image of the High Priestess in the position of the immediate outcome).

It was clear to me that in Gordana's case, Spirit itself was looking for ways to be recognized and acknowledged by Gordana as though she forgot her traditional ancestry, so strong in Latino culture, and needed to reconnect, to find a way home, to metaphorically return to the land of her soul.

The two numbers seven nearby each other manifested a sense of completion, if not of a current life cycle, then of a phase: the Seven of Cups in the fourth position of the "past" indicated that Gordana let her past illusions be carried into the present. She had not only built castles in the air, but continued to live in them. The Seven of Pentacles in the fifth position of the potential future suggested that at a subtle level there existed a feeling of wasted effort while Gordana had been unconsciously assessing her relationship and everything she invested in it. What if all was in vain, was the essence of her despair and depression, especially since consciously she was concerned with the issue of giving and receiving equally (the Six of Pentacles in the seventh position of Gordana's mental outlook) in their relationship.

The overall, fourteenth, card was the Major Arcanum The Sun, which in Rodney's reading depicted the root or the foundation of the matter in question. The duality of its nature projected the idea that it might be erroneous to structure and regulate feelings according to logic, as Gordana was manifesting. However the imagery of The Sun also carried the necessity and the natural "goodness" for Gordana to learn its lesson, to go through its challenge, as one often learns by one's mistakes. In fact, The Sun in this position reflected on Plato's allegory of the Cave in his *Republic*. It is just that in Gordana's case, awakened by the Holy Spirit, she would not be blinded by the rays of the Sun, like the prisoner in the cave, but will succeed in adjusting her symbolic "vision" so as to integrate the unconscious into consciousness, thereby starting the process of individuation.

Was Gordana's concern with the problematic issue of the equality in her relationship (The Six of Pentacles) the subject of arguments, I asked, and received a reluctant but positive answer. The constellation of the Major Arcanum The World next to the Six of Cups (in the supplementary eleventh and twelfth positions) indicated a vicious circle of endless discussions in an attempt, on Gordana's behalf, to create a relationship based on mutual trust, unconditional regard and intimate conversation. The World is also a symbol for the actualized Jungian archetype of the Self as the ideally integrated personality in harmony with her life-world. It was clear from the layout that Gordana's individuation was long overdue. The image of The World in this respect was the voice of Gordana's individuated Self that, even if only present *in potentia*, still called on her to become aware of her unconscious as displayed in the layout. The proximity of the Nine of Pentacles assured Gordana that she should feel comfortable and confident with her being self-sufficient and capable of relying on herself without becoming overwhelmed with emotions. Gordana was quite capable of maintaining peace of mind even if her dreams of having a family had not yet come true.

Three other powerful Major Arcana in addition to The World and The Sun pointed towards Gordana having approached a very important, karmic, stage in her life. The eighth position, taken by The Emperor together with The High Priestess – the very essence of Shekhinah – in the sixth position of Gordana's immediate future, indicated that for Gordana there might have happened a confusion of roles regarding the masculine and feminine principles in her psyche. According to The Emperor, The Jungian archetype of Animus was overpowering Anima in Gordana's psychic template, and her mind was projecting the Logos side at the expense of Eros. She lacked femininity in its deepest sense while in the meantime longing for a child. At this point Gordana interrupted me, angrily saying that her choice of not being a so-called stereotypical woman was quite conscious and based on contemporary societal requirements. What seemed to be above and over her conscious awareness, though, was the deep internalization of this idea so that the male archetype of the Animus mode of thinking and acting in accordance with "The Law of the Father" totally possessed her psyche. So an apparent feminist, Gordana had para-doxically internalized the image of the ultimate patriarchal consciousness. Trying to control her emotions, she blocked them as if staying in control of them, but they were showing nonetheless, bringing her to the verge of a nervous breakdown and depression (The Nine of Swords as the core of the problem).

What was Gordana's relationship with her parents? (Since she was in psycho-analysis, as Rodney said earlier, this issue was definitely discussed.) What was the image of her mother in her memory? "Like an army general (The Emperor)," I asked. Gordana answered yes. She did not want to be like her mother, did she? "Yes." Thus Gordana pushing childhood memories about the "wicked mother" out of her mind has "succeeded" in totally blocking the necessary feminine aspect in her own psyche so that Animus filled the vacuum represented by the absence of Anima. But The High Priestess, a spiritual healer who embodied the return of the Goddess able to put into practice the relational, feminine, ethics of care (Noddings, 1984), was none-theless responding to Gordana's desire to have a child by calling for Gordana to wake up, to feel herself a woman, a Goddess, to recognize her own value as a human being, irrespective of being a doctor of philosophy or a university professor. And Gordana's awakening was about to manifest, according to the Death card in the tenth, outcome, position as a symbol for the start of the individuating, transformative process.

If Gordana continues in the present state of a "tug of war" (the Five of Swords in the ninth position) with her partner regarding the issue of children and family, it would be a pointless battle, like banging her head against a brick wall: she would not win. It would only hurt more, as per the Nine of Wands in the same position, this card's imagery depicting a figure with a bandaged head, much in the framework of what often happens when getting into arguments with a passive-aggressive person whose sole aim is to create a battlefield. And Rodney himself, as per previous case, acknowledged his ability to provoke significant others.

The only bearer of good news for Gordana, the Page of Wands, indicated the change of attitude that would inevitably happen during the new transition she was about to enter. The transformation for Gordana would mean changes in her thoughts, feelings, and the whole of her value system – everything that constituted her world view. Would she still want a child? Importantly, would she want a child with the same partner? These questions seemed to be premature as only Gordana herself would be the person to answer them, providing she first meets the challenge of The High Priestess and uncovers her hidden potential as deep femininity. The awakening of a woman – the death of an old personality and the birth of a new one – would bring light to the development of feminine powers, so before a baby is born, a new Gordana is to be re-born; such was the message of Death and The Sun together in the same layout.

When answering the questionnaire, Gordana said that this reading partially contributed to achieving her purpose. It was precisely what the spread conveyed: that at the psychological level, Gordana's inquiry into motherhood seemed to precede certain stages in her personal development in accordance with her individual dynamics. I felt that this reading was a challenge for her, as well as for me. Gordana provided the following explanation: "Several of the characteristics of my situation that came out of the reading were known to me. The suggestion that being more feminine is a necessary step for me to achieve and the prediction of a major transformation in the future are new for me – I wonder about their validity." She was not sure if she wanted a follow-up session. "I need some time to check out if what came out helps me and I find the new information I got from it, valid." Gordana indicated that this reading was significant and meaningful for her, and she wrote, "It was interesting and I am open to consider the suggestions, the possible insight that came out of it." Gordana's overall comment was "Interesting experience. I will be able to judge the validity of the method by seeing how my personal life develops. I will remember this conversation and will see if what came out helps me in my future choices."

CASE 15. ANITA

Anita told me she had just enrolled in Pacific Oaks College to study. She was a black woman who indicated her age group as between thirty and forty. Her main reason for this reading was a personal problem that she specified as a family/financial situation. She asked me if the reading would reflect on her husband, as he was her main concern. The purpose of this reading for Anita was to gain insight into present, future and significant others, to focus on solutions and to feel empowered. Anita's layout is shown in Figure 8.15.

The spread indeed centered on Anita's husband, as male energy was a theme reflected in the first card, the Major Arcanum The Emperor. The Ace of Swords in the second "crossing" position indicated a constant struggle in trying to overcome many current obstacles. Driven by the Father archetype, as projected by the image of The Emperor, it was extremely important for Anita's husband to maintain his status as the head of the family and breadwinner, but according to the Ace of Swords, it was becoming increasingly difficult. While perceiving himself as omnipotent, this was not the case anymore. Anita's husband needed to compensate psychologically and to prove

141

Figure 8.15. Anita's layout.

himself by projecting the image of the King of Swords, that is manifesting strength of character, especially under the conditions of adversity of the Ace of Swords.

What were the circumstances that created the adversity in the first place? Did he have a feeling that he was unjustly treated, as suggested by the Seven of Swords in the third position of the root of the matter? Anita confirmed that a job he expected to get was taken by someone else. Thus the root of the presenting problem was her husband's feeling of defeat, that, in view of his desire to be the one to support his family, wanting desperately to keep it safe and secure (the Ten of Pentacles in the fifth position), was a truly emotional issue. While her husband was trying to carry the load of his responsibilities (the Ten of Wands in the eleventh position) on his own shoulders, Anita – in sharp contrast with the rest of the cards – manifested total gloom and hopelessness as depicted by the Ten of Swords in the overall, fourteenth, position in the layout. It appeared from this card's imagery that she was overwhelmed with the feeling of their family being ruined, as if they had been cursed with bad luck.

Unable to contain her negative emotions, she manifested destructive behavior, reflected in the Five of Swords in the fourth position. Was she fighting with her spouse, blaming him for all misfortunes instead of supporting him under the circumstances? Anita confirmed that they argued, in fact she did blame him and accused him of having been cursed. The negative energy projected by Anita was making her spouse's burden even heavier, and his endurance was at the point of becoming unbearable (the Ten of Wands), as if one more straw would break his back! Did he threaten to leave but stayed at home because of the children? The Knight of Swords (in the supplementary position) manifested a hastily thought and impulsive action, his chaotic behavior, though, contained by the boundaries provided by the Page of Cups in the same position that embodied the image of the children in Anita's family.

The Ten of Swords suggested that while the collective unconscious acknowledged Anita's feelings of being overwhelmed with strong emotions, her view of the situation was nevertheless counterproductive to the wellbeing of her family. She needed to accept the limitations of the present and to hold on tightly to what was very dear to her (the Four of Pentacles in the sixth position), namely her family. Anita was to be the one to organize her willpower in order to get out of the current family conflict. The Major Arcanum The Chariot in the sixth position encouraged her that she would have the quality of positive energy to counter her own negative emotions and almost uncontrollable destructive instincts. Right now it was imperative to concentrate on the long-term implications, as suggested by The Magician, and it was in Anita's power to make all the good possibilities ahead manifest. The Magician was a guardian angel who protected their family, despite the circumstances of the present. Anita should listen to his subtle message and use the tools on the Magician's table that he made available for her.

The position of the immediate future, occupied by The Magician, was a reassurance for Anita that she will indeed get a feeling of clear purpose and will be able to collect her willpower. Controlling her emotions (as per the imagery of the reins of the Charioteer in the same position) should enable her to overcome obstacles and get out of the self-imposed feeling of being in a vicious circle (The World in the seventh position) of continuous bad luck. At this point Anita, free-associating with the reading, said that her husband's misfortune started with the death of his father recently (indeed, The Emperor embodies the Father archetype that may manifest as an actual father in real life) and that she was now getting an insight with regard to what really presented the problem. The necessity of Anita's being there for her husband and providing emotional support to him at a time of the great stress – the central message of the collective unconscious represented in the pictures comprising Anita's spread – thus became further reinforced by her associative process.

Anita said at this point how important it was for her to hear her own voice, thus manifesting the therapeutic quality of the here-and-now of the reading. The position of hopes carried the message of love and happiness. The Ten of Cups represented the image of a happy family life that would last, based on mutual interests and spouses supporting each other. The tenth card, the Four of Cups, provided important advise for Anita with regard to her behavior modification so that her husband would reciprocate accordingly: in case of a job opportunity, instead of putting pressure on her husband and thus increasing his tension and anxiety, Anita should let go, thus preventing it becoming an issue if even the job is not offered to him at the time. By doing this she would definitely help in easing the weight of issues on her husband's shoulders (the Ten of Wands).

How could she get out of the blackness of her current state of mind (the Ten of Swords), asked Anita. She picked up a card from the deck, thus getting the message of the collective unconscious, this card being the Page of Pentacles. New ideas, studies, and the whole process of learning would enrich Anita's mind, and not only that – the school (Pacific Oaks Colleage) itself would function as a support system: the Page on the Tarot card was carefully holding the golden pentacle of the new cognition that Anita would acquire while studying.

Anita then filled out the questionnaire. She answered yes to the question if this reading contributed to achieving her purpose, adding that it was "very insightful into how my behavior affects the feelings of spouse." She was not sure about the need for a follow-up session and said that this reading was significant and meaningful to her by being "very positive". Her overall comment: "I do feel empowered by a very simple message from Tarot."

CHAPTER 9

THE CULTURAL PEDAGOGY OF TAROT

The fifteen readings described nearly verbatim in the preceding chapter together with the participants' immediate feedback on their readings represent the Tarot hermeneutic method in practice and not only in theory. We can see that symbols render themselves interpretable at the everyday level of our regular lives, and we do not have to employ an esoteric vocabulary at the level of practice. Tarot hermeneutic is egalitarian and is able to reach people in the middle and muddle of their actual lives. Yet, because it represents our confrontation with the unconscious it will surely "challenge deeply held beliefs or ways of life" (Noddings, 2006, p. 1) by virtue of transformative learning that leads us out of our old habits of thinking and acting in the world.

The art of interpreting Tarot images requires a developed intuition in conjunction with analytic thinking. The field of Gnostic knowledge is greater than a single truth of linear deductive reasoning. The discovery of deep meanings implicit in the unconscious occurred as much for each participants as for me, confirming Noddings' observation that we should understand "the fragility of *facts* – those peculiar statements wrenched free of context and speaker" (Noddings, 1993a, p. 144; italics mine). Sure enough, "there is no other truth than the creation of the New: creativity, emergence" (Deleuze, 1989, pp. 146–147) embedded in the construction of self-identity on the basis of the existential meanings enfolded in experience that we (re)create in our praxis.

It is only when our thinking "accedes to the infinite movement that frees it from truth as supposed paradigm [that it] reconquers an immanent power of creation" (Deleuze and Guattari, 1994, p. 140). It is under the condition of synchronicity or projection that the infinite movement, the flow of the unconscious, instantaneously collapses and we become conscious of the depth of implicit archetypal meanings as they unfold in front of our very eyes.

Tarot bricolage and the Deleuze-inspired "methodology of the fold" (St. Peirre, 1997a) lead to questioning our assumptions about what constitutes data. The sympathetic approach encompasses both the researcher and the researched, subject and object, consciousness and the unconscious in the process of producing "folded subjectivity" (St. Pierre, 1997a, p. 178) amidst ambiguous, transgressive, "corrosive, painful emotional data" (St. Pierre, 1997a, p. 181) that exceed the reductive method of positivist science. Tarot hermeneutic thus demonstrated itself as a specific technology of the self "that people use to create themselves as the ethical subjects of their actions" (St. Pierre, 1997b, p. 365).

To sum up the information provided by the participants in their subsequent verbal protocols and move from qualitative descriptive terms to quantitative, 80% of participants answered "yes" to the question of whether the reading contributed to achieving their purposes (whatever their individual presenting problem and the purpose for the reading happened to be); 7% answered "partially" and 13% answered "not sure"; none answered "no". 93% percent answered "yes" to the question of whether the reading was meaningful and significant for them, and 7% were "not sure"; none provided a negative answer.

The role of cultural, post-formal, pedagogy, irreducible to formal instruction, the value of learning from experiences, both individual and collective, both conscious and unconscious, should not be underestimated in the area of human development focusing on the process of self-formation: Tarot hermeneutic creates an alternative pedagogy of images that transgresses the boundaries of a formal classroom or the borders of solely cognitive knowledge alike. It expands these learning spaces to encompass the world of experiences via their symbolic, pictorial, representations that enable us to integrate the unconscious into consciousness.

The reading and interpretation of images and symbols as the projections of the archetypal dynamics contribute to people starting to learn from their experiences, thus stepping on the road to individuation. Although in many cases described in chapter 8 the individual experiences were traumatic, or repressed, or even denied and not dealt with, these issues were brought to the surface of the person's consciousness, hence *confirmed*. Reciprocally, the potential and as yet future Self implicit in the unconscious was also *confirmed* by the array of symbolic representations of the many experiences.

Confirmation is one of the pillars of Nel Noddings' ethics of care in education. Confirmation manifests in the ability to envisage the best possible motives belonging to the other's acts, therefore it can only be performed under the conditions of the self-other relation, hence defying the long-standing attitude that identifies moral agents with their acts and by implication holds them solely responsible for their actions. Initially belonging to Martin Buber, who emphasized its ontological sense, the idea of confirmation refers to an act of affirming and encouraging the very best in somebody's actions even if such a better Self is present only potentially.

For Buber, one's resources will have to be known only in the totality of a specific situation as a mutual event connecting two people. Indeed in Tarot hermeneutic neither a reader nor a person seeking a reading can possibly know in advance what to expect: Tarot bricolage simply presents the material at hand. Confirmation sustains a continuous connection, a healing relation, between the two people, as well as between an individual and the greater world. The fact of my not possibly having any agenda, before the very process of interpretation embedded in the caring relation of collaborative partnership has actually begun, enriched it with the element of novelty and creativity.

For Buber, achieving one's authentic existence, that is becoming a whole person, is more than a relation to oneself; it is only possible by virtue of the relation to others. Importantly in the majority of cases described in the preceding chapter, the readings involved "the other" either implicitly or explicitly, thus highlighting Jung's position that our confrontation with the depth of the unconscious is "not only bringing the conflict to consciousness: it also involves an experience of a specific kind, namely, the recognition of an alien 'other' in oneself" (Jung, CW 13, 481). This "other" appears to be doomed to remain always already foreign, strange, alien, and nearly impossible to communicate with.

Mutual decision making appears equally impossible because the sole means of verbal communication bypass the collective unconscious as a home for archetypal meanings and values *shared* by humankind. Unless the eternal alienation between self and other is overcome and integrated into consciousness, gaps and breakdowns in communication will still persist. In the material provided by the individual cases analyzed and described in chapter 8 we have seen the great potential of Tarot hermeneutic not only for individual but also for couple and relationship counseling. When verbal communication between parties becomes dysfunctional and counterproductive to the relationship, the integration of the non-verbal mode leads to repairing the whole situation in which both a generic "self" and a generic "other" are integrated. Taking a self-other relation as a starting point brings to the front the reciprocal and reflective way of knowing that since antiquity distinguished true pedagogy from plain sophistry.

This chapter considers Tarot in its function as a post-formal cultural pedagogy not only at the level of personal growth, identity and meaning-making but also as an educational aid for the whole of culture, when the re-symbolization of the Self becomes a means for overcoming the alienation at the social level and transgressing cultural differences amidst the folds of cultural unconscious. Relationship counseling, conflict resolution, mediation and real-life problem solving pertain as much to individuals as to, as Deleuze would say, *collective assemblages* functioning as the "minimum real unit" (Deleuze, 1987, p. 51) of anti-Oedipal, anti-Freudian, schizoanalysis.

Deleuze (1987) referred to the conversation between Freud and Jung when Jung was pointing out to Freud the importance of multiple elements constituting a particular context and appearing in the unconscious. Deleuze also reminds us of Freud's not paying attention to the assemblages within the totality of experiential situation in the famous case of Little Hans:

> Freud ...takes no account of the assemblage (building-street-nextdoor-warehouse-omnibus-horse-a-horse-falls-a-horse-is-whipped!); he takes no account of situation (the child has been forbidden to go to the street, etc.); he takes no account of Little Hans's endeavor (horse-becoming, because every other way out has been blocked up...). The only important thing for Freud is that the horse be the father – and that's the end of it (Deleuze, 1987, p. 80).

If we stick to a single conventional meaning of the images in dreams or in Tarot symbolism alike, the images will have been "deprived of their authority as mythic images and persons and reduced to...conventions and moralistic stereotypes" (Hillman, 1989, p. 25). In this way, Tarot hermeneutic will have been reduced to a mere repetition of pre-established superficial interpretations that forces the archetypal dynamics "into doctrinal compliance" (Hillman, 1989, p. 25). But, using Deleuze's example of the Little Hans case, his horse cannot be reduced to a single master-symbol with only one fixed meaning in terms of the Freudian father-figure;

rather it is a constituting part of the whole relational dynamics embedded in the collective assemblage determined by

> a list of...affects in the context of the individuated assemblage it is part of...These affects circulate and are transformed within the assemblage... Hans is also taken up in an assemblage: his mother's bed, ... the house, the café across the street, the nearby warehouse, the street, the right to go to the street, the winning of this right, the pride of winning it, but also the danger of winning it ... These are not phantasies or subjective reveries ... Is there an as yet unknown assemblage that would be neither Hans's nor the horse's but that of the becoming-horse of Hans? ... And in what way would that ameliorate Hans's problem, to what extent would it open a way out that had been previously blocked? (Deleuze and Guattari, 1987, pp. 257–258).

The implications for solving or ameliorating problems and decision-making, which is habitually framed in terms of the reasoning of a moral agent independent of her socio-cultural environment and who thereby presents categories in the form of either/or dualistic opposites such as good versus bad or right versus wrong, should not be underestimated. But the anti-Oedipal, collective, unconscious functions as "a productive machine...at once social and desiring" (Deleuze, 1995, p. 144) and is constituted by "races, tribes, continents, history, and geography, always some social frame" (Deleuze, 1995, p. 144). Freud's merely sexual overtones give way to libido as psychic or spiritual energy motivated by Eros, that is, the desire for knowledge-in-depth, for inner Gnosis.

Respectively, new, intensified and expanded, cultural *consciousness* will have been produced "not through any external determinism but through a becoming that carries the problems themselves along with it" (Deleuze, 1995, p. 149). Becoming is affect, as we said in chapter 6, and it is the diversity of affects such as those embedded in Tarot Arcana that produce multiple becomings-other, thus leading to amelioration and problem-solving in the context of a larger "social frame". In this way we become open to new ways of thinking, feeling and acting in the world. Such is the task of Deleuze-Guattarian schizonalaysis that, as we pointed out in chapter 2, effectuates bricolage as a mode of production at both individual and collective levels.

A genuine bricoleur who puts into practice the Tarot hermeneutic allows the image to project the depth of meanings in the context of the presenting problem, emphasized in chapters 7 and 8. In agreement with Hillman's archetypal psychology, it is image itself that is "the true iconoclast...which explodes [with plural] allegorical meanings, releasing startling new insights" (Hillman, 1989, p. 25). It is the Tarot hermeneutic that connects us with Corbin's *Imaginal* world, to which we referred in chapters 1 and 3, and which is projected into our very reality that therefore functions as a virtual foundation for deep Gnostic knowledge in the form of the collective memory gained by humankind over the course of its history. Such knowledge, always already exiting at the soul level, is being actualized within the "imaginal method" (Hillman, 1989, p. 24) that necessarily embodies a self-other, caring, relation.

Imagination, intuition and insight, as the pre-conditions for practicing Tarot hermeneutic, become three necessary components of an alternative pedagogical model that I want to call "3I" education versus the reductive "3R" approach, thus providing us with an unorthodox "ground of certainty" (Hillman, 1989). It is on the basis of this virtual yet real (chapter 6) ground that we can make ethical decisions and choose a particular course of action not as isolated agents but in harmony with universal, archetypal, dynamics.

The process of ethical decision-making embedded in relations rather than founded on a pre-determined rule for action demands, according to Noddings (1993a), concretization rather than abstraction. In chapter 7 we pointed out that the metaphor of the Kabbalistic Tree of Life demonstrates the downward movement from abstract to concrete that "ends up" in the reality of our material world, at the level of the body, that is exactly where, as Romanyshyn would say, "psyche *matters*, ... as evidenced, for example, by synchronicity" (2007, p. 38; italics mine).

It is by means of the embodied psyche that the concretization is achieved. Tarot hermeneutic as reading and interpreting images and symbols that unfold, in the narrative form, the deep meanings of significant events in human culture and history constitutes a practical art that can and should contribute to an enhanced capacity for all people to make intelligent connections to the *spiritual* realm and to learn from their experiences. Yet, it is in the form of *material*, paper-and-paint pictures when the abstract, virtual, reality of the archetypes is made concrete and actual that the mind-body split is overcome.

Discovering in practice deep meanings of, and value for, our collective experiences and events functioning as humanity's existential lessons overcomes the self-other dualism as well. However, have the existential lessons been learned? It was in 1942 when Europe was immersed in war that Jung presented his introductory address at the Zurich meeting of the Swiss Society of Psychology (Jung, 1947). Jung thought not only that the leading psychopaths in Germany were dragging the whole nation plus countless millions in other nations into a slaughterhouse but also that at the time Germany was representative of "the first outbreak of mental alienation" (Jung, 1947, p. 66), or a "peculiar psychological disturbance" (Jung, 1947, p. ix), the outcome of which was what Jung called the *indescribable* events of 20th-century Europe.

The equally indescribable events of September 11 at the start of the 21st century demonstrate that the many lessons inscribed in the process of collective, global, individuation still haven't been learned by humankind. Jung was explicit that the process of individuation, contrary to extreme individualism, naturally produces "in man a consciousness of his relation to the community, just because it brings into consciousness the unconscious which is the common factor uniting all mankind" (Jung, 1947, p. 33). But the Fool, standing at the edge of the abyss, may be still far away from the ideal destination symbolized by the final Arcanum The World as a symbol of the individuated Self in harmony with the World, in harmony with the Other.

Addressing the advances made by new psychotherapy, Jung pointed to the problem of opposites, "a problem which is profoundly characteristic of the psyche. The structure of the psyche is in fact so radically contradictory or contrapuntal that one can scarcely make any psychological statement without immediately having

149

to state the opposite" (Jung, 1947, p. 37). For Jung, the collective psyche fully individuates only when it has embraced the totality of its archetypal dynamics. The conflict of opposites still persists and demonstrated its full force at the start of the 21st century with the destructive event of September 11 followed by the chain of other related events that have been unfolding across the globe ever since.

For the reason that individuation means becoming "one with oneself, and at the same time with mankind, since after all one is a human being" (Jung, 1947, p. 33) it is clear that global individuation in terms of the actualized archetype of wholeness has not been reached. The ruling Jungian archetype of Wotan, like The Devil in the Tarot deck, did not disappear; it is still buried deep in the collective unconscious while simply having shifted its presence on the geopolitical map.

Trying to understand what was happening with Germany as regards its National Socialism movement, Jung invoked the mythology of the Nordic God Odin or Wotan, the master of storm and frenzy, and commented that Wotan was changed into *devil* by Christendom. The symbolic Wotan usually awakes to a new activity as "he releases...the lust of war" (Jung, 1947, p. 4) while going underground now and then and remaining invisible but still dormant in the collective unconscious, thus affecting the collective psyche.

Amidst the mass movements, "all human control comes to an end...when the archetypes begin to function" (Jung 1947, p. 13) on the greater political scene; and human development cannot be defined solely by its personal dimension in terms of the individual growth. The symbolism of The Devil, as we said in chapter 4, relates to the Jungian Shadow, a symbol of fear, bondage and denial. A particular constellation of images that follow each other in a natural progression in the deck, The Devil, The Tower and The Star, is very significant, especially as regards their interpretation at the socio-cultural level in the context of the collective psyche.

At the collective level, the Shadow encompasses those outside the norm of the established order and social system, such as "criminals, psychotics, misfits, scape-goats" (Samuels, 1985, p. 66). It is not only that they appear to stand outside culture, but importantly culture itself fails to assimilate its own Shadow. Jung commented that the

> whole rationally organized crowd, called a state or a nation, [appears to be] run by...terrific power...This ghastly power is mostly explained by fear of the neighbouring nation, which is supposed to be possessed by a malevolent devil. As nobody is capable of recognizing where and how much he himself is possessed and unconscious [of this condition], one simply projects [it] upon the neighbour, and thus it becomes a sacred duty to have the biggest guns and the most poisonous gas. The worst of it is that one is...right. All...neighbours are ruled by an uncontrolled and uncontrollable fear just like oneself (Jung, 1947, p. 78).

The venomous quality of The Devil is to be recognized. It represents a moment of psychological denial and the implementation of a scapegoat policy by the dominant culture or nation, while in the meantime projecting its own shadowy qualities to the culture perceived as "the other".

Human aggression is not only a psychological but also a "moral problem – the problem of dealing with the Shadow without becoming possessed by it" (Stevens, 1983, p. 227), that is, with the problematic of our choice of actions. For Noddings, it is fundamentalism that constitutes "the biggest stumbling block to educating for intelligent belief or unbelief" (Noddings, 1993a, p. 140). She comments that the "devilish...develops right along with goodness" (Noddings, 1993a, p. 32).

The scapegoat psychology is associated with what Jungian psychologist Erich Neumann called old ethics, and it is an ethical attitude indeed that is central with regard to the Shadow archetype. While the ego-consciousness focuses on indubitable and unequivocal, fundamental, moral principles, these very principles crumble when the unconscious Shadow begins to act out. Jung pointed to the compensatory significance of the shadow in the light of our ethical responsibility, the neglect of which tends to precipitate multiple evil consequences in the world:

> The complications arising at this stage are no longer egotistic wish-conflicts, but difficulties that concern others as much as oneself. At this stage it is fundamentally a question of collective problems, which have activated the collective unconscious because they require collective rather than personal compensation. We can...see that the unconscious produces contents which are valid not only for the person concerned, but for other as well, in fact, for a great many people and possibly for all (Jung, CW 7, 5).

Old ethics is grounded in the dualism of either/or thinking with its adherence to an ideal perfection and absolute Good that necessarily leads to the appearance of its binary opposite, absolute Evil. This ethics is "partial" (Neumann, 1969, p. 74) and not whole because the realm of the unconscious remains unrecognized or denied; hence any decision-making is the sole prerogative of the conscious Ego and not of the wholly integrated Self. But the new, relational, ethics demands recognizing our own dark side and, by integrating the Shadow, becoming conscious of our own darkness.

The individuated Self emerges only when the opposites exist as a harmonious whole and neither side is suppressed or eliminated. The perpetual presence of the shadow must be recognized and made visible otherwise it will fall into the very depth of the unconscious where it will continue to crystallize until it starts to break out from the "false consciousness" the symbol for which, as we said in chapter 4, is the next picture in the deck, The Tower that in some decks is called The Tower of Destruction, or The House of Destruction. Indeed, the opposite of the creative Eros that "drives" the human Psyche and fills it with desire is the destructive Thanatos, a powerful death-drive.

Hederman (2003) warns of a danger to ourselves and others if and when we remain unconscious of the Shadow. If history and culture have taught us anything, it is that in the 20th century The Devil fully manifested as "a hell on earth and that this hell was a human creation. It was a hell of cruelty and mayhem resulting from the incapacity of powerful people to decipher their unconscious motivation" (Hederman, 2003, p. 21). And the uncanny symbolism of The Tower can be perceived in the far more recent events of September 11 that marked the beginning of the 21st century.

CHAPTER 9

Jung pointed out that it is the excess of pride and passion that "raises a man not only above himself, but also above the bounds of his mortality and earthliness, and by the very act of raising him, it destroys him. This 'rising above himself' is expressed mythologically in the building of the heaven-high tower of Babel that brought confusion to mankind" (Jung, CW 5, 171). Thunder and lightning in the imagery of The Tower convey the mythological wrath of the gods that brings swift and painful alteration at the level of collective consciousness in the aftermath of the destruction of the self-erected unstable structure.

However, the enforced evacuation from The Tower, breaking all defenses, frees the Hero from being symbolically confined within outlived psychological, ideological, cultural, or any other belief system. Any unforeseen cataclysmic event that suddenly brings people down to earth by disturbing the existing norm and order of things through an abruptly terminated current psychological state or a break-up in a set of values privileged by a given culture necessarily raises the level of consciousness.

It is precisely because the transformation into becoming-other is involuntarily, not by our volition and conscious will, but by virtue of the confrontation with the unconscious, that the *creative* becoming-other takes place. For Deleuze, "once one steps outside what's been thought before, once one ventures outside what's familiar and reassuring, once one has to invent new concepts for unknown lands, then methods and moral systems break down and thinking becomes…a 'perilous act', a violence, whose first victim is oneself" (Deleuze, 1995, p. 103). It is oneself who has to undergo a symbolic Death, as we said in chapter 4, so as to effectuate becoming-other.

The breakdown in existing order simultaneously creates the conditions for the potential production of a new order. Natural disasters notwithstanding, cultural conflicts manifest the archetypal dynamics in the natural progression from the image of The Devil to the subsequent image of The Tower. But, as we said in chapter 4, the next picture that follows The Tower in a Tarot deck is The Star. Thus the image of The Tower indicates not just a breakdown but an important *breakthrough* with its "seeds of light broadcast in the chaos" (Jung, CW 8, 388) when the darkness embodied in the preceding image of the Shadow-Devil is illuminated by lightning; hence brought to consciousness in the imagery of The Star with the divine sparks indeed shining in the skies.

Deleuze (1983) commented that culture usually experiences violence that serves as a shock which forces the formation of our thinking and refers to Plato's famous metaphor of the cave: a prisoner is forced to start thinking. Human thought thinks "by virtue of the forces that are exercised on it in order to constrain it to think… A power, *the force of thinking,* must throw it into a becoming-active" (Deleuze, 1983, p. 108; Deleuze's italics). And because "Force itself is an act, an act of the fold" (Deleuze, 1993, p. 18), becoming-active is by necessity equivalent to becoming-other due to the process of unfolding when the destruction of The Tower is followed up by The Star with its image of the female figure.

Significantly, in Jung's dreams, as he wrote in his only recently published magnum opus, *The Red Book*, as well as in his letters to Wolfgang Pauli, the figure of Philemon, his male guru, was often accompanied by a female figure, his very psyche or soul, advising him to tap into inner images as a source of creativity and healing. The imagery of The Star, with the naked female figure stripped of her clothes as if from outlived habits and old values, connotes the field of meanings that include hope, healing, inspiration, creativity, and the realization of our spiritual dreams.

Therefore we do understand the symbolic message that "The Tower of Destruction" as a prequel to The Star was only a temporary stage in the forward-directed evolution of consciousness and human development. While the ruins of The Tower are still spread out across the globe with the continuing wars in Afghanistan and Iraq and the persistent threat of global terrorism, we should have by now learned the moral lesson implied by its symbolism as the clash of cultural value systems.

The presence of The Star in the deck, as the natural progression from The Tower, is a symbolic message that the destruction of the tower(s) was a precursor to the renewal of human spirit and the creation of new psychic space. The image of The Star conveys the natural oneness of pure (naked) soul with Nature or a potential unity of human psyche with *Anima Mundi*, the ultimate re-collection of fragmented holy sparks. The vessels in the picture are red, this color representing full flesh-and-blood humanity in unity with its spiritual essence symbolized by the blue color of water, that is, our conscious awareness of the streams and flows of the unconscious.

The Star embodies the meaning of hope, inspiration, healing and reconciliation at the dawn of the new Aquarian Age that implies a critical reversal of values. In the current global climate permeated by diverse beliefs, disparate values and cultural conflicts, when different ideologies compete with each other leading to destruction on the scale of The Tower, the universal value of hope is paramount. In fact, this Arcanum is often called The Star of Hope, the hope for new awareness and an expansion of human consciousness.

We don't need to wait indefinitely for a far-off messianic age but can reclaim the holy sparks at the level of worldly affairs. We can bring about a revolution (as Neumann called it) in the societal value system if we step into our own symbolic process of evolution and transform the potentiality into our very reality by virtue of the lived-through meanings embodied in Tarot hermeneutic as our ultimate cultural pedagogy.

The level of social praxis as encompassing human behaviors, decision-making or choosing a particular course of action or policy is of utmost significance! Jung was adamant that the presupposed universal rules of human conduct are

at most provisional solutions, but never lead to those critical decisions which are the turning points in a man's life. As the author [Erich Neumann] rightly says: "The diversity and complexity of the situation makes it impossible for us to lay down any theoretical rules for ethical behaviour."... The formulation of ethical rules is not only difficult but actually impossible because one can hardly think of a single rule that would not be reversed under certain conditions...Through the new ethic, the ego-consciousness is ousted from its central position in a psyche organized on the lines of a monarchy or totalitarian state, its place being taken by *wholeness* or the *self,* which is now recognized as central" (Jung, 1949 in Neumann, 1969, p. 13; italics in original).

To achieve such wholeness, we have to evaluate real-life social situations as they arise in our very praxis and learn the lessons embodied in the Tarot archetypal journey through the school of life. Only as such can we bring together the holy sparks of the original broken vessels and to discover the meaning and direction of our lives as our very ethos.

The real core of the ethical problem, for Jung, is the problem of how to achieve the union of conscious and unconscious that historically "was projected in the form of a drama of redemption" (Jung, 1949, in Neumann, 1969, p. 18). The symbolic drama replays itself again and again, not only in the context of the aftermath of World War II in Europe that Jung envisaged as "a mere prologue" (Jung, 1947, p. 90) but globally in the here-and-now of our socio-cultural reality. However the 21st century which, as the aftermath of The Tower, is presently illuminated by The Star is symbolic of a New Age indeed.

We remember from chapter 4 that the last Arcanum, numbered *twenty-one* and called The World, represents the archetypal image of us, fully individuated Selves, capable of living in harmony with Others and taking ethical responsibility for the social and natural World we inhabit. Robert Place (2005) reminds us of the twelfth-century monk Joachim of Flora who had an epiphany in which he saw all history ascending through several levels, each associated with one aspect of the Christian Trinity. In the Age of the Father, the world was created and the Old Testament written. In the Age of the Son, Christ was born and has died on the Cross, the New Testament was written and the Church began.

The New Age, envisaged by Joachim, would be ruled by the Holy Spirit. This promised Golden age of reconciliation will be infused with love and, according to Joachim's vision, humankind will be able to communicate with the divine directly, not via an official Church, which would thus be dissolved. The divine will be found within and not without, not unlike Hasidic cleaving to the God within. Analogously, a divine Eros and a human Psyche will form one organic whole.

A similar story is told in Jewish mythology when Shekhinah, a feminine principle, the bride of God – itself a symbol of dispersed light – can return from her exile to reunite with her beloved, and it is "then [that] the holy spark leaps across the gap" (Buber, 1963, p. 139) enabling the re-symbolization of the collective Self representing "cultural transformation into a new age" (Wexler, 1996, p. 63). It is the divine spark of The Star that "leaps from one soul to another [and] traces the design of an open society, a society of creators" (Deleuze, 1991, p. 111): the symbolism of The Star conveys such spiritual creativity. And this creativity can fully manifest only when our old modes of thinking are overcome in the process of becoming-other, even if this happens forcefully.

The archetypes embodied in Tarot images represent various aspects of the individual and collective personality that bridge the natural and cultural, the mental and material, the sexual and spiritual; ultimately embracing the alchemical Sophia, a feminine principle of wisdom embodied in the image of The High Priestess as mediatrix in the form of the Holy Spirit permeating both nature and culture

(Semetsky and Delpech-Ramey, in press), whose role is indeed to *mediate the conflict* between the opposites.

Shekhinah's "presence", while only potential in the symbolism of The High Priestess is being realized in The Star, the imagery of which conveys the brightness of sparks as symbolic of the forthcoming transformation towards new understanding, new age, new culture. The imagery of The Star is permeated with symbols of nature. For Buber, we are "educated by the elements, by air and light, and the life of plants" (Buber, 1971, p. 90). It is the task of the cultural pedagogy of Tarot hermeneutic to provide us with an empirical method to learn from nature and culture alike, to learn from life experiences, even if this empiricism is radically transcendental, as we said in chapter 6. In fact, without the presence of self-transcendence the very concept of learning would be meaningless.

While so far in this book we have been focusing on the practical *art* of Tarot hermeneutic and its role as a cultural pedagogy in the process of subject-formation, in the next chapter we will explore a new approach to *science* that makes this art functional.

CHAPTER 10

TAROT AND A NEW SCIENCE

This chapter has a story of its own. Back in 1994, when I was close to completing this research in the area of behavioral sciences, I started thinking more and more about a naturalistic, scientific, paradigm that could explain the phenomenon of Tarot. It was obvious that mechanistic science based on linear causality was insufficient. Indeed in chapter 7 of this book I commented that our verbal language is equally inadequate to reflect the full richness of human experience as exceeding the propositions of the conscious mind but encompassing the psychic reality of the archetypes "situated" in the collective unconscious and expressing itself in the language of images. The premise of the Jungian *unus mundus*, the one world enveloping body, soul and spirit, demands however that there should be naturalistic explanation of the functioning of the archetypes and, respectively, Tarot, even if this practice is usually considered esoteric hence *ipso facto* unscientific. The world as a *whole*, however, includes our very being-in-the-world thus transcending the visible physical nature as empirically given.

In April 1996 my poster titled *On the Nature of Tarot* was presented at the interdisciplinary conference *Toward a Science of Consciousness* in the University of Arizona, Tucson, and Mary Greer contacted me to reflect on the topic of the paper. The full text of the paper has been subsequently published in 1998 in the journal *Frontier Perspectives*, the voice of the Centre for Frontier Sciences, Temple University in Philadelphia, in the "Invited opinion" section of the 7 (1) issue, pp. 58–66. The issue provoked a lovely debate, notably with Martin Gardner, who subsequently republished his reflections in the 2000 book *Did Adam and Eve have Navels? Debunking Pseudoscience.*

In the chapter titled "What's going on at Temple University" Gardner criticized the Centre's research program, focusing specifically on the Fall/Winter 1998 issue of the journal with my article in it, among others. He referred to the exchange of letters that followed the publication of the issue and his rejoinder that first appeared in *Skeptical Inquirer.* In relation to my article, Gardner commented that "Inna Semetsky is irked because I called her defense of Tarot card reading 'funny' without giving my reasons for rejecting such fortune-telling...That a magazine claiming to discuss matters on the 'frontiers' of scientific research would publish her paper is...not funny but sad" (2000, pp. 229–230).

What is sad, however, is that public opinion holds to the habit of reducing Tarot hermeneutic to what it perceives as merely a fortune-telling exercise, which is *a priori* suspect, especially considering the odd case of this phenomenon attempting to get out of its pop-culture corner, to which it has been traditionally confined, and starting to lay claims to academic research. What is missing in Gardner's critique is the understanding of the bricolage mode of the production of knowledge and an exceptional new rigor (Kincheloe, 2001) in research together with an ethical stance as this type of research demands. In what follows I present a modified and updated version of my 1998 article *On the Nature of Tarot.*

The last decades of the 20th century have been marked by scientific discoveries that suggest the presence of a single unifying principle. Systems theorist Erich Jantsch described this fundamental principle as the unity of the macro and micro aspects of mind and evolution, and physicist David Bohm enriched its meaning by postulating the concepts of the implicate order and the quantum potential. Biology, chemistry, physics, and the social sciences have, quite synchronistically, manifested "a spectacular transition", using the words of Nobel Laureate Ilya Prigogine (Foreword to Laszlo, 1991), towards unification within the paradigm of complexity science and dynamical systems theory. Ludwig Von Bertalanffy, a founder of general systems theory, acknowledged the insufficiency of analytical procedures of classical science based solely on linear causality; rather, knowledge is not reduced to given facts but becomes a function of dynamic transactions in the field "between knower and known" (1972, p. xix).

This hypothetical field exceeds the currently known four fields in physics (gravitational, electromagnetic, and strong and weak nuclear fields). It is a field that would account for the much talked-about actions-at-a-distance, synchronistic events and morphic resonance (Sheldrake, 1988) and one that appears to organize chaos into order, thus contributing to its own self-organization. This field seems to manifest animated properties, it appears to know both how to learn and how to teach, and it renders invalid the habitual dichotomies transcending "the usual distinctions between...concepts of the physical and the mental" (Naess, Foreword to Laszlo, 1995).

For systems scientist Ervin Laszlo, the systematic exploration of this field would constitute a milestone in research on consciousness. Recently Laszlo (2004/2007) referred to this field as informational and conceptually equivalent to the Akashic field, the word *Akasha* in Sanskrit meaning the all-pervasive space that encompasses, in addition to the four elements of nature, also the fifth, quintessential, element. The fifth field is thereby a field from which emerges all that we can perceive by our senses.

Tarot hermeneutic indeed points to the existence of such a field. While typically either "elevated" to the status of an esoteric, hence magical, craft outside science or "reduced" to the level of fortune-telling, Tarot is neither. In fact the process of reading and interpreting the Tarot pictorial symbolism demonstrates properties that implicate the presence of a common foundation between this ancient art and the new science of self-organization (Dalenoort, 1994) pertaining to complex, multi-leveled, systems. Back in 1975, Jantsch had already included Tarot in his systematic overview of approaches and techniques of the "inner way" to knowledge, placing Tarot at the mythological level among genealogical approaches, yet acknowledging the relation of such a mythological level to the level identified as evolutionary. Jantsch claims that it is at this particular level where the human mind becomes potentially capable of "tuning in ... to the evolutionary wave-form [and] developing a consciousness capable of relating to a four-dimensional reality" (1975, p. 150) rather than staying outside of the three-dimensional physical world as its impassionate observer.

The evolutionary wave-forms refer to the interference patterns within the field. As for the complicated task of tuning into such a field, Jantsch anticipated, among other things, a dynamic "communication mechanism, which is at work across the... levels of perception, so that, for example, 'insight' from the evolutionary level may be received in some other form at the mythological level, e.g., in the form of intuition, or dreams, or general vibrations felt as quality" (Jantsch, 1975, p. 149). Such a communication mechanism is provided by means of the Tarot hermeneutic method when the spiritual realm of the universal mind becomes projected into the mental and emotional aspects of an individual mind. In turn, those aspects manifest in the material form of the geometrical layout of Tarot Arcana as the particular pictures are the projections, as we said in chapter 7, of the mental and emotional contents displayed in the here-and-now of our physical reality in their concrete, material, form. Pointing out that the organization of complex dynamic systems proceeds through self-realizing and self-balancing processes, Jantsch envisaged that the "Tarot cards...may be seen as embodying [and] mapping out the field of potential human response" (1975, p. 163). In a self-organizing process "characterizing the system and its relationship with the environment ...mind...is no longer the opposite of matter, but...co-ordinates the space-rime structure of matter" (Jantsch, 1980, p. 14), not unlike the universal *Nous*.

It is at the new level of complexity, as if along the paths displayed on the Tree of Life, that new knowledge *emerges,* as if from nowhere but in fact from the Akashic, fifth, field of invisible information when it is being transformed and made visible. Systems science does not therefore depart from the Hermetic world view because both consider an individual mind to be an intrinsic part of the universe and part of nature. Nature is not dead but *animated* by the self-organizing dynamics, and the archetypes projected in the material medium partake of mind and nature alike. They are "located" in Corbin's *Imaginal* world in-between. Indeed "phenomena of 'cultural synchronicity' require a naturalistic interpretation of the notion of archetypes... Archetypes, and the collective unconscious that frames them, are not just 'in the mind': they are 'in nature'" (Laszlo, 1995, p. 135). The deepest, *psychoid,* level represents the fundamental reality of the unification of *psyche* and *physis* as *Unus Mundus.*

Jungian synchronicity is therefore just another name for the property of non-locality posited by contemporary physics. For David Peat, an acausal connection may manifest itself in the form of non-local correlations that appear to lie outside the normal confines of space and time (Peat in Rubik, 1992). Jung himself is viewed as a systems theorist by contemporary post-Jungians, and "a systemic ...view implies that...inner and outer...interpersonal and intrapsychic can be seen to be [a] seamless field of references" (Samuels, 1985, p. 266) that unite in a holistic manner the otherwise binary opposites of mind and matter, the knower and the known.

Nobel laureate Wolfgang Pauli who collaborated with Jung on their work on synchronicity envisaged the development of theories of the unconscious as outgrowing their solely therapeutic applications by being eventually assimilated into natural sciences. The *field* of the collective unconscious is not unlike a field in physics, it however extends the reductive "old narrow idea of 'causality' … to a more general form of 'connections' in nature" (Pauli, 1994, p. 164). Synchronicity is responsible for the invisible communication link at a subtle level of perception, and the communication mechanism that Jantsch was looking for is displayed in the tangible reality of the Tarot layout that forms a bridge through which the invisible information comprising the fifth field is being transmitted and, importantly, *transformed* into visible.

The Hermetic postulate of translating the invisible into the visible that we addressed in chapter 3 is therefore not just a myth but agrees with the dynamics of complex systems characterized by new properties emerging at levels that appear to not be directly connected with preceding ones but are nevertheless continuous with the latter by virtue of effects produced at a new level, along a metaphorical bridge – a non-local connection – between the levels. The Hermetic law of correspondences upon which Tarot rests thus resembles, in terms of contemporary physics, non-linear or circular causality. Even in Newtonian times "sympathies" were paid their dues. The property of non-locality and entanglement pertaining to the fifth field that Ervin Laszlo equated, in physical terms, with the so-called quantum vacuum and David Bohm qualified as the "zero-point field" allows for a particular constellation of pictures to appear in specific positions that connote a field of meanings (chapter 7).

David Bohm's theory thereby provided a framework for a psychophysical model of the unified world. The field of information that "lies deeply behind/under our consciousness which is unfolded in space-time" (von Franz in Friedman, 1986, p. 117) serves as the background for this unity. Physics contends that a quantum vacuum is not empty but is "filled" with virtual particles. It is out of the vacuum that an actual (positively charged) particle emerges; while a virtual (negatively charged) particle remains hidden in the field. As Laszlo comments, this invisible Dirac-sea (named after physicist Paul Dirac) of virtual particles is everywhere, while the observable visible world just floats on its surface. We can see that Deleuze's philosophical insights into the virtual-actual interactions that we addressed in chapter 6 were visionary indeed.

According to contemporary science (Lucadou, 1994), complex living systems manifest the property of non-locality also at the macro level, analogously to the effect of Bell's correlations at the micro level. The information that is enfolded within the energetic field delocalizes itself and unfolds at the physical level of the system. The informational content of each picture, or group of pictures corresponding to a particular archetypal constellation, describes a state of consciousness in a specific moment through a set of discrete packets of information. When the information transmitted by the imagery is interpreted by a reader it creates a feedback loop. Specific contents become accessible through insight into the meaning of the pictorial symbolism. This insight triggers the flow of associative thoughts and feelings, and the person may decide to act upon the acquired knowledge, thus creating as yet another feedback loop.

According to information theory, it is the presence of feedback circuits that characterizes a system as having potential for self-organization and self-regulation. Jung indeed envisaged the self-regulating quality of the psyche. The Tarot hermeneutic thereby functions in a double manner: initially as an amplifier by making the subtle aspects of the psyche vivid and substantial, and subsequently in creating multiple feedbacks that direct the amplified information back into the system, thus expanding its boundaries to accommodate qualitatively new, potentially meaningful, information. As Jean Gebser would say, our consciousness *intensifies*, and the entire system, by assimilating the acquired knowledge, *reorganizes itself at a higher level of complexity*. Such is the process of human development and the evolution of consciousness.

This is what happens in the course of the archetypal journey marked by the stopovers symbolized by Tarot Arcana: the fifth field filled with information – as yet a theoretical concept created by Laszlo – becomes available to our awareness in its visible form as a living reality that emerges in the patterns of the Tarot layout and, as such, is experienced through the hermeneutic process. It is not only the experience of past evolution "but also the experience of anticipated future [that] vibrates in the present…The present of a dynamic system not only has a present which consists of the immediate experiences of the moment, of the horizontal processes, but also a past…which includes the vertical evolution process which has led to the present structure of the system, and the future…which corresponds to the options in further evolution" (Jantsch, 1980, p. 232). We are actively involved in communication with the fifth field, with our past, present and the potential future, via a dialogue, at once symbolic and literal, created along the lines of Gilles Deleuze's *transversal* communication as a bridge that connects different levels of a complex system.

This is the experiential reality of being on the verge of some kind of communication breakthrough (cf. Abraham, McKenna, and Sheldrake, 1992). Due to the irreversible process of Tarot hermeneutic, a person goes through the actual experience of accessing the field of the collective unconscious via its symbolic representation in the layout and becomes empowered with new awareness, thus acquiring greater degrees of freedom in the form of Gnostic knowledge. The process is never an instantaneous one: the physical world is forever bound by the arrow of time and thus by a temporal duration. For the fifth field of consciousness, however, time – as we understand it, in its linear chronological form – is but one of its own projections, an aspect of the *timeless* archetypal reality.

The law of correspondence as applied to space – as above, so below – has its analogy also in a temporal sense: that which was is as that which will be, and that which will be is as that which was. Rupert Sheldrake (1988) connected the latent state of his morphogenetic (form-generating) fields with a state that comes into being in the future. Jungian psychologist Michael Conforti, introducing his concept of the archetypal field theory (2003) referred to Jung's notion of the structural elements of the psyche and concluded that the archetypal and morphogenetic fields appear similar. In David Bohm's view time is a derivative of a higher order, as such it is enfolded into the whole of time at any present moment. His idea of the holomovement underlying all physical reality appears to relate to yet another esoteric law, that of periodicity, which states that the universe is forever in a series of periodic manifestations, cycles of flux and reflux. It is this very "process [as] the energetic flux of the universe [that] underlines time, change, and becoming" (Abraham, McKenna, and Sheldrake, 1992, p. 28) as we perceive as such in the physical world.

The human figure that appears in the majority of Tarot images is a symbol of the psyche depicted in a series of transformations as the instability and fluctuations that comprise human life contribute to the individuation of the Self. While the psyche may encounter everywhere a range of fluctuations, evolution, and diversification (Prigogine, in Laszlo, 1991), the chaotic state of it eventually becomes organized into order due to the effect of the self-organizing principle of developing order through fluctuations as a feature of complex, multileveled, systems. Each Arcanum represents a missing element that, when suddenly discovered, impels one to cry out "Eureka" at the birth of the idea; it is the long-awaited insight, the ever-present potential catalyst that transforms the spiritual life of an individual into a creative autopoietic process. What happens at the physical plane in the reality of our three-dimensional space and linear chronological time, though, is another matter, as free will is a variable that can either help or hinder the course of events.

The self-organizing process of Jungian individuation is catalyzed only if the authentic symbols of the Arcana become activated and the subject of the reading is ready to perceive them due to hermeneutic process that makes the information which was yet implicit in the Akashic field – the field of the collective unconscious – available at the level of human cognition. The situations and events that people go through are accompanied by an energetic spectrum of feelings, thoughts, emotions, and actions. This dynamics leads to the appearance of behavioral patterns that are archetypal in principle; each pattern is reflected in the imagery of the pictures and becomes the constellation of the psychic energy in the form of the spectrum of material representations (Abraham, McKenna, and Sheldrake, 1992). When one or another archetype is actualized, it is projected into the sequence of pictures in the layout, thus manifesting the a-causal connection grounded in the synchronicity principle.

An intensified and expanded consciousness, in which the unconscious has been integrated, can transcend the limits of space and time and perceive it simultaneously as the projected wave packets of the past, present, and future. The fifth field is un-differentiated, with no division between past, present, and future. The fragmented aspects of past, present, and future of the lower, most dense level of the whole spectrum of orders, are becoming unitary at the highest, most subtle and rarefied level, reaching out as such to the ultimate *unus mundus*. So the difference in various levels is specified by the frequency or intensity of their expression: matter turns into energy which turns into consciousness or information, always evolving toward ever finer frequencies, in the same way that matter itself once was just the simplest condensation of energy in the form of hydrogen.

While in the physical world the validity of the law of conservation of energy is still valid, in relation to the fifth field of consciousness, its meaning appears to be extended: in a Hermetic sense there should also be the law of conservation of consciousness, of information. According to Einstein's relativity theory, we exist in a four-dimensional world of space-time rather than proceed through time in three-dimensional spatial existence. New physics goes even further: the undifferentiated consciousness, the fifth field, incorporates time in itself. That is why there can be a sense of gazing into the future during Tarot readings that are infamously perceived as spooky fortune-telling. Yet action-at-a-distance not so long ago was also perceived as spooky!

Certain positions in the layout, as we said in chapter 7, signify the element of time, which is but a projection of the fifth field. And on its physical plane of mani-festation, time splits into its three dimensions that thus paradoxically coexist within one and the same layout. The apparently strange phenomenon of reading into the future as well as picking up past events derives from the fact that, in accordance with "Bohm's point of view, the real event is enfolded in the timeless implicate order and unfolds into the explicate order, thereby creating time in our three-dimensional world" (Friedman, 1994, p. 74). That is, the future as well as the past is the fifth field's eternal present. Laszlo (2004/2007) comments on the experiences of the *Apollo* astronaut Edgar Mitchell. Mitchell pointed out that information "is present everywhere...and has been present since the beginning" (Laszlo, 2004/2007, p. 67). This information signifies "a subtle...connection between things at different loca-tions in space and events in different points in time. Such connections are... 'nonlocal' in the natural science and 'transpersonal' in consciousness research" (Laszlo, 2004/2007, p. 68).

The here-and-now quality of the reading evokes the always present state of the fifth field that, just like the Akashic field, contains all there is to know and that nevertheless may project both past and possible future events that display themselves in the specific positions of the pictures in the layout. According to quantum physics, what we call an event is the actualized possibility of just a potential tendency: all the energetic/informational quantum potential of the fifth field expressed in its wave-function may manifest. The fifth field is the arena of the potential reality; all events of the past, present and future coexist within this field as virtual potentialities. Which probability, though, will become an actuality, which one out of all possible events will actually manifest in the physical realm, is a different matter. At any moment only part of a whole is being "read" therefore "giving rise to activity" (Bohm and Hiley, 1993, p. 36). The information is potentially active everywhere, "but it is actually active, only where and when it can give form to the... energy" (Bohm and Hiley, 1993, p. 36) that, in the context of Tarot hermeneutics, is the material form of the pictures.

The fifth "field produces *effects*, and these can be perceived" (Laszlo, 2004/2007, p. 73; italics mine) literally, by our very eyes. Is the layout a symbolic representation, a sort of a topological, or rather a holographic, model of the informational wave-form of the field of the collective unconscious? Is it the psyche's "flux arrested for the time being? [or] coming to balance for the time being, coming into relevant closure, like the vortex that closes on itself though it's always moving" (Bohm in Friedman, 1994, p. 64). Is the human mind a sort of measuring device and a highly sensitive one indeed so as to pick up the most subtle frequencies constituting the fifth field, the field filled with information?

The layout presenting us with the archetypal dynamics gives explicit expression to the unfolding of the enfolded, implicit potentialities of David Bohm's "Undivided Universe" (Bohm and Hiley, 1993). The explicit manifestations of the contents of the *mind* are being further unfolded into the form represented by the material substance of the pictures, at the level of the body or *matter*. Laszlo's assertion that form emerges out of the fifth field and the information transforms into matter thus acquires a practical, visible manifestation in the format of the Tarot spread. The evolutionary properties of the field of information or consciousness and its un-orthodox intentionality become obvious: the implicate order, as yet non-manifest, which permeates the field in question unfolds to create the explicate order and re-enfolds to give guidance to itself in a truly self-organizing manner. As such, the dynamics described by Tarot hermeneutic resonate with the universal dynamics of the fifth field of a *transcendental* realm, and in a holographic sense the fifth field itself is *immanent* in a layout in accord with Deleuze's method of transcendental empiricism (chapter 6).

As matter acquires *a new informational content*, it is being re-enfolded back into what has been called by Bohm (1985) the unbroken wholeness of the universe by means of the holomovement in a process of self-regulation. The movement along the levels of order creates different dimensions, and consciousness moves inward and outward in a psychological sense. *Inward* means into the depth of the unconscious realms, or into the realm of ideas "located" in the Kabbalistic worlds of formation and creation. *Outward* means into the material realm, into physical reality, and into the Kabbalistic world of action. According to the Hermetic tradition, the attributes or qualities of existence along the movement of consciousness are connected by twenty-two pathways comprising a network of relationships, just like the twenty-two Major Arcana of the Tarot deck.

The archetypes that according to Jung constitute the structure and dynamics of the psyche provide an analogous structure to the informational, Akashic, field. In the Bohmian holomovement there is *no direct causal connection* other than the *relationships between events*. The universal field is being interwoven into a whole by means of, according to Bohm, the interconnecting network of quanta, which there-fore constitute the archetypal patterns that manifest in the discrete constellations of pictures at the physical level. A *static* display of the holomovement, the Tarot spread is a projection that "contains" the *dynamics* of the process. Biophysicist Fritz-Albert Popp proposed a novel approach to evolution as the expansion of coherent states. Popp introduced the evolutionary principle as providing predictability of the development. Nevertheless he stated "the content of information that can be transferred by increasing development on this extending basis remains, however, unpredictable" (Popp in Rubik, 1992, p. 249). The modality of Tarot hermeneutic, however, facilitates the predictability of not only the dynamics of development but also of the informational content, however within the limitations of so-called deterministic chaos.

The value and applicability of the concepts of the mathematics of complexity to psychology has been recently addressed (Barton, 1994), including an explora-tion of the relationship between non-linear dynamics and Jungian therapy

(Abraham, Abraham, and Shaw, 1990). As long ago as 1946, Kurt Lewin, a pioneer in psychology, asserted that behavior depends on motivational forces comprising a psychological field. A dynamic system approach to the development of cognition and action has been elaborated in a monumental work by Thelen and Smith (1995). At the conceptual level archetypes have been equated with the imagery of the strange, or chaotic, attractors of the psyche (Van Eenwyk, 1997) that set forth the appearance of the "recognizable patterns [which] represent the emergence of order from chaos and, if correctly interpreted, give insight into the status of the [un-conscious] process" (Van Eenwyk, 1997 p. 10). What seems to be predicted in the course of Tarot readings is the objective tendency for a particular event to occur or the probable state of the system *together with* its corresponding informational content. Henry Stapp is adamant that "if causal anomalies [such as Tarot hermeneutic] actually do appear then the veil has apparently been pushed aside; we have been offered a glimpse of the deeper reality (Stapp, 1993, p. 181; brackets mine).

Autopoietic, self-organizing, archetypal patterns are embodied in the material form of Tarot images. Individual transformations contribute to what, in the esoteric language, is called the alchemical process of liberating the spirit from the confines and limitations of the physical world, or – in the context of education, learning and human development – from the narrow-mindedness caused by the boundaries of individual consciousness. The evolution of consciousness is really taking place. The spiritual quest thus becomes quite literally associated with personal growth, and achieving spiritual health is equivalent to acquiring a greater number of degrees of freedom along a developmental path. The degrees of freedom in any system reflect its evolutionary development or the levels of order. Indeed, the esoteric law of identity refers to the unifying principle underlying all manifested phenomena, not unlike what the contemporary science of complexity has been investigating all along.

What follows from this law is that the only difference between any two phenomena is the degree of their evolutionary development in space-time. Even more important is a particular corollary in terms of the law of Karma – the Cycle of Necessity – that, according to Schueler (1989), defines the specific nature of each object's evolutionary process. In other words, there is a peculiar mixture of determinism and probabilities (Prigogine, Foreword to Laszlo, 1991) describing the geometry of behavior for complex systems that undergo transitions when they are "unbalanced", that is, exist in a state far from equilibrium. The human psyche develops through a self-organizing process, although our conscious mind may remain unaware of this activity. The unconscious processes, however, are typically marked by tensions or bifurcations that signify "a fundamental characteristic in the behavior of complex systems when exposed to high constraint and stress" (Laszlo, 1991, p. 4). Tarot hermeneutic, as we saw in the preceding chapters, often indicates the presence of a highly unstable situation or a state of mind at disequilibrium, such a situation being a prerequisite for a sudden bifurcation, which occurs when the systems are stressed beyond their current state.

The outcomes of such "stressing out" may vary: similar to bifurcations being classified according to their degree of manifestation as well as the dynamic regimes in which the system will potentially settle, the Major Arcana may symbolically indicate

CHAPTER 10

either subtle (Wheel of Fortune), catastrophic (Death), or even explosive (The Tower) bifurcations. What chaos theory describes as fluctuations is presented in a symbolic form in the imagery of the pictures. They may appear either as the unfinished business of one's past, the current conflicts of the present, or an upcoming crisis that may take place in the future. Those unstable situations are practically "nucleated" (Laszlo's term) in the constellations of the cards, metaphorically indicating a point of transition, a sudden discontinuity within the otherwise continuous process, or a singularity of the dynamic regime that can be formally described by means of catastrophe theory (Thom, 1983).

The spontaneously created feedback loops comprise the Tarot dynamics, thereby satisfying the dynamic world view that focuses on the interactions situated in the network of relations which unfold due to continuous feedbacks "including reflection and self-reflection... in all manifestations of human life" (Jantsch, 1975, p. 149). The quality of self-reflexivity is simultaneously the condition for a system's self-transcendence as "the creative overcoming of the status quo" (Jantsch, 1980, p. 91), that is, the system's *learning* and becoming aware of new information. The feed-backs, what Bohm called "injections" (of *information*) influence the system's very *transformation*. It is due to feedbacks that unorthodox causal relations exceed *direct* cause-effect links. Jung's synchronicity in the form of a-causal connections thus represents just *another type of* (non-mechanistic) *causality* thereby allowing for the inclusion of synchronistic phenomena within the new scientific paradigm of self-organization.

In fact "all causation is 'vertical', from the bottom up (projection) and then from the top down (reinjection)... So-called precognition would really involve only the resonance of an event that is explicate *now* with an event that is *later* – from the view-point of the explicate order, which orders events sequentially – to become explicated" (Griffin, 1986, p. 129). The implicate aspects localize and become explicate, literally, in front of our eyes due to a synchronistic, *non-local*, indirect connection between the individual mind and the universal field of which this mind is a holographic part. The hermeneutic approach contributes to human development in terms of the mental, emotional, and spiritual growth and the integration of the unconscious into consciousness. Laszlo (1991) makes a similar point, stating that the actors participating in the dynamics of many fluctuations are conscious human beings and can create alternative patterns of behavior by steering the process in which they act, but only *if they come to know the nature of this process*.

It is by virtue of Tarot hermeneutic that the knowledge of the nature of the process becomes accessible to us so that we can become conscious of our own evolutionary process! The healing and educational process of Tarot readings renders new meaning and significance to the seemingly random and senseless coincidences that pervade human life.

Even as the universe inspires us with evolution and progress, it also warns us about chaotic periods that must exist so as to create new order, not unlike The Tower preceding The Star that we addressed in chapter 9. The unfolding of the evolutionary process is permeated with the nonlinear dynamics of human experience, and the Tarot layout demonstrates this non-linearity.

The symbolic imagery may indicate, for example, the presence of a stagnation period (The Hanged Man), the need to recognize and work through an individual or collective Shadow (The Devil), the necessity to learn the art of listening to one's intuition (The Hermit), or being prepared to face an unexpected crisis, whether in the form of a shock (The Tower) or temporary mental pressure (The Moon), as we said in chapter 4. The imagery may also encourage a person with hope (The Star) or teach a lesson of moderation (Temperance).

Each layout is comprised of a constellation of pictures representing archetypal patterns which in turn reflect combinations of many variables in the psychodynamic processes. Our conscious awareness of those patterns during the reading process leads to the ordering of information and its potential organization at a higher level of intensified consciousness. When we perceive the meaningful patterns and not just some disconnected events, then, as Laszlo affirms, "therein is the possibility of extrapolation. Whatever the nature of the pattern, it provides a handle for grasping something about the way it will unfold in the future" (Laszlo, 1991, p. 50). The enriched vision provided by Tarot hermeneutic not only reflects upon one's current state of being but also on the likelihood of states that are in the process of becoming. The information becomes available during the reading and instantaneously, according to quantum mechanics, acts as a source of guidance, facilitating and transforming the person's perception of this information.

However the quantum laws are valid in the quantum field. As for the macro world, it might take a long time before the material "hiding" in the unconscious reaches the level of consciousness in reality and even longer to manifest by our intentional actions. The higher-evolved a person is, however, the more accelerated the process of acquiring awareness becomes and the lesser the difference between the subtle frequencies of the individual mind and the universal *Nous*. Do both eventually resonate? If yes, is it a level at which intuition turns into telepathy? Is it this level at which mystics or prophets find themselves? In any case, the information is coming from within, from the depth of the person's psyche, who is at once the observer and the observed, embedded in what otherwise would be called *participation mystique.*

Yet, mutual participation and the abolition of dualisms now becomes a prerogative of science; science cannot be positioned in opposition to art because of the element of creativity embedded in self-organizing dynamics. Human insight and intuition become the means of perception embedded in a double-sided, dialogic, communication due to which "symbolic expression becomes possible, first in the form of self-representation…and later as a symbolic reconstruction of the external reality and its active design" (Jantsch, 1980, p. 14) in accord with our very decision-making. This is the ultimate feedback loop that enables the self-organization of consciousness: the person is becoming aware of the mental and emotional contents of her own mind by means of literally looking as if inside, by seeing the past, present and future which is taking shape right here and now in front of her eyes. All the information, "all this knowledge, and this is a crucial point, is available *within* ourselves" (Jantsch, 1975, p. 146) even if hiding in the unconscious before being brought to another level, that of conscious awareness.

The question arises as to how to treat the information that becomes available to us as a result of Tarot hermeneutic. Nel Noddings' relational ethics of care and David Peat's approach of "gentle action" (in Rubik, 1992) encompassing an extra-ordinary quality of mind complemented by our intensified perception based on care, love and respect become a necessity. And it seems that the ultimate purpose of the intelligent universe is to create such a quality of mind and to intensify an individual consciousness to the finest level of perception so that human mind resonates with the universal *Nous* in a mutual harmony and the human soul regains its home in *Anima Mundi* as the goal of human development and learning in the school of life.

QUESTIONNAIRE

1. I am
   ☐ male
   ☐ female

2. My age group
   ☐ under 20
   ☐ between 20 and 30
   ☐ between 30 and 40
   ☐ above 40

3. My main reason for this reading is (check one or more if applicable)
   ☐ personal problem
   ☐ professional problem
   ☐ relationship problem
   ☐ no problem at all
   ☐ other (please specify):

_____

_____
_____
_____
_____

4. The purpose of this reading for me is as follows (check one or more)
   ☐ to gain insight into
      ☐ past
      ☐ present
      ☐ future
      ☐ myself
      ☐ significant others
      ☐ something else (please specify):

_____
_____
_____
_____

□ to analyze feelings
□ to clarify issues
□ to interpret behavior
□ to focus on solutions
□ to feel empowered
□ to gain self understanding
□ to get counseling
□ to find out more about Tarot
□ to have somebody to talk to
□ other (please specify):

_____

_____

_____

_____

_____

5. This reading contributed to achieving my purpose.
   □ yes
   □ no
   □ partially
   □ not sure (please explain):

_____

_____

_____

_____

_____

6. I would like to have a follow-up session.
   □ yes
   □ no
   □ not sure (please explain):

_____

_____

_____

_____

_____

7. This reading was significant and meaningful to me.
   ☐ yes
   ☐ no
   ☐ not sure (please explain):

_____

_____

_____

_____

_____

_____

8. My overall comment:

_____

_____

_____

_____

_____

_____

BIBLIOGRAPHY

Abraham, F. D., Abraham, R. H., & Shaw, C. D. (1990). *A visual introduction to dynamical system theory for psychology.* Santa Cruz, CA: Serial Press.

Abraham, R., McKenna, T., & Shedrake, R. (1992). *Trialogues at the edge of the West: Chaos, creativity and the resacralization of the World.* Santa Fe, NM: Bear & Company, Inc.

Abt, L. E., & Bellak, L. (Eds.). (1959). *Projective psychology: Clinical approaches to the total personality.* New York: Grove Press, Inc.

Anonymous. (2002). *Meditations on the Tarot: A journey into Christian Hermeticism* (R. Powell, Trans). New York: Jeremy P. Tarcher/Putnam.

Auger, E. (2004). *Tarot and other meditation decks.* Jefferson, NC, and London: McFarland & Company, Inc. Publishers.

Barton, S. (1994). Chaos, self-organization, and psychology. *American Psychologist, 49,* 5–14.

Bateson, G. (1979). *Mind and nature: A necessary unity.* New York: E. P. Dutton.

Belenky, M. F., Clinchy, B. M., Goldberger, N. R., & Tarule, J. M. (1986). *Women's ways of knowing.* New York: Basic Books.

Bergin, A. E., & Lambert, M. J. (1978). The evaluation of therapeutic outcomes. In S. L. Garfield & A. E. Bergin (Eds.), *Handbook on psychotherapy and behavior change* (2nd ed., pp. 139–189). New York: John Wiley.

Bertalanffy, von L. (1972). Foreword. In E. Laszlo (Ed.), *Introduction to systems philosophy: Toward a new paradigm of contemporary thought* (pp. xvii–xxi). New York, London, Paris: Gordon and Breach Science Publishers.

Blank, W. (1991). *Torah, Tarot and Tantra.* Boston: Coventure.

Bohm, D. (1985). *Unfolding meaning.* London: Ark Paperbacks.

Bohm, D., & Hiley, B. J. (1993). *The undivided Universe. An ontological interpretation of quantum theory.* London and New York: Routledge.

Bolen, J. S. (1979). *The Tao of psychology: Synchronicity and the self.* New York: Harper & Row.

Bosteels, B. (1998). From text to territory, Felix Guattari's cartographies of the unconscious. In E. Kaufman & K. J. Heller (Eds.), *Deleuze and Guattari: New mappings in politics, philosophy, and culture* (pp. 145–174). Minneapolis, MN: University of Minnesota Press.

Brown, D. J., & McClen Novick R. (1993). *Mavericks of the mind, conversations for the new millennium.* Freedom, CA: The Crossing Press.

Bruner, J. (1966). *Toward a theory of instruction.* Cambridge, MA: Harvard.

Bryden, M. (Ed.), (2001). *Deleuze and religion.* London & New York: Routledge.

Buber, M. (1963). *Israel and the world: Essays in a time of crisis.* New York: Schoken Books.

Buber, M. (1971 [1965]). *Between man and man* (Seventh printing) (R. G. Smith, Trans.). New York: The Macmillan Company.

Casey, E. (1976). *Imagining: A phenomenological study.* Bloomington, IN: Indiana University Press.

Cohen, R. J., Swerdlik, M. E., & Smith, D. K. (1992). *Psychological testing and assessment: An introduction to tests and measurements* (2nd ed.). Mountain View, CA: Mayfield Publishing Company.

Conforti, M. (2003, June 1). *Field, form and fate: Patterns in mind, nature, and psyche* (Rev. ed.). Spring Journal, Inc.

Corey, G. (1991). *Theory and practice of counseling and psychotherapy* (4th ed.). Pacific Grove, CA: Brooks/ Cole Publishing Company.

Corsini. R., & Wedding, D. (1989). *Current psychotherapies* (4th ed.). Illinois, IL: F. E. Peacock Publishers, Inc.

Crawford, M., & Rossiter, G. (2006). *Reasons for living: Education and young people's search for meaning, identity and spirituality.* Australia: Australian Council for Educational Research.

Dalenoort. G. J. (Ed.), (1994). *The paradigm of self-organization II.* Gordon and Breach Science Publishers.

de Souza, M. (2008). The roles of conscious and non-conscious learning in impeding and enhancing spirituality: Implications for learning and teaching. *Education and Spirituality*. Melbourne: Australian College of Education.

de Souza, M. (2009). Promoting wholeness and wellbeing in education: Exploring alspects of the spiritual dimension. In M. de Souza, L. Francis, J. O'Higgins-Norman, & D. Scott (Eds.), *International handbook of education for spirituality, care and wellbeing* (pp. 677–692). Dordrecht, The Netherlands: Springer Academic Publishers.

de Souza, M., Francis, L., O'Higgins-Norman, J., & Scott, D. (Eds.). (2009). *International handbook of education for spirituality, care and wellbeing*. Dordrecht, The Netherlands: Springer Academic Publishers.

Deleuze, G. (1983). *Nietzsche and philosophy*. London: Continuum.

Deleuze, G. (1986). *Cinema 1: The movement-image* (H. Tomlinson & B. Habberjam, Trans.). Minneapolis, MN: University of Minnesota Press.

Deleuze, G. (1987). *Dialogues* (with Claire Parnet), (H. Tomlinson & B. Habberjam, Trans.). New York: Columbia University Press.

Deleuze, G. (1988a). *Spinoza: Practical philosophy* (R. Hurly, Trans.). San Francisco: City Lights Books.

Deleuze, G. (1988b). *Foucault* (S. Hand, Trans.). Minneapolis, MN: University of Minnesota Press.

Deleuze, G. (1989). *Cinema 2: The time-image* (H. Tomlinson & R. Galeta, Trans.). Minneapolis, MN: University of Minnesota Press.

Deleuze, G. (1990a). *The logic of sense* (M. Lester, Trans.). New York: Columbia University Press.

Deleuze, G. (1990b). *Expressionism in philosophy: Spinoza* (M. Joughin, Trans.). New York: Zone Books.

Deleuze, G. (1991). *Bergsonism* (H. Tomlinson, Trans.). New York: Zone Books.

Deleuze, G. (1993). *The Fold: Leibniz and the Baroque* (T. Conley, Trans.). Minneapolis, MN: University of Minnesota Press.

Deleuze, G. (1994). *Difference and repetition* (P. Patton, Trans.). New York: Columbia University Press.

Deleuze, G. (1995). *Negotiations 1972–1990* (M. Joughin, Trans.). New York: Columbia University Press.

Deleuze, G. (1997). *Essays critical and clinical* (D. W. Smith & M. Greco, Trans.). Minneapolis, MN: University of Minnesota Press.

Deleuze, G. (2000). *Proust and Signs* (R. Howard, Trans.). Minneapolis, MN: University of Minnesota Press.

Deleuze, G. (2001). *Pure immanence: Essays on a life* (A. Boyman, Trans.). New York: Zone Books.

Deleuze, G. (2003). *Francis Bacon: The logic of sensation* (D. W. Smith, Trans., and with an Introduction). Minneapolis, MN: University of Minnesota Press.

Deleuze, G., & Guattari, F. (1987). *A thousand plateaus: Capitalism and schizophrenia* (B. Massumi, Trans.). Minneapolis, MN: University of Minnesota Press.

Deleuze, G., & Guattari, F. (1994). *What is philosophy?* (H. Tomlinson & G. Burchell, Trans.). New York: Columbia University Press.

Deleuze, G., & Guattari, F. (1972). *Anti-Oedipus* (R. Hurley, M. Seem, & H. R. Lane, Trans.). London and New York: Continuum.

Delpech-Ramey, J., & Harris, P. (Eds.). (2010). Spiritual politics after Deleuze. *SubStance #121, 39*(1).

Downing, C. (2005). *Preludes: Essays on the lucid imagination, 1961–1981*. New York: iUniverse.

Dummett, M. (1980). *The game of Tarot: From Ferrara to Salt Lake City*. London: Gerald Duckworth & Co. Ltd.

Faivre, A. (1994). *Access to western esotericism*. Albany, NY: State University of New York Press.

Faivre, A. (1995). *The eternal Hermes: From Greek God to alchemical magus* (J. Godwin, Trans.). MI: Phanes Press.

Frank, L. K. (1939). Projective methods for the study of personality. *Journal of Psychology, 8*, 389–413.

Friedman, N. (1994). *Bridging science and spirit: Common elements in David Bohm's physics, the perennial philosophy and Seth*. St. Louis, MO: Living Lake Books.

Gad, I. (1994). *Tarot and individuation: Correspondences with Cabala and Alchemy*. York Beach, ME: Nicholas-Hays, Inc.

Gardner, M. (2000). *Did Adam and Eve have navels? Debunking pseudoscience*. New York, London: W.W. Norton & Company.

Garrison, J. (1997). *Dewey and Eros: Wisdom and desire in the art of teaching*. New York & London: Teachers College Press.

Gearhart, S., & Rennie, S. (1981). *A feminist Tarot*. Watertown, MA: Persephone Press.

Gebser, J. (1991). *The ever-present origin* (N. Barstad & A. Mickunas, Trans.). Athens, OH: Ohio University Press.

Gidley, J. M. (2009). Educating for evolving consciousness: Voicing the emergency for love, life and wisdom. In M. De Souza, L. Francis, J. O'Higgins-Norman, & D. Scott (Eds.), *International handbook of education for spirituality, care and wellbeing* (pp. 533–561). Dordrecht, The Netherlands: Springer Academic Publishers.

Goodchild, V. (2001). *Eros and Chaos: The sacred mysteries and dark shadows of love*. York Beach, ME: Nicolas-Hays Inc.

Greene, M. (2000). *Releasing the imagination: Essays on education, the arts, and social change*. Jossey-Bass Education.

Griffin, D. R. (1986). Bohm and whitehead on wholeness, freedom, causality, and time. In D. R. Griffin (Ed.), *Physics and the ultimate significance of time* (pp. 127–153). Albany, NY: State University of New York Press.

Grumet, M. (1991). The politics of personal knowledge. In C. Witherell & N. Noddings (Eds.), *Stories lives tell: Narrative and dialogue in education* (pp. 67–77). New York: Teachers College Press.

Guattari, F. (1995). *Chaosmosis: An ethico-aesthetic paradigm* (P. Bains & J. Pefanis, Trans.). Bloomington & Indianapolis, IN: Indiana University Press.

Guirdham, A. (1993). *The Great Heresy: The history and beliefs of Cathars*. England: Saffron Walden, the C.W. Daniel Company Ltd.

Hardt, M. (1993). *Gilles Deleuze: An apprenticeship in philosophy*. Minneapolis, MN: University of Minnesota Press.

Hederman, M. P. (2003). *Tarot: Talisman or Taboo? Reading the World as symbol*. Dublin: Currach Press.

Hillman, J. (1972). *The myth of analysis: Three essays in archetypal psychology*. New York: Harper Colophon Books/Harper & Row, Publishers.

Hillman, J. (1989). *A blue fire: Selected writings by James Hillman* (T. Moore, Ed.). New York: Harper Collins.

Hillman, J. (1997). *The Soul's code: In search of character and calling*. New York: Warner Books Edition.

Hopcke, R. H. (1992). *A guided tour of the collected works of C. G. Jung*. Boston: Shambhala.

Husserl, E. (1962). *Ideas* (W. R. Boyce Gibson, Trans.). New York: Macmillan.

Idel, M. & McGinn, B. (Eds.). (1999). *Mystical union in Judaism, Christianity, and Islam: An ecumenical dialogue*. New York: Continuum.

Jantsch, E. (1975). *Design for evolution: Self organization and planning in the life of human systems*. New York: George Braziller.

Jantsch, E. (1980). *The self-organizing universe: Scientific and human implications of the emerging paradigm of evolution* (Systems Science and World Order Library). New York: Pergamon Press.

Jung, C. G. (1972). *The structure and dynamics of the psyche*. London: Routledge.

Jung, C. G., & Pauli, W. (1955). *The interpretation of the nature and the psyche*. New York: Pantheon Books (Bollingen Series LI).

Jung, C. G. (1947). *Essays on contemporary events* (E. Welsh, B. Hannah, & M. Briner, Trans.). London: Kegan Paul.

Jung, C. G. (1949). Foreword (R. F. C. Hull, Trans.). In E. Neumann (1969), *Depth psychology and a new ethic* (E. Rolfe, Trans.) (pp. 11–18). New York: Harper & Row Publishers.

Jung, C. G. (1953–1979). *Collected works* (R. Hull, H. Read, M. Fordham, G. Adler, & W. M. McGuire, Trans., Eds.). Princeton University Press (cited as CW).

Jung, C. G. (1954). *Psychology and education* (Vol. 17). Princeton, NJ: Princeton University Press.

Jung, C. G. (1959). *The archetypes of the collective unconscious*. London: Routledge.

BIBLIOGRAPHY

Jung, C. G. (1963). *Memories, dreams, reflections* (R. Winston & C. Winston, Trans., A. Jaffe, Ed.). New York: Pantheon Books.
Jung, C. G., & Kerenyi, C. (1951). *Introduction to a science of mythology: The myth of the divine child and the mysteries of Eleusis* (R.F.C. Hull, Trans.). London: Routledge & Kegan Paul.
Kerslake, C. (2007). *Deleuze and the unconscious*. New York: Continuum.
Kincheloe, J. (2001). Describing the Bricolage: Conceptualizing a new rigor in qualitative research. *Qualitative Inquiry, 7*(6), 679–692. (SAGE Publications)
Kincheloe, J. (2005). On to the next level: Continuing the conceptualization of the Bricolage. *Qualitative Inquiry, 11*, 323–350.
Kincheloe, J. (2008). *Knowledge and critical pedagogy: An introduction*. Dordrecht, London: Springer.
Kincheloe, J., & K. Berry (2005). *Rigour and complexity in educational research: Conceptualizing the Bricolage*. London: Open University Press.
Koestler, A. (1972). *The roots of coincidence*. New York: Random House.
Laszlo, E. (1991). *The age of bifurcation: Understanding the changing World. The World futures general evolution studies* (Vol. 3). Philadelphia: Gordon and Breach.
Laszlo, E. (1995). *The interconnected universe: Conceptual foundations of transdisciplinary unified theory*. Singapore: World Scientific.
Laszlo, E. (2004/2007). *Science and the Akashic field: An integrated theory of everything*. Rochester, VT: Inner Traditions.
Lévi-Strauss, C. (1966). *The savage mind* (J. Weightman & D. Weightman, Trans.). University of Chicago Press.
Main, S. (2008). *Childhood re-imagined: Images and narratives of development in analytical psychology*. Routledge.
May, R. (1991). *The cry for myth*. New York: W.W. Norton & Company.
Mayes, C. (2003). *Seven curricular landscapes: An approach to the holistic curriculum*. University Press of America.
Mayes, C. (2004). *Teaching mysteries: Foundations of spiritual pedagogy*. University Press of America.
Mayes, C. (2005). *Jung and education: Elements of an archetypal pedagogy*. Rowman & Littlefield.
Mayes, C. (2007). *Inside education: Depth psychology in teaching and learning*. Atwood Publishing.
Murphy, M. (1993). *The future of the body: Explorations into the further evolution of human nature*. New York: Putnam Publishing Groups.
Murphy, T. S. (1998). Quantum ontology: A virtual mechanics of becoming. In E. Kaufman & K. J. Heller (Eds), *Deleuze and Guattari: New mappings in politics, philosophy and culture* (pp. 211–229). Minneapolis, MN: University of Minnesota Press.
Neumann, E. (1969). *Depth psychology and a new ethic*. New York: Harper & Row Publishers. English Translation by Eugene Rolfe. Copyright by Hodder and Stoughton Ltd and C. G. Jung Foundation for Analytical Psychology.
Neville, B. (2005). *Educating psyche: Emotion, imagination and the unconscious in learning*. Australia: Flat Chat Press.
Neville, B. (in press). The polytheistic classroom. In I. Semetsky (Ed.), *The Jungian currents in education, special issue of educational philosophy and theory*.
Nichols, S. (1980). *Jung and Tarot, an archetypal journey*. York Beach, ME: Samuel Weiser, Inc.
Noddings, N. (1984). *Caring: A feminine approach to ethics and moral education*. University of California Press.
Noddings, N. (1989). *Women and evil*. Berkeley, CA: University of California Press.
Noddings, N. (1991). Stories in dialogue: Caring and interpersonal reasoning. In C. Witherell & N. Noddings (Eds.), *Stories lives tell: Narrative and dialogue in education* (pp.157–170). New York: Teachers College Press.
Noddings, N. (1993a). *Educating for intelligent belief or unbelief*. New York & London: Teachers College, Columbia University, Teachers College Press.
Noddings, N. (1993b). Excellence as a guide to educational conversation. In H. Alexander (Ed.), *Philosophy of Education Society* (pp. 5–16). Urbana, IL.

Noddings, N. (1998). *Philosophy of education*. Boulder, CO: Westview Press.

Noddings, N. (2002). *Educating moral people: A caring alternative to character education*. New York & London: Teachers College Press.

Noddings, N. (2006). *Critical Lessons: What our schools should teach*. Cambridge: Cambridge University Press.

Noddings, N., & Shore, P. (1984). *Awakening the inner eye: Intuition in education*. New York & London: Teachers College, Columbia University.

Ouspensky, P. D. (2008). *Symbolism of the Tarot: Philosophy of occultism in pictures and numbers*. Samhain Song Press; First Samhain Song edition.

Paul, G. L. (1967). Outcome research in psychotherapy. *Journal of Consulting Psychology, 31*, 101–188.

Pauli, W. (1994). *Writings on physics and philosophy* (C. P. Enz & K. von Meyenn, Eds., R. Schlapp, Trans.). Berlin: Springer Verlag.

Pearce, C. (1977). *Magical child*. New York: E. P. Dutton.

Place, R. (2005). *The Tarot: History, symbolism, and divination*. New York: Jeremy P. Tarcher/Penguin.

Roberts. R. (1987). *The original Tarot and you*. San Anselino, CA: Vernon Equinox Press

Romanyshyn, R. (2007). *The wounded researcher: Research with soul in mind*. Spring Journal Books.

Romanyshyn, R. (in press). Complex education: Depth psychology as a mode of ethical pedagogy. In I. Semetsky (Ed.), *The Jungian currents in education, special issue of educational philosophy and theory*.

Rubik, B. (Ed.). (1992). The interrelationship between mind and matter. In *Proceedings of a conference hosted by a Center for Frontier Sciences*. Temple University, PA.

Ryce-Menuhin, J. (1992). *Jungian Sandplay: The wonderful therapy*. London: Routledge.

Samuels, A. (1985). *Jung and the post-Jungians*. London and Boston: Routledge & Kegan Paul.

Sargent, C. (1988). *Personality, divination and the Tarot*. Rochester, VT: Destiny Books.

Schueler, G. J. (1989). *Enochian physics: The structure of the magical universe*. St. Paul, MN: Llewellyn's New Times.

Schwartz, H. (2004). *Tree of souls: The mythology of Judaism*. New York, Oxford: Oxford University Press.

Semetsky, D. (1994). "The Night". In B. Janssen, et al. (Eds.), *Journeys to the point: Poetry by young Australians* (p. 79). Melbourne: Express Media Inc.

Semetsky, I. (2006). *Deleuze, education and becoming*. Rotterdam: Sense Publishers.

Semetsky, I. (2008). *Nomadic education: Variations on a theme by Deleuze and Guattari*. Rotterdam: Sense Publishers

Semetsky, I. (Ed.). (in press). *The Jungian currents in education, special issue of educational philosophy and theory*.

Semetsky, I. (1998). On the nature of Tarot. *Frontier Perspectives, 7*(1), 58–66. The Center for Frontier Sciences, Temple University, PA.

Semetsky, I., & Delpech-Ramey, J. (in press). Jung's psychology and Deleuze's philosophy: The unconscious in learning. In I. Semetsky (Ed.), *The Jungian currents in education, special issue of educational philosophy and theory*.

Sheldrake, R. (1988). *The presence of the past: Morphic resonance and the habits of nature*. New York: Times Books.

Singer, J. (1985). The education of the analyst. In M. Stein (Ed.), *Jungian analysis* (pp. 367–385). Boston: Shambhala.

St. Pierre, E. A. (1997a). Methodology in the fold and the irruption of transgressive data. *Qualitative Studies in Education, 10*(2), 175–189.

St. Pierre, E. A. (1997b). Nomadic inquiry in the smooth spaces of the field: A preface. *Qualitative Studies in Education, 10*(3), 365–383.

Stapp, H. P. (1993). *Mind matter and quantum mechanics*. Berlin: Springer-Verlag.

Steinberg, S. R., Kincheloe, J. L., & Hinchey, P. H. (1999). *The Post-Formal reader: Cognition and education*. New York and London: Palmer Press.

Stevens, A. (1983). *Archetypes: A natural history of the self*. New York: Quill.

Sullivan, H. C. (1953). *The interpersonal theory of psychiatry*. New York: Norton.

BIBLIOGRAPHY

Sullivan, H. C. (1972). *Personal psychopathology*. New York: Norton.

Sullivan, H. S. (1950). The illusions of personal individuality. *Psychiatry*, *13*, 317–322.

Tarkovsky, A. (1989). *Sculpting in time, reflections on the cinema* (K. Hunter-Blair, Trans.). London: Faber and Faber.

Tarnas, R. (1991). *The passion of the Western mind: Understanding the ideas that have shaped our World view*. New York: Ballantine Books.

The California Therapist. (1992, November-December). 4:5.

Thelen E. & Smith, L. (1995). *A dynamic systems approach to development of cognition and action*. Cambridge, MA: The MIT Press.

Thom, R. (1983). *Mathematical models of morphogenesis*. Chichester, England: Ellis Horwood Ltd.

Van Eenwyk. J. R. (1997). *Archetypes & strange attractors: The chaotic World of symbols* (Studies in Jungian Psychology By Jungian Analysts). Toronto, CA: Inner City Books.

Viorst, J. (1992). *Necessary losses*. New York: Fawcett Gold Medal.

von Franz, M. (1992). *Psyche and matter*. Shambhala: Boston.

von Lucadou, W. (1994). A new experiment suggesting non-local correlations in macroscopic complex systems. In G. J. Dalenoort (Ed.), *The paradigm of self-organization 11*. Gordon and Breach Science Publishers.

Watson, J. (1985). *Nursing: The philosophy and science of caring*. Boulder, CO: Associated University Press.

Weil, S. (1951). *Waiting for God*. New York: G.P. Putnam's Sons.

Wexler, P. (1996). *Holy sparks: Social theory, education and religion*. New York: St. Martin's Press.

Wexler, P. (2000). *Mystical society: An emerging social vision*. Boulder, CO: Westview.

Wexler, P. (2008). *Symbolic movement: Critique and spirituality in sociology of education*. Rotterdam: Sense Publishers.

Whitmont, E. (1984). *Return of the Goddess*. New York: The Crossroad Publishing Company.

Whitmont, E. C. (1985). Recent influences on the practice of Jungian analysis. In M. Stein (Ed.), *Jungian analysis* (pp. 335–364). Boston: Shambhala.

Witherell, C. (1991). The self in narrative: A journey into paradox. In C. Witherell & N. Noddings (Eds.), *Stories lives tell: Narrative and dialogue in education* (pp. 83–97). New York: Teachers College Press.

Witherell, C. & Noddings, N. (Eds.). (1991). *Stories lives tell: Narrative and dialogue in education*. New York, London: Teachers College, Columbia University.

Yates, F. (1964). *Giordano Bruno and the Hermetic tradition*. Chicago: The University of Chicago Press.

INDEX

Lightning Source UK Ltd.
Milton Keynes UK
UKOW041951280812

198194UK00005B/10/P